HIGHER EDUCATION AND THE

AMERICAN RESURGENCE

A CARNEGIE FOUNDATION SPECIAL REPORT

Higher Education and the American Resurgence

FRANK NEWMAN

WITH AN INTRODUCTION BY

ERNEST L. BOYER

THE CARNEGIE FOUNDATION FOR THE

ADVANCEMENT OF TEACHING

5 IVY LANE, PRINCETON, NEW JERSEY 08540

Library of Congress Cataloging in Publication Data

Newman, Frank. 1927-
    Higher education and the American resurgence.
    (A Carnegie Foundation special report)
    Bibliography: p. 237
    Includes index.

    1. Education, Higher—United States.   2. Competition, International.
3. Research—United States.   I. Title.
II. Series.

LA227.3.N46   1985   378.73   85-21357
ISBN 0-931050-28-6

Copies are available from the
PRINCETON UNIVERSITY PRESS
3175 Princeton Pike
Lawrenceville, N.J. 08648

CONTENTS

vi

ACKNOWLEDGMENTS

THE WORK of shaping the ideas of this report has been done with remarkable insight, energy, and skill by a panel that includes Alden Dunham, Russell Edgerton, Walter Leonard, Margaret MacVicar, Michael O'Keefe, Alan Pifer, and Frank Rhodes. The panel has engaged in intense discussions, reviewed multiple drafts, searched out sources of information, and provided new insights, all with a deep concern for careful analysis. While the responsibility for both the writing and the ultimate decisions with regard to positions is mine, the quality of the report is due to the work of the panel. In this sense, the term "we" as it is used in the Prologue refers to the sense of the panel.

The hard work has been done by a research team of Mary Jeanne Buckley, Josephine Lee, Ann Spruill, Dennis Stout, and David Woolwine, a team that was both diligent and imaginative, willing to challenge each assumption with careful scholarship and yet able to see the larger view.

Throughout the life of the project, we depended on discussions with literally hundreds of people around the country—groups of faculty from many universities, researchers in particular fields, business leaders, government officials, students, librarians, administrators of programs—people who had the answers to the questions we were asking. They were generous with their time, their sources of data, and their ideas. What was made evident to us over and over again was the willingness of those in the academic and policy making communities to address openly the issues facing higher education and to participate in the search for ways to improve it.

The task of support and production was accomplished through the ever cheerful, willing, and able efforts of the Carnegie Foundation staff—Robert Hochstein, Warren Bryan Martin, Jean Van Gorden—and the support staff—Lisa Cziffra, Tom Doyle, Marissa Endicott, Anne Groom,

Arlene Lamar, Carol Lasala, Lane Mann, Nancy Mihalik, and Cecile Wall. I am particularly indebted to Verne Stadtman for his wise and patient counseling on all aspects of the report.

Finally, while the sole responsibility for the report rests with me, I have been greatly aided by discussions with the Carnegie Foundation Board and particularly by repeated exchanges of ideas with the president of the Foundation, Ernest L. Boyer.

FRANK NEWMAN

INTRODUCTION

by Ernest L. Boyer

I N APRIL 1985, the Board of Trustees of The Carnegie Foundation for the Advancement of Teaching issued a special report entitled *Sustaining the Vision*. This statement highlighted the essentialness of the federal role in higher education and the equally crucial role colleges and universities play in the nation's life.

The Trustees urged increased federal support for colleges and students in order to empower the coming generation and to strengthen America's technological and scientific leadership in the world. There also was an urgent call to expand access for minorities and to insure that all students are economically independent and civically prepared.

To regard American education as somehow unrelated to national concerns is as grievous as it is dangerous in a complex, interrelated world. To fail to provide students with a perspective beyond self-interest is to fail the nation.

The unique partnership between Washington and higher education was seen by our Trustees as essential to the advancement of key national objectives: social justice, economic growth, civic and cultural enrichment, and the security of the nation.

As the Carnegie Trustees said: "This nation's greatest strength is not its weapons, but its people. Our greatest hope is not technology but the potential of coming generations. Education is, as it has always been, an investment in the future of the nation."

In *Higher Education and the American Resurgence*, Dr. Frank Newman, President of the Education Commission of the States and a member of our Board of Trustees, supports and extends these essential themes. He takes a searching look at our interconnected world. He concludes that our colleges and universities can, once again, play a central role in national renewal. Our system of higher education is the world's best, he argues. It must be even more effective since "New and powerful forces are re-shaping American society, increasing the demands placed upon higher education."

In a world where we were once technologically far ahead of most other nations, we now find ourselves in serious competition with nations considered "emerging" only a few years ago. And Dr. Newman argues that, "Our financial system, telecommunications, and countless other aspects of today's life are so intertwined with the rest of the world as to have changed permanently."

Today's economic competition is a far cry from what it was just 25 years ago. "Not only have Japan and Western Europe become more sophisticated in manufacturing and technology, but newly industrialized countries—Taiwan, South Korea, Singapore, Hong Kong, Israel—are hard on their heels," Dr. Newman writes. "The result is a dynamic world market, a never ending economic race, which the United States leads, followed by Japan, then West Europeans, who are in turn pressed by emerging countries such as Brazil or Mexico."

In this report, Dr. Newman argues persuasively that colleges and universities have a crucial role to play in helping America meet emerging competition. But beyond confronting the realities of a global economy is the issue of whether the United States can provide moral leadership as well.

Frank Newman describes the new demands. They include the quest for world peace; the securing of our neighborhoods and cities from crime, drug use, and violence; and the need to protect our environment from toxic wastes and senseless despoliation.

Graduates of American colleges, he says, "must see themselves as able to help shape the world in which they must adapt." And he gives great priority to creativity, to educating students who are concerned not just about the quality of our products but also about the quality of our lives.

We need more science and more technology to meet the nation's future needs. But we need more wisdom, too. In every field of endeavor, we need men and women who are willing to think creatively, and to act with conviction and concern.

This means changes within the nation's colleges. A coherent general education program is required, one that gives students a basic understanding of the world we all share. It also means more independence in the classroom, with less telling and more asking and critiquing.

Preparing the coming generations also is achieved by service, a central theme in this provocative report. Dr. Newman points out that "When students participate in (service and jobs) they become colleagues in the educational process rather than objects upon which teaching is practiced. When students take responsibility, they learn to be responsible."

In what may well be the most important and interesting ideas in the report, Dr. Newman proposes that young people who engage in public service become eligible for financial assistance when they enroll in a college. In one variation of this notion, he suggests that students receive a federal scholarship if they agree to teach in the public schools after graduation.

What's at stake here is the proposition that federal aid is something to be earned, not automatically awarded.

Work and service programs will not, of course, make all other forms of student assistance obsolete. Some students will still need special grants and loans in order to complete their higher education. This is especially true for students now underrepresented on the nation's campuses. There is, quite correctly, a call for more federal support for programs that improve the preparation of minority students for higher education and improve their persistence after they enroll.

Frank Newman concludes by focusing on the role of the American university in the advancement of new knowledge and the development of new technology. Increasingly, the lines between "basic" research and "applied" research have become blurred and lines of authority have become blurred as well. Newman argues persistently that the university, not government, should dominate the research agenda of the nation.

In his penetrating, well-written paper, Dr. Newman forces us to look at ourselves and at our institutions. He prods us, raising issues that certainly will stir discussion and debate.

The Carnegie Foundation for the Advancement of Teaching deeply appreciates the important contributions Dr. Newman's study and report have made. Thanks to him, his advisory panel, and his colleagues, our understanding of the vital relationship between higher education and the nation's leadership in an increasingly competitive world is deepened and enlarged. Our national destiny inevitably will be influenced by the way the issues he has raised ultimately will be decided.

ERNEST L. BOYER
President
The Carnegie Foundation
for the Advancement of Teaching

A Matter of Will

HIGHER EDUCATION in the United States is entering a period of questioning of its purposes and its quality. The searchlight of educational reform, which has been focused on elementary and secondary schools, is now moving to include colleges and universities. My colleagues on the panel and I welcome this challenge, encourage it, believe it will be positive in its effects. This report is intended to extend and deepen that debate.

Our confidence in encouraging public scrutiny stems from a simple yet important observation—the American system of higher education is the best in the world. Our motivation to do so flows from another observation—despite its high quality, American higher education must be even more effective if it is to meet the needs of this country in the decade ahead. New and powerful forces are reshaping American society, increasing and changing the demands placed upon higher education.

The most visible new demand is the need to be more effective in an economy that for the first time is truly international; an economy in which the traditional hierarchical approach to organization is rapidly being displaced by a more decentralized, entrepreneurial approach. The jolt of growing competition, most notably from Japan, has already turned the attention of the nation toward the roles that education plays: the importance of research and new technologies to the growth of jobs; the need for scientific and technical talent; the adequacy of our base of elementary and secondary education. The states have already made plain their determination to focus on these issues.

At stake is more than simply the issue of the health of the American economy. At stake is the fundamental issue of the place of the United

States in the world, whether it will define itself as a country moving ahead or as a country drifting into a lesser role. We believe that the United States is gearing up for an economic renewal. Education at all levels is expected to play a major role.

If the need to respond to the new world economy were the only force for change, it would be essential that higher education respond. As important as this is, we do not believe that it is the most urgent issue. The most critical demand is to restore to higher education its original purpose of preparing graduates for a life of involved and committed citizenship. It is a need which arises from the unfolding array of societal issues of enormous complexity and seriousness—issues such as how to accelerate the integration of growing and diverse minorities, how to control the continuing proliferation of nuclear arms, how to reduce the dangers of toxic wastes. Toxic wastes, to use one example, are now recognized as not merely an annoying issue of pollution confined to certain areas but a widespread problem potentially lethal to society in which the critical issue is not technological but political—the ability to fashion solutions acceptable to the community.[1] Not only are new issues added regularly to an already formidable list, but those issues that have been visible for several decades remain maddeningly intractable, if anything, revealing themselves as even more complex than anticipated.

This growing complexity adds greatly to the tasks of citizenship at the very time that the capacity for citizenship seems to be declining. How, in these circumstances, can the public avoid becoming tired of its civic responsibilities, avoid the temptation to accept simplistic solutions? The need to resolve complex problems intelligently places an ever greater demand on higher education—a demand for graduates who have a profound understanding of what it means to be a citizen; graduates capable of an interest larger than self-interest; graduates capable of helping this country to be not simply a strong competitor but a responsible and effective leader in a complicated world. Yet by every measure that we have been able to find, today's graduates are less interested in and less prepared to exercise their civic responsibilities. Colleges and universities are less willing to recognize the teaching of civic skills as part of their missions.

How, then, can higher education transform the experience of going to college so that it fosters a sense of civic responsibility?

In a period when resources are tight, enrollments are declining, and the programs of the federal government for higher education are in disarray, there is a tendency to argue that this cannot be a period of change but must be a period of holding on. Such an approach makes transformation from within difficult and decline inevitable. But this is not the only choice.

In a period when interest in economic development is high, there is a tendency to focus exclusively on the role that higher education plays in supporting the economy. Such an approach only adds to the excessive specialization and career focus already prevalent today.

We would be wise, instead, to make this a period of purposeful renewal. Times change. In the United States, a liberal education has always been important. It is essential that the purpose of a liberal education be transformed so that it provides not only a broad base of knowledge and the requisite intellectual skills, but that it develops an entrepreneurial spirit and a sense of civic responsibility, subjects that are seldom discussed on campus. Research universities exist in every area of the country. Today, successful research *and* technology universities are needed, but most research universities still resist this transformation. Transformations are difficult, and we recognize that all institutions resist change.

In this, national policy toward higher education can play a critical role. National policy is not a result of some vast impersonal forces beyond our control. It is the sum of conscious decisions by policy makers, by institutional leaders, and by students. It is a matter of will. Both in terms of the formation of national policy and the education of the individual, what is needed is the belief that one can make a difference.

Policy makers must be willing to examine whether current programs and policies are achieving their educational and scholarly goals, not just whether they are meeting their financial and administrative requirements.

Colleges and universities must be willing to examine how successful each is in meeting the goals espoused—for a truly effective liberal education, for active involvement of students in their own learning, for the development of research and technology that is at the cutting edge of world scholarship.

Students must be willing to recognize that learning is more than preparation for a career, more than sitting in a class, and more than piling up the credits needed for graduation.

We must all recognize the demands that the American role of leadership in the world places on higher education—leadership in the best and fullest sense of that word. Economic leadership is involved, as is scientific and technological leadership. But more is involved—cooperative efforts at home and abroad, a willingness to face the difficult social and political problems, and a determination to work toward constructive solutions. In short, what is needed is more than just an economic renewal; what is needed is a true American resurgence.

Within this resurgence, higher education should not take its present status for granted. An American resurgence requires that the country challenge itself to change and improve in many dimensions. While higher education has a unique role in helping to articulate that challenge, it has a special responsibility to question *its own* effectiveness. It is toward the fostering of this spirit of reexamination that our proposals are intended.

For the debate to address the issues of importance, many of the current assumptions about higher education need to be reframed:

- Access: Many assume that the great gains in broadening access to higher education made in the 1960s and 1970s have done the job. But concern for access must include concern for outcomes as well. Both economic development and civic integration require the full participation of more than just an elite, particularly just a white elite. The enduring and honorable American tradition of opportunity through education must function for the whole of the population. This requires higher education to do a better job of drawing people from all segments of society into those programs that lead to positions of leadership in the life of the country.

- Oversupply: With the arrival of the high technology economy, a question has emerged as to whether there will be enough good jobs for all college graduates. The debate as to whether there is an oversupply or undersupply of college graduates is misleading. Not only do the current trends of jobs and degrees indicate an improving market for graduates, but the significant issue is whether education makes a difference in the quality of the lives of those who attend college; whether graduates feel empowered— ready to help remake the world they find.

- Expertise: Much attention has been focused on whether higher education is graduating a large enough pool of technically trained manpower to meet the needs of an advanced technological society. We believe the answer is probably yes. A more urgent question is whether graduates, in all fields, have the ability to be innovative, the will to take the necessary risks, the capacity for civic responsibility, and the sensitivity to the international nature of the world to be effective in today's society. All too often, the natural tendencies in students toward creativity and responsibility are stifled by a classroom approach that makes them passive objects of learning rather than active colleagues in the learning process.

- Research: There is a strong feeling within the academy as to the importance of leadership in basic research. The urgency of being at the forefront in *both* research and technology demands a reexamination to find the most effective means of achieving leadership in each. Universities have accepted their role in the generation of research, but have been slower, except in a few selected fields, to accept their role in the development of new technologies. Yet today this is a crucial task if the United States is to remain competitive.

- Funding: Within the higher education community, primary concern is still focused on the need for greater funding. While more funding is surely needed in many areas, a more pressing problem is the use of the resources already available. Difficult choices are required. Resources are more constrained than they were at the time of the last debate about higher education policy. Many of the problems cannot be solved by the application of more money alone, for what must be addressed are questions of how things are done more than how much is to be attempted.[2]

We propose a series of steps that we believe will help American higher education meet its expanded responsibilities. The following is a listing of the recommendations that have been put forward in the body of the report. They are repeated here for emphasis and convenience. The purpose of these recommendations is not to address all or even most of the current problems of national policy as it relates to higher education. Rather, they focus on what we perceive to be the most significant task—encouraging those transformations necessary to meet the emerging demands of American society. A critical task of national policy is to provide the incentives, the encouragement, and the appropriate social pressure to bring about the needed changes.

- Students must become more actively involved in their own learning. The resources and opportunities already exist to make learning on every campus more active. Many colleges and universities have created successful model programs for writing fellows, undergraduate teaching assistants, peer tutors, and undergraduate research assistants. Opportunities for actively involving students also are to be found beyond the academic process itself, in the provision of work opportunities and internships.

- In order to encourage students to engage in community service as well as to meet critical social needs, more student aid should be given in return for community service. A number of programs should be created based on the model of the ROTC program. A program that meets the shortage of math and science teachers and the shortage of teachers willing to work in central urban areas should be created—a Public Service Fellows Program for teaching.

- The use of merit (measured by test scores and grades) as a means to select students to receive aid should not be allowed to detract from other forms of aid, particularly need-based and service-based aid.

- Contrary to current proposals (and the actual practice of the past few years), the sum of student aid programs should be expanded, not contracted. The Pell grants and the current work/study programs should be the cornerstone of the student aid programs in order to insure access to those of limited income.

- The balance among the differing types of student aid programs should be altered so that public service programs are increased; Pell grants increased; work/study expanded in both volume and in the scope of the jobs provided; and loans reduced as a means of financing students.

- Work/study funds are often not used as fully or as effectively as they can be, yet work can be an important educational experience. The program should be expanded so that a larger share of those receiving aid work; the significance of the jobs students perform is increased; and colleges and universities are encouraged to use at least 20 percent of their work/study funds for public service on and off campus. In addition to the program in its present form, a modest-sized system of competitive grants to colleges and universities, much along the lines of the FIPSE Program, should be added in which institutions would propose ways to employ undergraduate students in more active and responsible jobs.

- The rapidly increasing dependence on loans as a means of financing students is alarming and must end. Loan programs are needed to provide a degree of flexibility, but they should be maintained in a more measured amount.

- The traditional GI Bill was the country's most successful program of student aid, based on the concept of aid in return for military service. The GI Bill should be restored for military service and a new program should be created, based on the basic elements of the GI Bill, providing student aid in return for community service on the part of young men and women.

- To improve minority participation in higher education, we propose that a new agency be created, the National Opportunity Fund, modeled on the form of FIPSE, specifically designed to support competitive grants to programs for disadvantaged students. The Fund should support programs within colleges and universities and emphasize programs that link these institutions to high schools. We further propose that the funding and function of the TRIO programs be included in the Fund.

- The Fulbright program should be expanded to provide a greater range of fellowships for an exchange of undergraduate or immediate postgraduate students; for the exchange of high school teachers on a regular and continuing basis; and for more intense recruiting of faculty for the three areas of Latin America, Africa, and Southeast Asia. Universities and colleges should themselves create expanded summer programs of organized travel and study, on the alumni travel/study model, to extend the opportunity for study abroad to a wider share of students.

- In the debate over whether to centralize or "target" more of American research, the current balance between "targeted" and "competitive" research is appropriate. All federal support of any nature for university research should be based on careful measures of merit with primary dependence on peer review.

- The total support for basic research should continue to grow. Within that total, the *share* of all basic research funds devoted to economic development should be increased, that for health sciences should be held at its present level, and that for defense should be decreased.

- The basic diversity of research laboratories should be retained. However, a rebalancing should occur so that funding flows more toward the university laboratories and less toward federal laboratories. The need to reduce or eliminate questionable programs or centers should be recognized, particularly in those federal government laboratories which have proven ineffective over the years in generating high-quality research, or in those that have unclear or dubious missions.

- The National Science Foundation and the mission agencies should expand their support of university-based applied research. The

National Science Foundation should continue to fund new university/industry research centers, encouraging competing approaches—not only centers with differing types of linkages, but competing centers in the same fields, for example, multiple research centers in polymers, or in computer graphics. The National Science Foundation should support the implementation of existing studies which address the effectiveness of the various research approaches and fund sufficient further study to determine the most efficient approaches consistent with preserving the autonomy of the university. All parties—the universities, the government, and corporations—must be alert to the danger in any linkage that subverts the traditional functioning of the university processes.

- While the mission agencies, such as the Departments of Defense and Energy, should continue to carry on programs designed to help equip the laboratories that serve their needs, the primary responsibility to improve instrumentation and facilities should be assigned to The National Institutes of Health and the National Science Foundation. Some part of their program funding should be set aside for instrumentation for developing institutions (not, however, for the encouragement of new Ph.D. programs but rather for the improvement of instrumentation necessary for teaching undergraduate students). Funding agencies should also allow universities to set aside a fixed percent, up to 10 percent, of research overhead expenses to be placed in a fund for future instrumentation needs.

- Four regional periodical centers, run as consortia by the major research libraries of each area, should be established in order to provide immediate delivery, often electronic, of articles and other materials. A working group from the key academic, library, and governmental organizations should be formed and charged with the task of proposing the model for the next generation of scholarship information systems.

- The National Science Foundation program of grants for engineering, computer science, and related graduate fellowships should be funded for a period of five years. The grants should be concentrated on the first three years of the student's graduate experience. Many federal agencies, not just the National Science Foundation—Defense, Energy, Agriculture, Humanities, Arts, National Aeronautics and Space Administration, and National Institutes of Health—should establish programs similar to the Presidential Young Investigator Awards, for the same problem exists in all fields, not just the sciences.

- The federal government should allow each university to retain a sum of up to 3 percent of the overhead recovery of federal research grants, up to a maximum of $500,000, for the purposes of seed money to fund new researchers just getting started or those researchers beginning a new field of research and unable as yet to attract funds. Foundations and corporations also should concentrate some resources on small grants to assist new researchers as a needed antidote to the tendency to support only known people in established fields.

SECTION ONE

CHAPTER I

The Need For Debate

A REVIEW OF NATIONAL POLICY toward higher education is urgently needed. More than a decade has passed since the United States Congress and educational leaders last engaged in a major debate about the purposes of higher education and the best means to achieve them.[1] New forces, particularly the intense focus on economic growth and advanced technology, are pressing on society.[2] Other issues, such as the growing need for civic education, are, despite their urgency, largely ignored.

THE BREAKDOWN OF CONSENSUS

By and large, recent national arguments have been about how to reduce expenditures, which programs should be cut, or which ones must be saved.[3] A forty-year tradition of bipartisan consensus about higher education has come to an end.[4] Early in the first term of the present administration, an attempt was made to reduce sharply appropriations for student aid. In real terms, efforts to achieve a steady growth in real dollar support for higher education ended. (See Chart 1.) Other valuable programs, such as Fulbright fellowships, programs for the educationally disadvantaged, and youth service programs such as VISTA or the University Year for Action, were targeted for reduction or elimination. Research priorities shifted toward defense needs.[5]

In recent months, we have seen the administration launch a new budget-driven attack on the concept of federal student aid, met by a determined resistance to such cuts from Congress and the higher education community.[6] As important as federal student aid is to preserve the opportunity

CHART 1

FEDERAL SUPPORT FOR HIGHER EDUCATION IN CURRENT AND CONSTANT (1967) DOLLARS AND AS A PERCENT OF THE BUDGET, SELECTED YEARS: 1952–1985 (EST.)

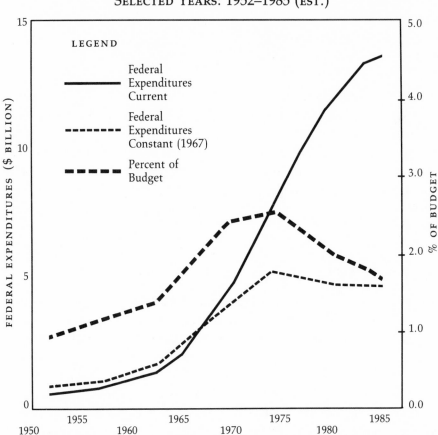

Federal expenditure data for FY 1952–1965 from National Center for Education Statistics (N.C.E.S.). *Digest of Educational Statistics (D.E.S.), 1968*, Washington, D.C., 107; for FY 1970, *D.E.S., 1970*, p. 109; for FY 1975, *D.E.S., 1976*, p. 165; for FY 1980, *D.E.S., 1981*, p. 181; for FY 1983–1985, *Budget of the United States, FY 1983–1985*, Washington, D.C.

SOURCE: Federal budget data for FY 1947, 1952, and 1957 from Bureau of the Census. *Historical Statistics of the United States, Colonial Time to 1970*, p. 1105; for FY 1963 and 1965, Bureau of the Census. *Statistical Abstract of the United States, 1969*, Washington, D.C., p. 375; for FY 1970, 1975, and 1980, *Statistical Abstract of the United States, 1981*, p. 245; for FY 1983, *Budget FY 1984, Special Analyses*, Table C–1; for FY 1984 and 1985, *Budget FY 1985, Special Analyses*, Table C-1. For calculating the federal budget in constant (1967) dollars, the Bureau of Labor Statistics Consumer Price Index was used from United States Bureau of the Census. *Statistical Abstract of the United States, 1984*, 104th edition, Table 796. 1985 is an extrapolation.

for wide access to higher education, it cannot be the only debate. It is more important than ever to the American concept of opportunity that each individual be able to make his or her own way. The *form* that federal student aid takes must be debated to insure that it meets the national needs as they exist now.

While Congress has preserved many programs, there is no longer a consensus on what national education policy should be or what kind of support for such policy the federal government should provide. The country should not drift into some new posture toward higher education without thoughtful consideration of the consequences. The current debate over funding is important, but a fundamental reexamination of the effectiveness of existing programs and the crafting of new policies to meet society's changing needs is critical.

BUILDING A NEW CONSENSUS

The United States does not fashion national policy in the way many European countries do. There, the typical mode is to create a national commission, conduct a debate *within* the government, and ultimately present proposed action to the legislature. Given the diversity and the federal nature of government in the United States, national policy is developed not just within the government but through a much wider forum.[7] The resulting consensus, which we choose to call "national policy," is implemented by a variety of means—federal and state programs, initiatives from individual colleges and universities, and the attitudes and actions of students and their parents.

In the United States, despite the postwar growth of the federal role, federal funds represent only 34 percent of all institutional sources of revenue in higher education. (See Table 1.) This situation is quite unlike that in Europe where, by the 1970s, the national governments had assumed almost all of higher education costs. Even today, despite a trend in Europe toward increasing the student contribution, students there still pay only a fraction of what Americans pay.

Since the end of World War II, three occasions have generated major debates about the role of higher education in our society—the Cold War,

TABLE 1

FEDERAL, STATE, LOCAL, AND PRIVATE SHARE OF HIGHER EDUCATION COSTS, 1980–81 (IN BILLIONS OF DOLLARS)

SOURCE	AMOUNT	PERCENT
Federal	$24.1	34
State	20.9	29
Local	1.8	3
Private	24.4	34
Total	$71.2	100

SOURCE: These data are calculated using National Center for Education Statistics' current-fund revenue of institutions of higher education. *Digest of Education Statistics*, Washington, D.C., 1984, Table 119, p. 137. Tuition and fees income and income from hospitals and auxiliary enterprises have been excluded. After dividing institutional revenue by federal, state, local, and private source, aid to students and student support from family, work, and savings were added in from Michael O'Keefe. "Incumbent and Challenger: The Future for Higher Education," unpublished MS, August 28, 1984, Figure 2, p. 8. Note that federal student aid includes total loan volume of the Guaranteed Student Loan Program, which is greater than federal cost and includes the private sources triggered by the federal expenditures.

Sputnik, and the civil rights revolution. In all three cases new needs of American society, external to higher education, led to changes in the universities and colleges. It might seem inappropriate to make higher education policy based on such large societal issues. A careful examination of the results indicates that it has been neither inappropriate nor ineffective. The outcomes of these adjustments—the creation of the GI Bill, the establishment of the federal government-university research system in response to the Cold War, the improvement and expansion of science in the universities and colleges in response to Sputnik, and the broadening of access to higher education for minorities and low-income students in response to the civil rights revolution—have permanently and positively transformed higher education.

Historically, once a consensus is established around a set of problems, various institutions, both governmental and nongovernmental, work out a division of responsibility for developing, financing, and implementing a range of solutions. An example is the widely shared understanding that access to higher education should be available to all who have the ability and the motivation. No single law spells out this policy, yet it is backed by varied forms of implementation: federal and state student aid programs, the establishment of colleges with open admissions, recruiting programs at universities and colleges, and hundreds of other decentralized decisions.

Another example of national policy is the understanding that research is important to the United States; that basic research is primarily, but not exclusively, housed in the universities; that the federal government supports much of the basic research for the country. It is further understood that research is, in general, both competitive and cooperative. (It is competitive in the sense that there is competition for research grants, for publication in journals, and for professional recognition; but it is cooperative in that information is open and facilities are often shared.) No law covers all of these activities. Federal laws established the National Science Foundation, and the federal budget includes the research components of the various mission agencies. States and the private sector created and maintain research universities. Individual faculty members decide whether to involve themselves in the research effort.

Once established, these national policies are powerful, but they are not fixed. They continue to evolve. For example, when the national research policy was first developed in the early postwar period, it focused, by common agreement, on research for national defense with only a modest bow toward the importance of medical research and research to support economic development.[8] Over the postwar years, however, medical research continued to grow in importance until today, over half of all federally supported basic research is in the health sciences.[9] Now, forty years after the original research proposals, in light of new concerns about American competitiveness, research for economic development is joining defense and health as a full partner in the research agenda.

7

Most federal funding in higher education serves two primary purposes: the improvement of access to higher education for needy students through grants, loans, and work opportunities; and support of research through competitive grants as well as support for larger research facilities. Although there are other federal roles, this report, where it addresses federal policy, focuses primarily on student aid and research support.

From 1937 to 1977, federal support rose from $50 million to $11.8 billion. In constant dollars, this represented an average annual increase of about 130 percent.[10] This growth in federal support coincided with the most rapid expansion of enrollments in higher education and the most thorough reorientation of higher education toward higher quality education and research in the nation's history.

THE CENTRALITY OF THE FEDERAL ROLE

Although national policy involves much more than federal programs, the federal role is central. Much of the current debate revolves around whether some federal programs should be reduced. That issue is often misstated as a questioning of the appropriateness of the federal role. That mistake needlessly confines the channels of discussion. What should be examined is not only how large but how effective each federal program is.

There is today a well-established rationale for a federal role. If the issue is truly national, if the costs or benefits of an action accrue to the country as a whole and not simply to a given state or institution, then it is appropriate for the federal government to be involved. This is the case in most research or graduate education. For example, Michigan cannot easily capture an exclusive benefit from the research in robotics or the education of a Ph.D. in electrical engineering that takes place at the University of Michigan.

Many of the proposals in this report will address changes in federal programs that will help move higher education toward desired national goals. More is at stake than funding. How much the federal government spends and how it goes about spending it are only clues to the effectiveness of programs. Under any administration, either by design or by accident,

8

the federal government is an important force in higher education. How can the country insure that it is a positive force?

A suitable federal role for any national policy will involve:

A national need

A means for federal action that is both effective and acceptable

An issue for which other parties cannot achieve a satisfactory resolution without federal involvement.

PRINCIPLES OF EFFECTIVE FEDERAL ACTION

Experience with federal programs has shown that certain methods are effective, some ineffective, and some dangerous to the autonomy and flexibility essential to institutions of higher education.[11] Each program, whether intended or not, reflects inherent values. A federal student aid plan that says to a student, "There is help available if you work," places work in service to learning. This is quite different from a program that says, "You may borrow money and pay it back out of the higher earnings you can expect." Such a program places learning in service to work. The values that each of these programs promotes are almost exactly reversed.

The GI Bill, or, in its formal title, the Serviceman's Readjustment Act, while intended as a counter to unemployment, a reward for veterans of World War II, and assistance in readjustment to civilian life, also had a major impact on the rate of college attendance. Before World War II, a minority of those with the academic ability to attend college by the standards of the times actually did go to college. The GI Bill convinced many that it was all right for them to aspire to a college education—"if the government thinks it is all right for me to go to college maybe then I should go." The result was an irreversible shift in the public perception of who ought to go to college. All federal programs, no matter how carefully constructed, encourage some values and discourage others; sometimes with conscious intent, often a result of inadvertent effects. No programs are value free.

Similarly, federally supported university research, which began as an

9

emergency program to help win the war, created a new partnership that continues today. The assumption is now well established that a wide range of national priorities should be advanced through research that is federally sustained. Thus, a productive bond has been forged between the federal government and higher education.

Despite how hard it is to make such an analysis, the public needs to question the effects of federal programs and the values they support. It is inappropriate for the federal government to try to affect by direct control the nature of teaching or other central components of the American educational system. Beyond this, when the effects of federal programs or values are considered, care and restraint are required to insure that one does not slip across the line from values to ideology.

What assumptions might be drawn from the experience to date? Federal efforts tend to function well when they are based on competitive grants (such as those of the National Science Foundation, the National Institutes of Health, the National Endowment for the Humanities, and the Fund for the Improvement of Post–Secondary Education), when they provide benefits to students and faculty (such as student aid programs like Pell grants, the GI Bill, or the Truman Scholarships, or through faculty programs like the Fulbright grants),[12] and when they use federal influence to raise issues and create debate, as was the case with the recent report, "A Nation at Risk."

- The federal government functions best when it uses its powers and resources—incentives, regulations, recognition, and the like— to encourage those within higher education to perform more effectively, or to undertake new and often pioneering roles. The Northwest Territories Act of 1780 and the Land Grant Act of 1862 remain perhaps the best known examples of this type of intervention.

- Much of the success of the modern federal role in higher education results from careful avoidance of programs that attempt centralized control. To continue that policy, the federal government should avoid block grants that provide permanent funding to projects or institutions.[13]

- It is essential for federal funding agencies to avoid political considerations when making decisions about the merits of individual projects. While it may not be possible to avoid such decision making in selecting large projects of the Corps of Engineers or setting farm subsidies, experience elsewhere in the world demonstrates that research and teaching function poorly in such political settings. So far, autonomy for higher education has come from three factors: the small size of most grants or programs,[14] the interjection of some form of peer review or expert decision making,[15] and a strong tradition of independent higher education that has constrained both the Congress and the institutions.[16] In the last few years, this principle has been challenged by those who argue for targeting of research efforts or by some universities that have lobbied for construction funds on selected campuses.

- One major role of federal funding is to permit program flexibility that allows for evolutionary change. As research needs require a change of direction, new grant awards can readily reflect the priorities; some projects close down, new projects start up. As colleges and universities improve in quality and reputation, they gain in grant funding and in attracting students (and thus student aid) or the reverse.

Gains have been made and lessons have been learned. But now the time has come to look ahead. The analysis and proposals set forth in this report are intended to help higher education strengthen its own tradition, meet the escalating needs of society, and enhance characteristics of its operations that are needed for the effective functioning of our society.

Not all changes in national policy or in higher education can or should be supported by federal programs.[17] Some are better served by private or state funding. Others are best achieved by reallocation of existing resources within the college or university. One of the advantages of the American system is that differing sources of support allow higher education great flexibility in responding to the changing needs of society. This flexibility and autonomy should be

11

vigorously preserved. In meeting this challenge, higher education has a crucial role to play. The nation's colleges and universities must not only be centers for the preservation and transmission of our culture, but centers for the development of creative thinking, too. Classrooms must be places where new ideas are encouraged, and federal policy should support innovation on the campus. At the same time, scholarship and research must be vigorously advanced. Federal support for university-based research must be strengthened not only to create centers of excellence but to provide new equipment and facilities for the advancement of their work. The program implications of these goals will be discussed later in this report.

CHAPTER II

The New Economy: American Education in a Competitive World

ODAY, in every region of the country, states are struggling to
bolster their economies. More than thirty state commissions have
reported their findings. The same themes run through these reports.[1] The time has come, they say, to:

Accelerate economic growth and job formation

Attract advanced technology industry

Improve elementary and secondary education in order to improve
the skills of the work force

Invest in the research universities in order to improve the research
base and the numbers of technically trained graduates

Create links between business and the universities and business and
the schools.

All of these proposals seem sensible and self-evident. What is significant, of course, is that education has become a central focus of concern.
In many states there already has been a sizable commitment of new
resources for colleges and schools. Welcome as this renewed attention to
education is, there are larger implications that go beyond the interests of
the separate states. Decisions for the future must be made in the context
of these new and important forces.

THE AMERICAN ECONOMY IN WORLD CONTEXT

Immediately after World War II, it was common in this country to think
and talk in terms of the movement toward an international world. The

13

American public understood and was committed. In time, that understanding and commitment slipped, in part because Americans seemed to lead their daily lives in a context that was largely domestic despite the headlines about the Cold War or Korea that reminded them about an international dimension. Today, the economy is as international as the post–World War II rhetoric implied.

In 1950, less than 6 percent of the GNP was involved in foreign trade. In 1984, it was more than 20 percent and growing.[2] Not only has the share increased, but the character has changed. There has been a large increase in the United States trade surplus in products of advanced technology.[3] In parallel, there was first a decline in exports and then a massive growth in imports of traditional manufactured products. Rows of Toyotas and BMWs available for sale and the omnipresent Japanese consumer electronics dramatically attest to this shift. The United States has become a huge exporter of advanced technology products and an even larger importer of traditional or mature products—the largest of each.

More than 70 percent of U.S. manufactured goods now face import competition[4]—20 years ago it was only 25 percent. The expanding international considerations and the increasingly dynamic nature of the economy affect more than just trade in manufactured products. The American financial system, telecommunications, and countless other aspects of today's life are so intertwined with the rest of the world as to have changed permanently.[5] From automobiles to rubber bands to banks, American companies are now involved in intense foreign competition.

This competition is not like the competition of the 1950s. Not only have Japan and Western Europe become more sophisticated in manufacturing and technology, but newly industrialized countries—Taiwan, South Korea, Singapore, Hong Kong, Israel—are hard on their heels. The result is a dynamic world market, a never ending economic race, in which the United States leads, followed by Japan, then the West Europeans, who in turn are pressed by the newly industrialized, who in turn are pressed by emerging countries such as Brazil or Mexico.[6]

To date, the United States has outperformed every other developed nation in the growth of new jobs and particularly in the growth of professional and managerial jobs.[7] Whether this growth can continue is not

14

preordained by already set economic imperatives, but is a function of conscious decisions.

VANISHING TRADE ADVANTAGES

The United States has had two advantages over the last thirty years. One advantage has been its skill as an industrial power, its ability to deploy massive amounts of capital coupled with production know-how. In 1950, the United States was the source of more than half of all the world's manufactured goods—a circumstance that could not last. By 1980, despite the tripling of the American GNP, the United States produced just over 30 percent of the world's manufactures.[8] Today many countries, including newly developed industrialized countries such as Korea or Taiwan, have both the necessary capital and production capability.

The second advantage has been a sizable lead in new technologies. This edge has been based primarily on university research, skill in the translation of this research into emerging fields of technology, and an informal system by which industry has been able to stay ahead by exploiting the fruits of research and technology, whether generated here or abroad, to develop new products. In the last decade or so other countries, most notably Japan, have learned the process of exploiting research (often American research) and have narrowed the technological gap, or in some fields gained the lead.

Even more intense technological competition is ahead. Contrary to earlier expectations,[9] technology has proven far easier to export than had been believed.[10] Not only have countries such as Korea or Malaysia become important industrial centers by adapting technologies developed elsewhere,[11] but a host of other countries from China to Israel are hard at work studying the American experience, creating industrial parks, and developing their universities in order to enhance their abilities both to do serious research and to create new technologies.[12]

Consequently, one cannot expect the American advantage in research and in technology to remain as pervasive as it has been in the past.[13] In research, the gap has narrowed considerably.[14] In technology, there is a struggle for leadership in many fields, including some that are critical.

15

The United States needs to reexamine the approach of its universities toward research and technology not because their effectiveness has begun to slip, but because the international competition has become so much more effective.

While both the research gap and technology gap have been narrowed, they are still integral to the primary American comparative advantage. That advantage comes from the ability to be at the cutting edge of new ideas, not just in developing new technologies but in exercising creativity in many dimensions—the creativity that pioneered supermarkets, car rentals, new forms of finance, even TV programming. New technologies are an increasing part of all products, but the central point is the need for creativity, flexibility, and entrepreneurial spirit if the United States is to continue to lead in a world of perpetual dynamism.

THE MATURING OF THE TECHNOLOGY REVOLUTION

The attention of domestic and foreign policy makers concerned about economic growth has been focused on high technology. Understanding the actual implications of advanced technology is critical in understanding the role of higher education. While the initial surge of interest was often unrealistic and narrowly focused (high tech often meant only computer and semiconductor chip manufacturers), the debate has since become more sober and realistic but no less urgent.

By any analysis, there is a revolution of advanced technologies: computers and semiconductors, of course, but also software, biotechnology, pharmaceuticals, new materials, scientific instrumentation, telecommunications, and many more. These diverse fields share two characteristics: dependence on advanced technology and the development of innovative new products through creativity in the application of those technologies. Policy makers have come to see the need to address both sides of the issue—increasing the already huge pile of technology and enhancing the ability of companies to create new products by the use of technologies selected from that pile.

While it is now apparent that computer and semiconductor firms by

16

themselves will not provide all of the new jobs the country needs (the Bureau of Labor Statistics estimates that only about 600,000 of the 20,000,000 new jobs of the past decade came from the manufacturers of computers, chips, and robots), these products are important beyond their direct job statistics. Taken in their broadest dimension, advanced technology firms add a critical growth segment to the economy. They are the products that the United States exports. They also are often the means for modernizing and improving productivity in traditional industries, such as textiles, or agriculture, or even banking. The U.S. is dependent on this rapidly growing segment for much of the vibrance in the American economy.[15]

One early response to the country's economic crisis was to argue for writing off what became known as the sunset industries, such as steel, autos, and textiles; give them up to Japan and Germany; and concentrate on "high tech." It soon became apparent that this was hardly rational, if for no other reason than that the traditional industries provide the large majority of manufacturing jobs.[16] Not only that, but the process of technological development is dynamic, and no country or industry or firm is safe. The Japanese and the Germans have themselves been losing jobs in these industries to countries such as Korea or Taiwan.[17]

Even new industries, such as computers, can soon become sunset industries unless the individual companies learn how to continue innovating as they grow in size and mature. Merely naming an industry *high technology* does not guarantee job growth.

The real issue for the United States is the need for all of industry to understand and master the concept of perpetual dynamism. The problems in doing so lie as much in the approach of management and labor as in the cost of American manufacturing. One response must be a consistent effort to modernize and automate in every industry, not just the automobile or steel industry. Another response must be an unremitting effort to improve the design and quality of the product or service.[18] Under the old rules, management sought to gain control of a market by heavy fixed capital investment in order to reduce costs. Now flexibility and imagination are the essential ingredients.

Companies that have been the most successful in capitalizing on ad-

17

vanced technology seem to function best in a supportive environment, such as the Silicon Valley in California, Rt. 128 outside of Boston, or the Research Triangle in North Carolina—areas that are centered on major research universities. Some states—Utah, Minnesota, and to a growing extent Michigan, New Jersey, Florida, and Texas—have managed to create emerging advanced technology areas. The economic success of these areas has sparked a determined attempt in state after state to replicate such growth by support for high technology. In each case, not only have the universities played a key role as a source of research and technology, of faculty who serve as sources of expertise, and of graduates who carry new ideas with them to industry, but they have helped create a progressive atmosphere within the surrounding communities. That atmosphere seems to be essential for nurturing the entrepreneurial spirit in dimensions that go well beyond technology.[19]

THE AMERICAN JOB MACHINE

A basic function of every economy is to provide enough jobs for everyone who wants one, jobs that pay enough for the standard of living desired, jobs that are desirable and respectable.[20] Jobs provide more than just wages. Our need to work is far deeper than just the need for money. Jobs provide a focus for our energies and ambition. In many ways our jobs define us.

Jobs are increasingly linked to education—to how much, of what sort, and at which institution. Jobs are similarly linked to technology—in its role in expanding the economy, in its capacity to replace workers with machines, and in the changes it brings in the education needed for given jobs. Therefore, higher education plays a central role in insuring that requisite skills are available, in the sorting that determines who gets which job, and in the creation of the technology necessary to provide the job growth. Higher education also plays a central role in the development of the attitudes of its graduates, attitudes that, over the long run, will determine the nature of the American resurgence.

The American economy has been extraordinarily effective at not only creating jobs, but creating good jobs. From 1950 to 1980, the civilian

18

labor force increased from 59 million to 99 million, and in the five years since to 108 million. Perhaps the most startling aspect of this rate of growth is that it exceeds that of all of the other major industrial countries. Just in the last decade, from 1970 to 1980, the number of jobs grew by 24 percent. The next best performance was that of Japan at 9 percent.[21]

Not only did the number of jobs increase, but the share of the work force in professional jobs grew rapidly. These jobs, largely embodied in the two census categories of "Professional and Technical" and "Mana-

CHART 2

AVAILABLE JOBS IN THE U.S. WORK FORCE: 1950–1984

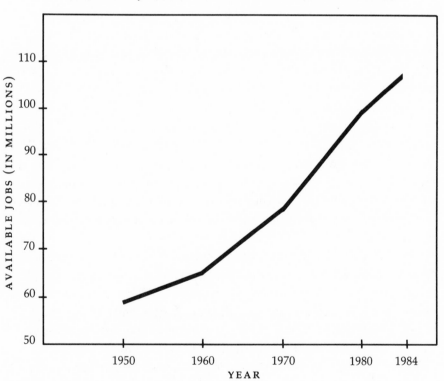

SOURCE: Provided by the Bureau of Labor Statistics.

19

gerial and Administrative," rose from 17 percent of the total work force in 1950 to 26 percent in 1980.[22]

By any measure, the performance of the United States economy over these 30 years is remarkable. The number of jobs grew by 67 percent; the share of professional jobs increased from about one-in-six to over one-in-four; and family income rose by 85 percent.[23]

Why then is there so much concern? Why, if the United States has done so well in the past, shouldn't the expectation be that it will do just as well in the future? In part it is because of the intensifying international competition, and the fear that the United States will lose jobs to new competitors. It is also because the nature of the American population is changing rapidly, both in terms of who wants jobs and how many want them. Despite the huge increase in the number of jobs, there has been an even larger increase in the number of people who want to work: a flood of women—now two-thirds of the women between 25 and 54; a rise in those turning 18 each year—from 2.5 million per year to 4 million; and the second largest influx of immigrants (legal and illegal) in our history.[24]

This huge flow of new entrants into the work force has now, however, run its course. Each year, from 1979 forward, a smaller number of young people turn 18. By 1994 the number will be back down to about 3 million. The number of women entering the labor force is already falling, not because fewer women want to work (on the contrary, younger women are closing in rapidly on males in the rate of work force participation) but because so many are already working. What will happen to the number of immigrants is uncertain. In the last year, immigration has been a subject of intense national and congressional debate. A reasonable assumption is that the level of immigration will not increase.

The next decade is likely to see, therefore, a continuation of the trend of the last few years—falling numbers of new entrants to the labor market.[25] If the rate of job formation continues at anything close to the lead of the 1970s, unemployment should continue to fall.

The rate of job formation is obviously critical. What has caused the growth to date? One major change has been the increasing share of all jobs in the service sector—government, education, communications, bank-

TABLE 2

CIVILIAN EMPLOYMENT BY SEGMENT OF THE ECONOMY

	1950 SHARE (%)	1980 SHARE (%)
Manufacturing	35	28
Service	51	69
Agriculture	14	3
Total	100	100

Manufacturing includes: mining, construction, durable and non-durable manufacturing.
Service includes: government, education, communications, banking, fire insurance, and real estate, transportation and public utilities, wholesale and retail trade.
Agriculture includes: farming, forestry and fishing.
SOURCE: Department of Labor. *Employment and Training Report to the President*, Washington, D.C., 1970; 1981.

ing, health care, and the like. As the economy matured (moved, in the terms of some, to a "postindustrial" or "knowledge" economy) the share of jobs in manufacturing has dropped.

Contrary to the widely held opinion, despite the drop in the *share*, the *absolute number* of jobs in manufacturing actually *rose* by 7,000,000. The United States is one of the few industrialized countries in which such an increase occurred. Just in the past ten years (1974–1984), the share of manufacturing jobs dropped from 25 percent to 20 percent of total jobs but rose in absolute numbers by 343,000. Contrast that statistic to the fall in manufacturing jobs in Japan (–70,000); France (–457,000); West Germany (–1,234,000); or Britain (–2,089,000).[26]

Only in agriculture has automation produced an absolute reduction in jobs. Despite the huge increase in farm output and the export success of American foodstuffs, employment fell by half over the three decades.[27]

There is a popular myth that the reasons the service sector has grown is because it has avoided automation. This is belied by word processors, electronic mail, and on-line information retrieval systems already widely used in this sector with more to come. The largest number of robots in

21

use today are not in automobile manufacturing. They are the automatic tellers in banking.[28] Some parts of the service sector, such as the telephone companies, have long been highly automated. The diversity of the service sector makes predictions as to its future makeup difficult. It probably will continue to grow, albeit more slowly, as even greater automation takes hold. The Bureau of Labor Statistics projects that the balance between manufacturing and service will remain roughly as it is now through the 1990s (agricultural employment is expected to remain at the same level, so its share will continue to fall).

What has kept these two sectors—service and manufacturing—growing in numbers of jobs in spite of intense international competition and growing automation has been a high rate of entrepreneurial activity. In the manufacturing sector, this has taken the form of the growth of small and medium-sized firms. The *Fortune 500* actually *lost* jobs over the last decade. In the service sector as well, new ideas and new programs have sprung up and grown—including new forms of financial services, medical services, communications, and trade schools. A significant part of the service sector expansion over the past three decades came from the growth in government, which has slowed dramatically in the last five years.[29] Yet, even here a remarkable share of the growth has come from new types of governmental services. Thus, job growth in every sector has been a function of entrepreneurial activity.

There remains a dual worry. While the economy has performed spectacularly in the past, it may be entering a new phase in which the accelerating rate of automation will slow or reverse the rate of new job creation; and intensifying international competition may lead to more jobs moving offshore. In weighing each of these threats, it is important to remember that this is not the first year of the computer age but the thirty-fourth; it is not the first decade of intensifying international competition but the fourth. Yet the rate of new job formation remains high.

Despite all the worry about whether there has been a decline in the work ethic, more people want to work and more people (that is, a greater share of the population—now 65 percent of those over the age of 16) are working than ever before.[30] Whether the United States can continue the dramatic growth in jobs of the last several decades is a function of decisions yet to be made, and particularly of the entrepreneurial skill of those in professional and managerial roles.

SKILLING OR DESKILLING IN THE AMERICAN WORK FORCE

Of equal importance to the *number* of jobs is the *kinds* of jobs that will be available. Despite the intrinsic value of being well educated, a college education is, for most Americans, the means for entry to the professional and managerial life of the country.

There is a growing argument as to whether the long, postwar pattern of increasing professionalization of the work force will continue. A number of economists now argue that while some growth in the higher level professional jobs will continue, the impact of technology will be to reduce the number of middle level jobs (those requiring skilled workers just below the professional and managerial level) and make most jobs less demanding and interesting, what has been termed "the deskilling" of the work force. Others argue exactly the reverse, that the advance of technology already requires more education and training at all levels and that it has generally added to the interest of jobs. The issue is important far beyond its manpower ramifications. The loss of the middle would have profound political and social implications, particularly coming at a time when women and minorities are aspiring to new and more prominent roles in society.

So far, the effects of the latest wave of automation are still controversial, with new research cited as evidence both for and against the deskilling argument.[31] Much of the deskilling argument is based on studies of the impact of automation on specific plants or office locations.[32] Here the evidence is mixed. The differences in the effects of automation from company to company demonstrate that much appears to depend on *how* the process of automation has been carried out. There is nothing inherent in the new technologies that prevents their use in a manner that enhances the worker's interest and the skills demanded in a typical job. It is not simply a question of which approach does the most to reduce the cost of labor. Rather, in light of the increased competition, particularly from

Asian countries, what matters as well is which approach provides the encouragement of full participation and enhancement of worker motivation and ingenuity now recognized as essential.

An interesting piece of evidence as to what corporate executives believe comes from a new Carnegie Foundation study of corporate education (formal education programs run by corporations for their employees). The study shows that industry is spending billions in the belief that the changes in the economy will require *better* educated employees.[33]

A related issue is whether the jobs for professionals (i.e., college graduates as opposed to "middle level" workers) will diminish. So far, the evidence based on the labor force taken as a whole, for example, the 1980 census figures, or even the estimates to 1984, demonstrate the continued professionalization of the labor force. In addition to the growth of the "professional/technical" and "managerial/administrative" categories, there is a continuing trend of upgrading middle level jobs toward a more professional role. An example is the changes that have occurred in the occupation of the policeman, with the expectation that applicants will have at least some college. There may yet develop a change of direction, but through 1984 there has been an ever larger share of a continuously growing work force in professional and managerial posts.

Another concern has been that the increasingly technological nature of many professional jobs may begin to restrict access except to a narrow elite. To date, however, except for the difficulty certain minorities have had in gaining adequate preparation for programs in science and engineering, access to the professions has not been restricted. On the contrary, more Americans than ever who are past the traditional college age are taking advantage of the openness of American higher education to sort themselves into the professional class. The enormous flexibility of the American system of higher education seems to have averted any major dislocations despite the magnitude of the changes occurring.

The question, then, is whether the multiple effects of international competition and technology will some time in the future reverse the post–World War II pattern of job growth and professionalization. Under any likely circumstances, the opportunities available to college graduates will be different, and better, in the 1990s than they were in the 1970s.[34] As

24

Charts 2 and 3 show, the massive increase in those graduating from college in the 1960s and 1970s simply overwhelmed the job market despite its remarkable growth in new jobs and the even more remarkable growth in the share of all jobs that are professional. The reverse will happen in the 1990s even with the most optimistic estimates of how many of each age cohort gain college degrees, with the most conservative estimates of job growth, and even assuming no further growth in the professionalization of the work force. The opportunities ahead for college graduates will improve simply because there will be fewer of them.

Enthusiasm for this development should not ignore a central point: the primary purpose of American higher education is not to prepare graduates for specific jobs. The purposes of a college education are broader than the provision of the skills necessary to gain an initial job. The central issue should not be lost in the technicalities of the argument. The shape of the work force will be determined by the collective decisions made about the American economy—decisions that depend on whether the managers, professionals, workers, and public servants feel empowered or feel over-whelmed; whether the new technologies are used in ways that enhance or diminish the role of the individual. Attempts at detailed manpower planning have always fared poorly, yet the skills necessary to run the economy have always been available. The nature of American society has always allowed room for multiple chances for an education and for many paths to advancement or self-realization. One goal of higher education must be to help future graduates develop the knowledge, intellectual capacities, motivation, and values so that each feels confident enough to help create his or her own opportunities.

CAN THE UNITED STATES BOTH COMPETE AND COOPERATE?

It would be easy to read the preceding argument as a call for U.S. leadership in all-out economic competition. Such a course, untempered by other public policy concerns, would, in the long run, be self-defeating. Over its two hundred years of existence, the United States has traditionally argued for competition that is both open and mitigated by larger goals.

CHART 3

AVAILABLE PROFESSIONAL AND MANAGERIAL JOBS
AND EARNED BACCALAUREATE DEGREES, 1960–1984

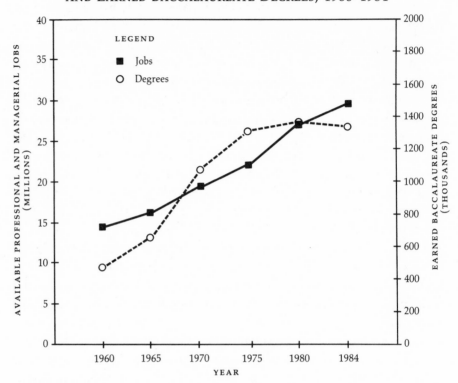

SOURCE: Professional and managerial jobs provided by the Bureau of Labor Statistics.

Baccalaureate Degrees come from American Council on Education. *Fact Book on Higher Education, 1981-1982* (New York: Collier Macmillan, 1982), Table 146. Figures after 1979 are projections.

Now that the international competition is intensifying, there are two dangers that must be addressed lest the process damage the world. The first danger is that the power of technology will simply allow the rich, albeit a larger group of those who are rich, to get richer. The second is that more competition based on technology will lead the major industrialized nations to a form of cutthroat competition that undermines open sharing of the fruits of economic development.

Viewed broadly, the increase in competition, particularly technological competition, has already provided some important advantages to the world—new and better products, greater productivity, and a spreading base of wealth across the world. For the future, much depends on how countries choose to use their technological skills, whether they choose to both improve their own capacity to compete, and their willingness to share the benefits. Over the postwar period, the United States has a record of doing both.[35]

Perhaps the most striking example has been the willingness to share agricultural technology. Despite the dependence of the United States on agricultural products for its balance of trade (in 1980, the United States exported $40 billion of agricultural products, almost 20 percent of total exports, making the U.S. the world's largest food supplier), a major effort has been mounted to help other countries. Many of these were customers of the United States.[36] Some have advanced enough to become exporters themselves and thereby competitors with the U.S.[37] The "Green Revolution" included programs of foundations (particularly Rockefeller), the U.S. Agency for International Development, the involvement of American universities, as well as the commercial efforts of American corporations selling seed, fertilizer, and other agriculture products. The results have been remarkable.

The other major example has been the American investment in research in the health sciences. It took over 50 years for international cooperation in health care to develop. The impetus and major funding on the program side was (and continues to be) from the United States. In terms of research, America devotes a far greater percentage of its total research and development dollars to health and health sciences than other developed countries.[38] The National Institutes of Health even fund some medical research projects in other countries. Some of this cooperation leads to commercial ends, as has been true with biotechnology, but most of it simply helps improve health care throughout the world.

There is always the danger that the willingness to share will be undercut by the pressures of competition. In any competition, there is pressure to break or rewrite the rules. There are constant demands to close borders to imports, to penalize imports by tariffs or restrictions, to restrict the open flow of research information, or even, as has been seen recently, to utilize technological espionage.[39] Here again, the quality of American leadership will be critical.

THE NEW CHALLENGE FOR HIGHER EDUCATION

The economic times have changed. Ours is a more technological, more international, but most of all more dynamic world. This country's ability to compete and to lead is dependent on the nature and quality of higher education. An understanding of technology is important to graduates, but so is the capacity to take initiative, to be creative, to understand the international nature of the world, and to comprehend the need to both compete and cooperate. In preparing for the future, it is important to see that the rate of growth of jobs and the growth in the share of those jobs that are professional and managerial have been unique to the U.S. We have gained both absolutely and relatively by our leadership in technological entrepreneurship. Yet our situation should be kept in perspective. We cannot be either Luddites or Technocrats. There are formidable tasks ahead.

At the same time, scholarship and research must be vigorously advanced. Federal support for university-based research must be strengthened and our centers of excellence must be given new equipment and facilities for the advancement of their work. The program implications of these goals will be described later in this report.

To meet this challenge, higher education has a crucial role to play. The nation's campuses must not only be places where the tradition is honored and the culture preserved, but where students are educated for creative thinking, as well. Classrooms must be places where new ideas and self-confidence are encouraged.

While the subject of the debate is the American economy, the larger concern is the quality of America's place in the world. At issue is whether the United States will move ahead in a sensitive role of leadership or begin a graceful retreat from the global social and political and economic

28

issues we confront; whether we remain a source of new ideas and new opportunities or allow a climate of bureaucracy and cynicism to settle in; and whether the United States can lead in the most profound sense—helping this country and others to a better world—or focus only on immediate economic self-interest.

To succeed in the fullest sense, the graduates of American colleges and universities must see themselves as able to help shape the world in which they live and not simply as living in a world to which they must adapt. In the discussion of the role of higher education, much of the focus until now has been on the need for greater expertise but it is clear that technical expertise alone is not enough. The graduates of American colleges and universities must be more entrepreneurial, more creative, more flexible, and they must be more internationally minded.

In the days ahead, higher education must not only contribute research, technology, and able graduates, but an enlightened and progressive atmosphere as well. Colleges and universities have a major role in developing the new civic responsibilities tomorrow's citizens must assume.

CHAPTER III

The New Politics: Civic Involvement in an Age of Self-interest

BEYOND the economic agenda, there is a more fundamental challenge to higher education and the nation. There is today a dangerous growing mismatch between the country's urgent need for civic mindedness and the parochial attitudes of its citizens. The intense demand for economic renewal or the even more pressing need for social and political renewal require a far greater sense of public purpose. Yet, in the face of the growing complexity and danger in the problems facing American society, there are clear signs that self-interest is undermining public interest.

A tension always exists between the centripetal forces of public interest and the centrifugal forces of individual interest. There are times, however, when individuals must take a broader and longer view in order to exercise power for the common good. The wise exercise of this power, the founding fathers argued, depends upon the education of the public.[1] If there is a crisis in education in the United States today, it is less that test scores have declined than it is that we have failed to provide the education for citizenship that is still the most significant responsibility of the nation's schools and colleges.

CIVIC INVOLVEMENT: THE NEW IMPERATIVE

The United States faces extraordinarily complex issues that demand of society a greater capacity for civic integration than ever before:

Peace in the face of the proliferation of nuclear arms

Protection from toxic wastes

31

Effective integration of the growing minority populations

Controls for genetic engineering

Economic stability without stagnation, inflation, or poverty

Reduction of crime, drug use, and violence

Effective cooperation among increasingly interconnected nations.

The list grows constantly as new issues are added each year and few are resolved.[2] All share a number of common characteristics: a complexity that grows with time and a long-term nature; no obvious or simple solution; a need for common action; and an international dimension— none can be solved within this country alone. The attempt to solve any of these problems requires, in the words of David Mathews, "a sense of shared objectives, common aspirations, and elemental cohesion."[3]

Traditionally, this country has looked toward education for building a sense of elemental cohesion. Education is an important factor in political involvement; according to some, it is the most important factor.[4] The Carnegie Foundation's earlier report, *Higher Learning in the Nation's Service*, argued, "This nation began with a conviction, at once deceptively simple and profound, that, for democracy to work, education is essential. When Thomas Jefferson was asked if mass opinion could be trusted, he responded, 'I know of no safe depository of the ultimate powers of society but the people themselves. And if we think them not enlightened enough to exercise their control with a wholesome discretion, the remedy is not to take it from them, but to inform their discretion.' "[5] The advancement of civic learning, therefore, must become higher education's most central goal.[6]

THE CHANGING POLITY

As the complexity of issues has increased, the burden on education also has increased. Not only are social problems more complex, but many of the changes in society have made the process of civic education far more difficult.

One change results from the shifting structure of the family.[7] Traditionally, the family has been the major institution that, along with the schools, is expected to provide education for civic responsibility. Not only does the family play a critical role directly in the development of values of the young, but it is the most influential factor in their educational aspirations.[8]

Many changes in family structure, the increase in parents who both work, for example, seem to have few measurable effects on the intellectual or personal development of children. However, the influence of single-parent families does have an effect. Too much of the effort to measure such impact has been focused on test scores. While children in single-parent families appear to develop, in terms of test scores, at the same rate as children in two-parent families, they are less likely to grow up with a socialization toward civic responsibility or with a strong sense of self-esteem. They are also less likely to finish high school or to enter college.[9] They are not only less likely to attend college, when they do attend they are also less likely to be affected positively in terms of their sense of responsibility. The significance of all this lies in the fact that the number of single-parent families is growing rapidly, from 9 percent of all families with children in 1960 to 21 percent in 1982. Almost one-fourth of all young children and, of most concern, over one-half of all black children now live in single-parent families.[10]

A second social change of great significance in the nation is the sharp increase in those immigrating to the United States. Legal immigration has more than doubled since 1950, to over 600,000 per year. Illegal immigration adds several hundred thousand more each year.[11] This requires the civic education of large numbers of people from a diverse array of cultures, many of whom do not share a similar tradition of civic involvement.

Both of these changes are complicated by the powerful role of the media, particularly television. While the influence of television on the attitudes of the young is still unclear, there is no question that its power to shape the culture is considerable. By the time the typical student graduates from high school, he or she has spent more hours with television (15,000) than with teachers (12,000). Television's ability to appear credible and its tendency to oversimplify require schools and colleges to provide a more effective liberal education for citizens, particularly in analytic and critical thinking skills. The most important point is not, however, what a child experiences while in front of the television set, but what he or she does *not* experience, for, increasingly, the child is cast as an observer rather than a participant in life's events. "Civilization," as one scholar put it, "has become a spectator sport to be watched at 6:00 P.M."[12]

All of these—the changing structure of the family, the rise in immigration, and the influence of television increase the burden on the schools and colleges to educate for civic understanding. And yet, ironically, while the need to strengthen social integration is increasing, many indicators point to a fragmenting of the body politic and a growing sense of alienation and cynicism.[13]

One troubling measure is the decline in trust in our governmental system. For the whole of the post–World War II period, and particularly since 1970, skepticism about government at all levels has been growing. The assumptions take many forms: "The government is run for the benefit of a few big interests"; "quite a few of the people running the government are a little crooked"; "the government wastes a lot of money"; "politicians are crooked"; "politics is so complicated that a person like me can't really understand what is going on"; "people we elect lose touch quickly; they are interested in votes but not opinions." The result is the same: a steady rise in skepticism and mistrust.[14]

One longitudinal survey measuring "Trust in Government" yields a distressing report that those who believe the government can be trusted to do the right thing "only some or none of the time" has doubled to 54 percent over twenty years. A survey by the Roper Organization showed that the number of people who feel that "things in this country are pretty seriously on the wrong track" now totals over 50 percent.[15] Half of all Americans no longer believe that the important national problems can be solved through the traditional political process.[16] Yet more troubling, this dissatisfaction with public life is not just a reflection of personal dissatisfaction. The same respondents were, in general, satisfied with the way things are going in their personal lives.

During the same period, there has been a continuing decline in the public's belief in other institutions of society—in business, where favorable ratings in the 1960s became unfavorable by the late 1970s; in labor unions and particularly labor leaders; in the press; in medicine; in the military; even in organized religion and education.[17] Perhaps most disconcerting is the decline in the public's belief in itself, in the ability of any one citizen to make a difference, or in the ability of the collective voice to be heard.[18]

These changes in belief or trust in our most basic institutions have been accompanied by action—or nonaction—by the people. While the public continues to believe that voting is important, actual voting has declined in every presidential election for the last twenty years, and the decline appears to be directly related to the rise in cynicism. In 1960, 63 percent of those eligible voted. In 1980, 52 percent voted for the president, while only 38 percent voted for members of the House of Representatives.[19] The presidential vote that year was 26.8 percent Republican and 21.6 percent Democrat; 47.5 percent did not vote.

One would have expected a *rise* in those voting as a result of the sharp rise in the educational level of the citizenry. Historically, both belief in the system of government and actual voting have been positively correlated with the level of education.[20] And yet, in 1984, despite a massive registration campaign by both parties, the estimates are that the share of those eligible who voted rose by only a fraction of 1 percent and the share of those registered who actually voted continued its 24-year decline.[21]

Another change has been the shift in the nature of political participation. Most estimates are that participation has increased, but the form has changed. The shift in political participation is from involvement in broader organizations to those with more narrow and special interests.[22] In an important sense, special interest groups are a means of educating the public and encouraging its involvement. New political organizations, often with remarkable skill and determination, abound—to stop the spread of nuclear power, to save the shoreline, to end the dumping of hazardous wastes. As laudable as these goals are, they are most often negative (for example, to stop harmful exploitation of one group by another) and of limited or specific focus (what is now called single-issue politics).[23] Such interests are essential—but not sufficient.

This country is distinguished by the sheer scale of what is undertaken on a voluntary basis and the fact that almost every segment of society, not just political life, is affected by public service organizations.[24] It is easy to understand how self-interest can provide the motivation for the devotion of time and energy to an interest group; it is more remarkable that there are so many voluntary organizations with broader, positive goals as diverse as those of The United Negro College Fund, Common Cause, the hundreds of major philanthropic foundations, or the Rotary Clubs.[25]

For a democracy to function, the role of volunteerism is absolutely crucial. Is the country pulling together or pulling apart? Is the spirit of reform and change keeping a balance between stopping what is unwanted and starting what is needed? As political action committees have grown (doubling the amount of funds they dispense in the last five years), as other special interest groups grow in numbers and in stridency, has the interest of the whole been lost in the battles over specific interests? Has the advent of the modern media and the widespread acceptance of litigation as a political tool made the interest of the whole impossible to reach? To some degree, the appeal of special interests is that they serve as an antidote to the fact that the "system" is so complex and entrenched that it seems no longer responsive to the people.[26] The irony is that the continued growth of such groups leads to what John Gardner has called the "paralysis of polarization,"[27] deepening the general sense of powerlessness.

THE CHANGING COLLEGE STUDENT

How much have these trends toward self-centeredness and isolation been reflected in the attitudes of the freshmen coming to higher education? Unfortunately, the evidence is clear. For fifteen years, there has been a continuing change in the knowledge and attitudes of incoming freshmen. For one thing, freshmen appear to know steadily less about the nature of the American political system. They are more confused about both factual information and the purposes of the system, about such issues as the rights of others, or the role of the courts.

Still more troubling is the transformation of student attitudes toward

36

their personal responsibilities. The annual ACE-UCLA surveys show a fifteen-year decline in expectation of participation in the political life of the country, in any form of altruism, or of concern for the interests of others. Over the same time, there has been a steady rise in student interest in those values associated with money, status, and power. The values showing the greatest increases since 1972 are: 1) being very well-off financially, 2) being an authority, 3) having administrative responsibility for others, and 4) obtaining recognition. The values which show the largest decline are: 1) developing a philosophy of life, 2) participating in community affairs, 3) cleaning up the environment, and 4) promoting racial understanding.[28]

How effectively has higher education overcome these attitudes? Historically, college seniors have shown substantial gains in their sense of civic responsibility compared to freshmen. The college years are a period of personal growth, including a growth in responsibility and awareness of the interests of others. For the traditional student it is usually the first experience of being away from home and responsible for oneself as well as the first exposure to voting.

However, recent studies have raised disturbing questions about the continuing ability of colleges to broaden the student view. While there still appear to be slight gains in the rate at which seniors vote, write to an office holder, participate in a partisan political effort, or undertake community service, their attitudes toward the political system or toward public interest versus self-interest closely resemble those of freshmen. Only about 31 percent of the freshmen men and 27 percent of the women expressed a strong desire to influence political structures and decisions, which improved slightly for senior men (31 percent) and actually declined for senior women (24 percent). In addition, such attitudes also seem to hold for recent graduates.[29]

Among college students, there has been a trend toward more intense focus on careers, a shift in enrollment toward those professions of high status and income, a shift away from the human services professions and the liberal arts. Education for the professions is a valued role of higher education, but the emphasis both students and institutions place on narrow

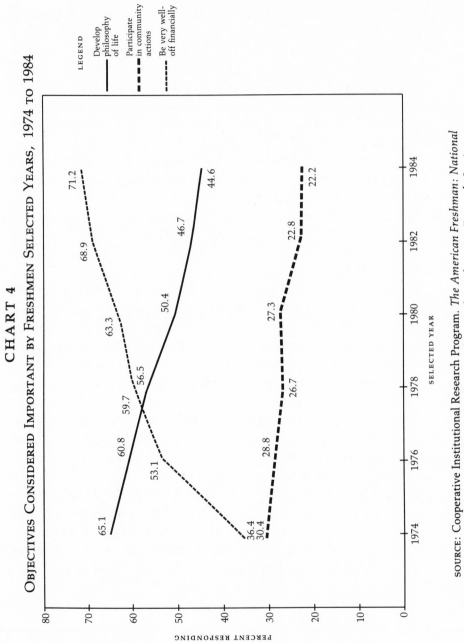

CHART 4

OBJECTIVES CONSIDERED IMPORTANT BY FRESHMEN SELECTED YEARS, 1974 TO 1984

LEGEND

Develop
philosophy
of life

Participate
in community
actions

Be very well-
off financially

PERCENT RESPONDING

SELECTED YEAR

SOURCE: Cooperative Institutional Research Program. *The American Freshman: National Norms, Fall 1974-1984.* (Los Angeles: Higher Education Research Institute, U.C.L.A., 1974-1984.)

vocationalism and narrow self-interest at the expense of the development of a broader civic view is a matter of concern.[30]

A recent Carnegie Foundation survey of student personnel officers at colleges and universities described the change in students from 1969–70 to 1977–78 as more career-oriented, better-groomed, more concerned with material success, more concerned with self, and more practical. Students were also less radical, less activist, and less hostile.[31] To some degree, this may be simply a process of "sorting out" values.[32] Perhaps it is partly a return to normality after a tumultuous period. Certainly such characteristics as being "well-groomed" may be considered an advantage.[33] Being less interested in the affairs of the nation is surely a disadvantage. A new survey by The Carnegie Foundation for a report soon to be released on the undergraduate experience confirms the continuing trend toward self-interest and away from a sense of broader responsibility.

There is a tendency within higher education to worry about these changes in students, but to feel that not much can be done, that one can only wait for another swing of the pendulum. This is an abdication of responsibility.[34] There is, in fact, a sizable task ahead for higher education in the civic education of its graduates. Such education must encourage a knowledge of how government works, a political awareness, as well as a willingness to take part and a scholarly skepticism but not cynicism, an awareness of the differing interests of those who share this world, and a general idealism, a broader view.

The college experience should also develop within each student a sense of country and community service and a desire to help others. Patriotism in the best sense means a willingness to believe in and work for improvements in the country. This must not be a welcome byproduct of a college education, but a central, urgent, and conscious purpose.

During this last academic year, a number of colleges and universities have reported a renewed interest on the part of many students in community service. Those that have given new visibility to internship programs or other service opportunities have seen a surge in applications. Even the increased scope of student protests can be seen as a turn away from self-interest. Here, then, is a window of opportunity when the awakening concern of students can be matched with the need to restore education for citizenship to its primary role.

We would do well to remind ourselves of the principles put forward two centuries ago in the Charter of the University of Georgia:

> As it is the distinguishing happiness of free governments that civil order should be the result of choice and not necessity, and the common wishes of the people become the laws of the land, then public prosperity and even existence very much depends upon suitably forming the minds and morals of their citizens.[35]

SECTION TWO

CHAPTER IV

The Supply of Technical Expertise

T HE MOST COMMONLY EXPRESSED CONCERN about higher education over the last several years is that it may not graduate enough engineers and computer scientists to meet the demands of the new high technology economy.

A *U.S. News and World Report* editorial argued: "We should be taking notice of the near-disastrous shortage of engineers in the country. . . . The engineering lag is related to a long-recognized falloff in U.S. research while Japan, West Germany and France scored gains based on increased effort in the field."[1] The American Council on Education's Business-Higher Education Forum reported: "Unless the clear inadequacy of the United States engineering manpower and education system is rectified, it jeopardizes the future competitiveness of our nation's technologically-based industries and defense."[2] As noted in Chapter II, essentially every state has developed a plan for economic revitalization, and the urgency of expanding engineering and computer science in the universities is a recurring theme.

Much of this concern seems misdirected. A recent report of The National Research Council, *International Competition in Advanced Technology: Decisions for America*, makes a more measured argument focused on the shortage of faculty. "Problems in training future scientists and engineers are apparent in U.S. engineering education. . . . The large number of unfilled engineering faculty positions . . . spells serious trouble for the quality of engineering education, particularly because undergraduate enrollments are at an all-time high."[3]

The focus is on four issues:

The need for more engineers and computer scientists

The low share of Ph.D. candidates in engineering who are U.S. citizens

The shortage of faculty in these fields

The quality of education being provided because of limitations of staff and facilities.

Quality of education is the most significant problem, but not in the sense that the traditional expertise of the graduates of American colleges and universities is wanting. Rather, it is a question of more fundamental attributes—the capacity to innovate, the willingness to take risks and to pioneer, the acceptance of personal responsibility for the functioning of the community.

ENROLLMENT AND GRADUATION RATES OF ENGINEERS AND COMPUTER SCIENTISTS

In the 1970s, undergraduate engineering enrollment was declining. Engineering undergraduate enrollment reached a nadir in 1973–74 at 187,000.[4] Four years later, the number of bachelor's degrees awarded hit bottom at 38,000.[5] Then, enrollments began to grow at a phenomenal pace. By 1981, enrollments were up by 107 percent over the 1973 figures and the number of degrees earned increased by 55 percent—both at all-time highs.[6] Because of the enrollment growth, the number of degrees granted also will continue to grow.

Enrollments in computer science at the bachelor's level show a roughly similar picture with two differences. There was no decline in the early 1970s because the field was so new, and the jump in enrollments and degrees granted has been even more rapid. In 1972, the number of bachelor's degrees granted in computer science was 359; by 1983 it had reached 2,643.[7] The number of computer courses being taught to nonmajors appears to have grown even faster.

These increases only partially reflect the general rise in college enrollments over this period. Primarily, they represent a major shift in the career interests of students. Some of them, however, represent the grow-

44

ing number of women and Asian Americans entering technical fields. Between 1970 and 1983, the proportion of bachelor's degrees in engineering held by women increased from less than 1 to over 13 percent.[8] An astonishing 9.3 percent of engineering Ph.D.s awarded in 1982 went to Asian Americans.[9]

The gross underrepresentation of blacks and Hispanics, currently 20 percent of all 18-year-olds, in engineering and computer science is disturbing.[10] Fortunately, there has been a slow but steady growth recently as joint university-industry programs have reached into the high schools and junior high schools to encourage science and mathematics preparation. (See Chapter VII.)

The problem is far worse at the doctoral level, where blacks made up only 1 percent, and Hispanics only 1.2 percent of full-time graduate students in doctorate-granting institutions in 1982.[11] Between 1975 and 1982, only four blacks and four Hispanics received doctorates in computer science.[12]

Clearly, enrollments in engineering and computer science are up sharply, but the question of *who* enters these fields remains a major problem.

THE EQUILIBRIUM BETWEEN SUPPLY AND DEMAND

Several major studies in the last few years have attempted to assess the balance between supply and demand.[13] Since engineers frequently move to careers in management, sales, government, or a dozen other fields, estimating demand is approximate at best. It is further complicated by the tendency of large employers, particularly defense contractors, to "stockpile" engineers if they feel a shortage is likely and to cut back when times are slow. This, plus the cyclical media reports of either "shortage" or "glut" has created an undulating enrollment pattern that is unique to this major. Actual employment has been far more steady.

In 1980, the National Science Foundation and the Department of Education jointly studied the demand for science and engineering graduates in this decade. They concluded that ". . . the supply of scientists and

45

engineers at all degree levels will likely be more than adequate to meet demands in all fields except the computer profession, statistics, and some fields of engineering, such as aeronautical and industrial. . . ." They also reported that there was and would continue to be an undersupply of Ph.Ds, but were uncertain whether the ". . . supply of engineers will exceed the demand, or whether there will be shortages in at least some engineering disciplines."[14] This reinforces, we believe, the point that supply and demand are in a rough balance.

The current supply of graduates is somewhat distorted by students' strong desire to cluster in two fields: electrical engineering and various computer options. The Massachusetts Institute of Technology, for example, found that over half of its freshmen in 1983 wanted to select these two fields.[15] The result is that student/faculty ratios have been particularly severe in these areas. In terms of employment this distortion is not severe because many jobs are suitable for an engineer or a scientist from any of a number of disciplines. Most graduates show a remarkable ability to shift and adapt.

The emerging trends are partly obscured by effects of the recession. One effect is slower enrollment increases. The rate of growth has declined each year since 1980.[16] A second effect is a softening of the market as seen by college placement offices. Uncertainty about jobs also surrounds prospects for the defense build-up. It may be that as the number of weapons systems now under construction move toward the later stages of development there will be a new burst of demand for technical manpower.[17] This would be the case particularly if the Strategic Defense Initiative (Star Wars) were to reach the size envisioned by the administration.

The number of engineering and computer science graduates are at an all time high. Despite continuing media predictions of a manpower "shortage" in engineering and computer science fields enrollments are not likely to increase much more. Moreover, a decrease in 18-year-olds each year is now anticipated, and it is likely that some sort of natural upper limit on the share of all students interested in engineering has been reached.

The supply and demand of engineers, meanwhile, appears to be in a rough balance, close enough for the traditional flexibility of the marketplace to resolve short-term shortages. We have been unable to find a field in which a shortage of technically trained personnel has seriously impaired industry's ability to turn out new products.

THE AVAILABILITY OF PH.DS

While there has been a tendency to talk in terms of falling numbers of Ph.Ds in engineering, the number of degrees granted in the field actually bottomed out in 1978 at 2,423. Each year since then the number has increased. In 1982, 2,644 Ph.Ds were granted in engineering.[18]

However, it must also be noted that the share of all Ph.D. candidates who are foreign nationals also has been rising, but the number of U.S. nationals receiving a Ph.D. has been roughly level. In 1982, the share of Ph.D. candidates in engineering who were foreign nationals reached 50 percent, but perhaps as many as half of them will remain in the United States after receiving their degree.

In computer science, the number of Ph.D. degrees granted has been static and the share of foreign recipients as high as in engineering. To a certain extent, we have been relying on the importation of graduate students to meet the demands of our technological economy. We also have been "re-exporting" the remainder overseas, where they make their skills and information available to our international economic competitors. This is offset, perhaps, by their better understanding of the country that gave them advanced education.

The shortage of Ph.D. degree holders in both engineering and computer science (Table 3) shows up most noticeably in the difficulty of recruiting faculty.

The number of open faculty positions in engineering has been declining (Table 4). While 9.8 percent, or even 8.5 percent, is a large number of open positions, particularly when enrollment is at an all-time high, it should be noted that since 1982 the situation has been slowly improving for engineering. Perhaps most surprising, the well-publicized loss of engineering faculty to industry and government is more than compensated for by the number of Ph.Ds in engineering leaving industry and government to join universities.

47

TABLE 3

PH.D. DEGREES IN COMPUTER SCIENCE

	1975	1976	1977	1978	1979	1980	1981	1982
Citizens	60	65	75	40	36	28	29	21
Non-Citizens	42	51	48	36	41	34	41	50

SOURCE: *Science and Engineering Doctorates 1960–82*, Washington, D.C., National Science Foundation, 1983, Table 2.

TABLE 4

PERCENT AUTHORIZED FACULTY POSITIONS UNFILLED

	1980	1981	1982	1983
Engineering	9.8	9.0	7.9	8.5
Computer Science	N/A	17.0	16.8	15.8

SOURCE: John Geils, "The Faculty Shortage: Review of the 1981 AAES/ASEE Survey," *Engineering Education*, November 1982, for years 1980 and 1981, and "The Faculty Shortage: 1982 Survey," *Engineering Education*, October 1983, for the year 1982. Paul Doigan, "ASEE Survey of Engineering Faculty and Graduate Students, Fall 1983," *Engineering Education*, October 1984, pp. 50–59, for the year 1983.

In computer science, a somewhat more severe but still slightly improving picture of faculty shortage has emerged.

The flood of new enrollments in the 1980s found the universities unprepared in terms of faculty, laboratory space, and instrumentation. One result has been a sharp increase in the student/faculty ratio and—by almost half—in the average class size, even at the better engineering schools.

The situation is gradually easing as faculty slots are filled. But universities, struggling to find enough candidates for existing positions, fear-

TABLE 5

CHANGE IN SIZE OF SECTION ENROLLMENTS
OF STUDENTS PER COURSE, 1977 AND 1982

| | 'TYPICAL CASE' CLASS SIZE | | | |
| | 1977 | | 1982 | |
	AVERAGE–HIGH		AVERAGE–HIGH	
Senior Level Professional	23	50	36	185
Senior Level Design	22	53	32	80
Senior Level Project	16	100	23	120
Junior/Senior Laboratory	17	70	24	100

SOURCE: John Geils, "The Faculty Shortage: 1982 Survey" *Engineering Education*, October 1983, p. 53.

ful of another down-swing in engineering enrollments, and hard-pressed to hold down expenses, are reluctant to add permanent staff.

The availability of state-of-the-art instrumentation, particularly for the use of undergraduate students, is an urgent problem. Students need direct, hands-on experience with such equipment as computer-assisted design systems or modern machine tools. One role graduates play is to carry to their new employers knowledge of the latest techniques as well as a willingness to adapt new techniques to their jobs. Each year this role becomes more difficult as undergraduate laboratories fall further behind the times. (See Chapter XI.)

The data indicate that there is not now, nor is there likely to be in the immediate future, a serious shortage of engineers or computer scientists. There *is* a shortage of Ph.Ds and consequently of faculty in these fields, but it could not be called a crisis. Contrary to the widespread assumption, the shortage of faculty is slowly being corrected. Action can and should be taken, however, to increase the number of U.S. citizens in these graduate programs. Action also must be taken to improve black and Hispanic enrollments. Even in technical fields a quality education must develop the capacities of creativity and prudent risk taking.[19] Weakness in these dimensions is where the greater risk to American economic and social renewal lies, not with any potential shortage of technical expertise.

CHAPTER V

Education for Creativity, Risk Taking, and Civic Involvement

M UCH OF THE ATTENTION of policy makers—and students—focuses on technical expertise necessary for today's careers. Such expertise is essential for the successful functioning of society, but, as we have seen, American higher education will, with continued support, provide that expertise in the depth and diversity required. More problematic is whether graduates will have those capacities beyond technical expertise, or even beyond intellectual skills, that are now critical—the ability to be creative, the willingness to take risks, and the desire to participate constructively in the civic affairs of the country.

Higher education in the United States is not less effective than elsewhere in developing these traits. On the contrary, compared with other countries, the United States system of higher education is more flexible, more accessible to the new ideas of faculty and students, and more influenced by the forces changing society. Compared with their counterparts in other countries, American students are more involved and responsible. They pay for a large share of their college costs, make decisions about their programs of study, and participate in extracurricular activities. Despite this, higher education in this country falls far short of what it can and must do to give students the capacities urgently needed for leadership in the 1990s.

For the remainder of the 1980s and beyond, the capacity for entrepreneurial activity cannot be a valued trait admired in only those individuals who seem to be naturally endowed with it. We need more than a few Henry Fords or Martin Luther Kings. We need to have the qualities they

51

embodied disseminated as widely and as deeply as possible throughout society. In international relations, in education, in local government, people are needed who are willing to explore new avenues and consider new approaches.[1]

If American industry is to be competitive in an increasingly interdependent changing world, its leaders must do more than grudgingly give ground to change only as necessary. Industry must move toward change, must see change as opportunity, challenge, excitement. It must be a society in which employers seek out the creative rather than the submissive to hire.

In this sense, change is as much social as technical. Can the leaders of the automobile industry accept women in management with as much enthusiasm as they have front-wheel drive? Can industry grasp the need to be responsible about toxic wastes? Can traditional firms move toward automation and computing? Can labor leaders understand the need to embrace the new forms of industrial organization that are emerging? Can a bank in Ohio or a police department in Texas grasp the newly international nature of today's world?

Clearly, it also is important to develop a sense of what we must conserve. Change only for the sake of change will lead only to faddishness or, worse, to dangers such as those inherent in unrestrained technology. The willingness to face change must therefore be informed and reinforced by a truly liberal education that develops a historical sense and the capacity to think critically. To educate future leaders who are ignorant of the past is a recipe for disaster. The times demand, in Roy Heath's term, "reasonable adventurers."[2]

ENCOURAGING CREATIVITY

Education, particularly higher education, plays a central role in encouraging—or stifling—a student's creativity. By *creativity* we mean the ability to create new concepts, to integrate differing forms of knowledge and experience in order to reach new understandings, and to be receptive to change. It has many forms, including:

52

Scientific creativity—the ability to conduct research and develop new knowledge in all fields

Technological creativity—the skill to utilize available information in new ways

Organizational creativity—the talent to form new human networks to better solve problems

Artistic creativity—the capacity to express personal insights and conceptions through art and literature.

Despite the growing body of research focused on creativity, the mental processes involved in the creative solution of problems or in the development of novel or original products are still unclear.[3] There are character traits that researchers agree are closely associated with creative personalities including independence of mind, desire for autonomy, self-directed acceptance of a task coupled with a sense of challenge, ability to connect diverse ideas to identified problems, and the capacity to act.

Studies of the upbringing of creative scientists show a childhood environment that valued independence of mind and intellectual activities, and one that encouraged imagination in problem solving.[4] Motivation and its companion, persistence, play key roles. That these are not words heard on campus everyday underscores our concern about the nature of the current educational debate.

Creative talent must be matched to willingness to act.[5] If the fear of change overwhelms the creative instinct, it is of little use. Therefore, the encouragement of the capacity to take risks intelligently is also central. At the very least, higher education should not teach students to avoid taking appropriate risks.

Can creativity be developed? Much depends on whether it is inherent or whether it can be nurtured. Available research finds that individuals vary considerably in their ability to be creative—in part due to their inherent capacity and in part due to their past environment. At the same time, each individual has a range of creative potential within which he or she can be encouraged or inhibited by the environment, including the environment represented by education. The experiences within higher education often are particularly significant. This argues for concern about both admissions practices and particularly about the nature of the educational experience.

THE STIFLING OF CREATIVITY

Despite the advantage that American higher education has over other systems of higher education, it far too often stifles the inherent creativity of the student. Students too frequently sit passively in class, take safe courses, are discouraged from risky or interdisciplinary research projects, and are discouraged from challenging the ideas presented to them.

We now know that the development of creativity in the student is discouraged by fear of censure, or distrust, or fear of failure; a stifling atmosphere; attempts to closely control behavior and thinking; restricted communication; the assumption, in the classroom and in texts, that there is one right answer to every problem; and a passive role.[6] Creativity and independence of mind are encouraged when students learn to question; select projects or research topics themselves (within whatever framework is necessary); and learn how concepts are related.[7]

The values teachers hold, and their ability to act as role models, also seem to play an important role in producing creative students. There is strong evidence that working closely with teachers who are themselves creative, or who value creativity and the character traits associated with it, tends to reproduce those characteristics in students.[8] Among other things, students are less likely to be stifled by those who encourage questioning and are not threatened by inquiring students.

Faculty members, judged by their peers to be creative, describe their own experience in graduate school compared to their colleagues in the following terms:

> Graduate instructors were less "authoritarian." Both competition and cooperation were encouraged.
>
> Skepticism and inquisitiveness were encouraged.
>
> Research involved more than normal independence and was not closely supervised.

54

They felt that they had more freedom of choice in regard to courses and research areas.[9]

In summary, their's was a less structured, more self-directed experience than that of the less creative control group.

As might be expected, a number of institutions have experimented with courses designed to teach creative problem solving.[10] Such courses have provoked a controversy as to whether it is possible for learning creativity to stand alone or whether it must be associated with learning a body of knowledge in a given field.[11] There is a danger, however, that students will be asked to spend 17 years accumulating a knowledge base before being asked to try applying that knowledge in creative ways. Clearly the student must learn both in parallel and must learn from more than just the curriculum, including experience in campus activities, off-campus internships, and in work experience.[12] A major task for American higher education is to change the relationship between faculty and student so as to encourage creative and challenging thought and to stop stifling these characteristics.

CREATIVITY AND ADMISSION TO SELECTIVE PROGRAMS

An additional question is whether grades or the standardized tests used for college and professional school admissions—SATs, GREs, LSATs, etc.—or other tests which measure *cognitive* abilities also measure *creative potential*. The answer appears to be no. Past a certain necessary minimum level, intelligence tests and grades do not seem to be correlated with creativity or risk taking.[13] Grades do not identify those students able to create novel solutions or those able to demonstrate "higher order" thinking skills.[14]

This point is particularly important at the graduate level. At the undergraduate level grades and test scores often determine who gains admission to selective programs, but able students somehow find their way. At the graduate and professional level, however, the admissions approach has considerable influence on which students enter a particular field. Ph.D.

programs, for example, are expected to produce graduates who will be judged on the basis of their original scholarship. Grades and test scores are not, however, the best evidence that the most creative, innovative, and risk-taking scholars have been selected.[15] The failure of most Ph.Ds to complete any research past their dissertation[16] is in part evidence that the selection process is not optimal. A key leverage point in improving the climate of higher education is to change the selection and experience of graduate students in ways that actively encourage creative thinking and divergent views, for it is from among those students that future faculty will be selected. Of similar importance to the business community is whether the capacity to take risks or to generate new ideas is adequately represented in the admission criteria of graduate programs in business, or to governments in public policy programs.

How can higher education judge in advance an individual's capacity to be creative if scores on traditional tests are not helpful? The traditional approach would be some form of new test. In the last decade, there has been growing interest in tests designed to measure creativity. Among them are the Watson-Glaser Critical Thinking Appraisal and the Cornell Critical Thinking Tests. As the experience with these tests grows, their usefulness increases as well, but there is a good deal of controversy about their validity in their current form.

New work on tests to measure creativity is underway at Educational Testing Service, the Council for Advancement of Experiential Learning (CAEL), and at various universities. Some of that research indicates that it is not only possible to select those who are more prone to be creative, but that students selected on this basis are likely to demonstrate all-around effectiveness.[17]

In the meantime, the most certain method is the examination of past creativity. Schools of fine arts have measured artistic creativity this way for a long time. If the goal of an educational institution is to graduate citizens who can be effective leaders and who can be effective at taking risk and innovating, then a student's prior record of independence of mind, willingness to take risks, and generation of new ideas is significant. It is not as easy as using the SAT, GRE, or LSAT, but it is more meaningful.[18]

56

The importance to the American future of the encouragement of creativity is clear. It is also clear that the colleges and universities can and should make a conscious attempt to structure the students' experiences in ways that enhance their creativity.

EDUCATION FOR CIVIC RESPONSIBILITY

Liberal education has always focused on more than the acquisition of knowledge. In ancient Greece, "liberal education" was for those citizens with the civic responsibility to govern. Its opposite, "servile education," was for those who needed education for their work but who did not share in the responsibility for public affairs.[19] American higher education, from the first, assumed that all of its graduates would participate fully in public affairs as well as in their own careers. Although higher education's commitment to education for civic responsibility remains undiminished, at least in the rhetoric of college catalogues, there has been an erosion in the practice.

Education for public responsibility includes but goes beyond a knowledge of how the system of governance works.[20] It encompasses the sensitive issue of values and, specifically, the value of moving from self-interest to larger-than-self interest. For the first two centuries of American higher education, the development of the character of the student was seen as the central task of the administration and faculty. For the last half century, it has declined in priority.[21] Despite the decline, the concept, as Ernest Boyer and Fred Hechinger argue, remains integral to the expectations of a college education:

> For all the nagging doubts of the contemporary age, the belief persists that the process most capable of holding the intellectual center of society together, preventing it from disintegrating into unconnected splinters, is education. It may not have lived up to this vision of cohesion, but, at its best, the campus is expected to bring together the views and experiences of all its parts, and create something greater than the sum, offering the prospect that personal values will be clarified, and that the channels of our common life will be deepened and renewed.[22]

The importance of universities and colleges in the development of values has grown for two reasons—the decline in the role of family and church, and the larger share of the population who now obtain higher education.[23]

The college years are ones of special significance. Students begin their life away from their families. They begin to vote. It is a time of a shift from the narrowly held views of adolescence to the more reasoned views of adulthood.[24] It is a time when students are led into a larger view of moral problems and decisions, and a time when they learn to move from the abstractions of moral theory to the dilemmas of moral action. The values that are developed at this time in their lives will persist throughout life.[25]

Despite the importance of this period in the student's life, and the concomitant urgency for building a sense of community in a society increasingly pressed by difficult problems (see Chapter III), there is little evidence to indicate that colleges and universities are interested, let alone effective, in encouraging value development. Students seem less and less interested in the civic life and less and less able to mobilize themselves to get involved in public issues.[26] Allan Bloom, after examining the university role in the teaching of values, argues:

> . . . students in our best universities do not believe in anything
> and those universities are doing nothing about it. . . . An easy-
> going American kind of nihilism has descended upon us, a ni-
> hilism without the terror of the abyss. The great questions . . .
> hardly touch the young . . . the universities, which should en-
> courage the quest for the clarification of such questions, are the
> very source of the doctrine which makes that quest appear fu-
> tile.[27]

Why have colleges and universities seemed to abdicate such a central responsibility? Some faculty members and administrators argue that it is the inevitable result of the growth in size of campuses. Size does make the task difficult. A recent Carnegie Foundation survey reinforces earlier findings that students at large universities feel the most isolated and the least involved.[28] Other studies suggest that students at such institutions

58

are substantially less involved in extracurricular activities than students at small colleges.[29] Still, size seems to us only a complication, not a root cause for the lack of value education.

Faculty attitudes are a more significant factor. Many described to us a slow shift in the attitudes of faculty (and administrators) that, over time, has come to treat warily at best and often reject outright the role of higher education in treating values. Many argue that higher education must be concerned with absolute truths and not deal in values. It does teach values, of course. To proclaim to students that the campus is neutral toward all ideas is in itself to propose a profound value. Besides, values are inherent in how the college treats the issue of honesty (prohibiting cheating) or merit (not everyone gets As).

At least one cause of the wariness is the fear that any attempt to address values will gradually slip over into indoctrination. There is a strong fear that an individual faculty member will begin to impose his or her personal ideology.

The logical answer is to draw a careful boundary rather than retreat altogether. It would seem worthwhile to spend as much time on this compelling issue as is spent, say, on the discussion of the academic calendar each year. Harold Shapiro, in an editorial in *Science*, argued that the university already espouses such values as the worth of knowledge, the benefit of fair and open inquiry, respect for other points of view, and the possibility of human progress.[30] To these should be added those values essential to the functioning of a democratic society: the value of personal freedom and the willingness to see the larger interest beyond only immediate self-interest. Without these, neither a free society nor the free university can function.[31]

The most common explanation of the gradual retreat from values is the increased focus on the academic disciplines. As fields become more complex, the temptation rises for faculty to stay within the limits of "factual" knowledge, to see one's task as teaching the methodology of physics, or sociology, and therefore to abdicate responsibility for the whole student. The faculty reward system has come to focus increasingly on publications and research grants.[32] It is expedient to concentrate on what is familiar and real—namely one's research—rather than on the messy, controversial, uncertain, and often unrewarding area of value development.[33] For the last 60 years as well, faculty also have become less involved in extracurricular affairs where values are often transmitted to students. These activities are now the domain of a new breed of professionals, the student affairs officers.

The faculty withdrawal from values was exacerbated by the deep involvement of many faculty in the debates over the morality and politics of the war in Vietnam. The experience left a mixed and often cynical legacy. Many faculty members are inclined toward skepticism about their role in imposing values on the young and instead seek refuge in the argument that values are each individual's own responsibility.[34]

Is the situation hopeless? Probably not. In fact, there seems to be a slowly emerging interest in addressing values once again. A group of universities and colleges has begun an effort to encourage students to undertake public service before, during, or after their college experience. Their assumption is that engagement in service to the community helps develop a fuller understanding of both the nature of American society and each citizen's responsibility. They have found an excellent response. Since 1970, 12,000 courses explicitly designed to explore practical moral questions have come into existence.[35] In light of the evidence available (see Chapter III), it is hard to argue that students are turning sharply toward a public interest, but it does seem as if there is now a moment in which the issue can again be addressed. How then can colleges and universities, with due regard for the risks of indoctrination that must be avoided, move toward the restoration of the teaching of civic responsibility to its rightful role?

ACTIVE LEARNING

As the need has been addressed to encourage each student's creativity and each student's sense of responsibility, the tendency of higher education to think in narrow terms about the process of teaching and learning has repeatedly been confronted. Too often, quality is assumed to be measured only in terms of selectiveness of admission and effectiveness only in terms of knowledge transferred to the student as measured by grades and test scores.[36] Of course, knowledge is an important outcome of education. But the focus of the student's interest cannot be just grades, which in turn lead to academic credit, which in turn leads—when enough credits have been accumulated—to a degree, and finally, as students and parents hope, to a job. Rather, education must be an opening to an exciting experience.

A number of authorities who have studied the growth and development of students were consulted to determine how colleges can encourage both creativity and civic responsibility. There was a wide variety of responses, but one recommendation was universal: the student must become more actively involved in his or her own learning.[37] Far too often, students are treated as the object of learning rather than as colleagues in the learning process.

Ironically, there is a danger that emphasis on a new rigor in American education may cause just the opposite to happen. The pressure to improve test scores may be translated into an emphasis on rote learning. Yet rote learning does not provide a base for higher order integrative thinking. Instead it inhibits creative potential and frustrates the learning of responsibility.[38] Therefore, emphasis must be more on understanding than on memorization of facts.

College education is nowhere near as exciting nor as effective as it could be. In many ways it is boring, particularly the classroom part. The student is expected to sit quietly in class, listen to a lecture, make notes with the purpose of memorizing not only the information about the subject being transmitted but the interpretation that is provided in a predigested form.

Students spend somewhere between 5 and 20 percent of their time in active participation in class.[39] Discussions with students and observations of undergraduate classes suggest that active classroom participation is probably closer to the 5 percent figure than the 20 percent. A new Carnegie Foundation survey shows that more than half of the undergraduates at large universities feel that ". . . most students are treated like numbers in a book." The recent Carnegie Foundation report, *High School*, as well as other recent reports on elementary and secondary education describe a similar pattern of teaching at those levels.[40] Theodore Sizer, in *Horace's Compromise*, argues:

> No more important finding has emerged from the inquiries of our study than that the American high school student, *as student*, is all too often docile, compliant, and without initiative. . . . Their harshest epithet for a teacher is "boring." There are too few rewards for being inquisitive; there rarely is extra credit for the ingenious proof. The constructive skeptic can be unsettling to all too many teachers who may find him cheeky and disruptive.[41]

A student cannot learn to reason solely by listening to a description of how a teacher or professor has reasoned. Lectures, at their best, transmit knowledge, but they are rarely inspiring. They seldom transform the experience of learning from the humdrum to a level of excitement that captures the student's attention. Students know that mastering data or a given professor's viewpoint is only peripherally related to the purposes of education but intimately related to the grades necessary for admission to selective programs. So the process breeds cynicism toward the teaching.

Beyond that, the passive process fails to accomplish the most fundamental goals of a liberal education. To become creative, one must practice being creative. To become a risk taker, one must try to take risks. Particularly in a world where constant change has become the norm, students must reject facile answers and pre-digested certainty. They must fashion their own conclusions, tentative as they may be, and their own plans for learning. Perhaps most crucial, if one is to understand the importance of judgment and the importance of responsibility, one must learn by attempting to make such judgments and acting responsibly.

There is no more critical task ahead for American higher education than to transform the undergraduate experience into a more active learning process. Research about higher education confirms that:

> Active involvement in the classroom adds substantially to the level of retained knowledge, the intellectual skills, and the personal development of the student.[42]

62

Involvement with faculty both in and out of class substantially accelerates the development of the student.[43]

Students learn as much from each other as they do from their classes.[44]

Participation in student government, the student newspaper, or other extracurricular activities is an important means for developing both intellectual and personal skills.[45]

Graduates of active learning education programs show a growth in those qualities of personal responsibility, public interest, self-confidence, and the capacity to achieve needed for civic leadership.[46]

If much of American classroom experience is passive, how is it that students still seem to gain at least some of the value of a liberal education? First, American higher education is *less* prone to passivity than the higher education systems of most other developed countries. In addition, students seem to have a remarkable ability to contrast *on their own* the approach taken in one course with that taken in another. They learn there are many pathways to salvation. In discussions among themselves, they experiment with the process of thinking. This is one reason students who live on campus develop intellectually more rapidly than their commuting counterparts.[47] Students also appear to generalize from limited contact with faculty in some courses to what they should be thinking about or how they might reason and learn in other courses.

Extracurricular activity, internships and work/study all provide students with opportunities for personal growth.[48] One hopeful sign is that the extracurriculum is thriving. There has been a recent boom in intramural athletics, for example. Both women and men now have the opportunity, through intramural and varsity athletics, to learn to take risks and to learn from both success and failure. Yet, faculty and administrators seem to have lost sight of the educational value of the extracurriculum. One result is that top administrators and faculty often tend to think of these activities as nice ways to keep students happy.

On the whole, students are good learners under modest circumstances both in and out of the classroom. They could learn a great deal more if the circumstances were better designed with that end in mind.

Why then does the passive mode persist so widely? The faculty members interviewed for this study gave several reasons. One is the strong belief that the role of the faculty is to teach and that the lecture is the appropriate mode for doing so. It is assumed that learning occurs *because* faculty teach. Another reason is that most faculty are not equipped to draw students into active class participation. Few have training in the process of teaching beyond instruction on how to create an effective lecture. The graduate training of most faculty members involved risk avoidance, not risk taking.[49] Unusual or interdisciplinary dissertations are discouraged. Graduate study has always been a period of intellectual subservience until one becomes a faculty member in turn.

Many have told us that drawing a student into active participation in the learning process is threatening. The student becomes a questioner, a prober, a challenger. Moreover, the investment of teaching energy in experiments or interdisciplinary courses or in imaginative off-campus internship programs are much less likely to help one's career than a narrow focus on disciplinary research and conventional teaching. Besides, it is simply easier to lecture.

Some students also object to a participatory mode. Some of them say they wish to hear the professor and not other students talk. Since freshmen have been socialized by 13 years of elementary and secondary school to the passive learning style, it is hardly surprising that they are uncomfortable at first with a new and riskier role. Many want "the facts" so they can be sure to be prepared for the exam.[50] When students become familiar with an active learning mode, however, many find it not only exciting but the most important classroom learning experience of their undergraduate years.

There are already many successful models for transforming the student's experience from passive to active.[51] On every campus there seem to be at least some faculty members whose classes deviate from the norm and who are skilled at drawing the student into an active dialogue as part of the classroom experience. There is also no reason for the classroom to be the only focus of education. More imaginative use of the library, laboratories and other learning opportunities can contribute greatly. One advantage of an active learning class (where students have been parties to the selection of the projects they will carry out, the methods that they will use to gather data, and the presentation of material to their peers) is that the amount of reading or laboratory use goes up significantly. More importantly, interest in and the retention of the content of the reading jumps up sharply.

A number of programs manage to achieve a powerful, active involvement on the part of the student.[52] Two of these are the Brown Writing Fellows Program and Beaver College's Cross-Disciplinary Writing Program. Across the country there is a recognition that undergraduates need more extensive writing experience. A major difficulty, however, is that if a faculty member assigns more than one paper, provides the student with a critique, and asks for the paper to be rewritten, his or her work load becomes extraordinary. At Brown, selected undergraduates are trained and assigned to assist a faculty member in this work. Students meet first with the writing fellow who offers a critique of the paper. The student then rewrites the paper and submits both the original and revised versions to the faculty member for grading. This process usually is repeated at least twice during a course. The program has proven to be a powerful learning experience for the writing fellows, and a critical force in changing the way that Brown students view learning to write, as well as learning to accept and even look for criticism.[53]

Writing cannot be confined within a single discipline or department. It is useful in all fields of study, from history to biology. Beaver College, in Glenside, Pennsylvania, has managed to overcome the tendency to confine writing within the English Department by using trained undergraduates as writing consultants who are available to respond to student papers while they are still in the draft stage. This program of "Writing Across the Curriculum" has attracted national attention. Its success is due in large part to the enthusiastic participation of the faculty, each of whom is given free reign in developing a personal style for teaching writing.[54]

A number of universities have also experimented with undergraduate teaching assistants. Where such programs have been carefully developed there has been a positive reaction and a positive evaluation by outside experts.

Several colleges and universities have experimented with peer tutoring. A study of peer tutors at Brooklyn College indicates that they not only show growth in social, intellectual, and emotional maturity, but seem to move toward an awareness that learning is not an autonomous process measured by an external authority. They learn to "deal with ideas in their fluid incomplete state of change, as developing emanations of human beings' minds. They receive ideas and engage in thought together, through the medium of personal and social exchange."[55]

Another approach is what has become known as collaborative undergraduate education, a process by which undergraduate students participate with the faculty member in course planning. One advantage of the collaboration is that it often leads to a more interdisciplinary approach than students normally encounter. Students, as one undergraduate dean reported, undergo a "shock of responsibility" when they are involved in peer tutoring or collaborative planning responsibilities. They suddenly realize that they are not just learning for themselves and take a much deeper sense of responsibility toward their work.

Hampshire College in Massachusetts makes collaboration a central feature of its education program. Undergraduates design their own majors in conjunction with one or more members of the faculty. There are no departmental requirements as such. To graduate, students must develop and complete an independent research project.

The clear connection between research and education has been recognized for years, but its benefits usually have been restricted to graduate education. Over the last decade a number of universities have involved undergraduates in the research process. The best known programs are at MIT, Worcester Polytechnic Institute, and the University of Delaware.[56] In each case the student participates in both the planning of the project and its execution. Utah State has gone so far as to fund a scholarship program for graduating high school seniors that allows them to participate in proposing scientific experiments that become part of the NASA space program. The combination of writing proposals, creating experiments,

66

watching them fail and, in increasing numbers, succeed, is a heady and powerful experience that goes a long way toward helping tranform the undergraduate experience.[57]

A more familiar way to actively engage students is in the use of internships. An advantage of internships is that they can be used in any discipline. Where the internship is coupled with traditional academic work, including research and a term paper, and faculty supervision, the gains are considerable.[58]

Opportunities for actively involving students also are to be found beyond the academic process itself. One of the most important is the provision of work opportunities.[59] About 40 percent of all full-time undergraduate students already work. Research indicates that such experience is generally helpful in developing students' capacity to take responsibility, interest in learning, and capacity to take risks. A number of colleges incorporate the idea of work to support campus functions as a regular part of the college experience. They believe that both the college and the student benefit. If the amount of work exceeds between 15 and 20 hours a week, however, it may undercut the academic interest of a full-time student.[60]

American higher education now enrolls a wide diversity of students. Because their experiences are different their needs are different. But all of them need to engage their minds, to take responsibility, to gain the benefit that comes from shared work and educational opportunity.

What is required to provide more active dynamic learning opportunities for undergraduates? Much can be done through changes in federal policy. More can be done as well to encourage corporate support of internships and work opportunities. In addition, resources and opportunities already exist to make learning on every campus more active. To exploit them requires a clear commitment from the president, from the administration, and from the faculty.

The issue for American higher education is not that it is turning out too few engineers, doctors, lawyers, or Ph.D.s, or too few graduates in the liberal arts. Compared with the other industrialized countries, the United States graduates twice as many professionals per capita. The most important issue is that the quality of education that college graduates receive can and must be better if the United States is to play an enlightened role of leadership in the world—economically, politically, and socially.

The opportunity exists for a vastly improved educational experience on the part of young people. Many of the following chapters spell out specific proposals for national action. To achieve success, they require the support of both policy makers and the campus. Taken together, these proposals represent an opportunity for change in American higher education.

CHAPTER VI

American Youth and the Ideal of Service

FEDERAL STUDENT AID PROGRAMS are often debated primarily in terms of how much aid should be made available to which classes of students. But the *form* of student aid is also important. By expanding the concept of student aid in return for service to the community, public policy can have an important effect on educational outcomes.

REORDERING PRIORITIES

In recent years, the primary goal of most student aid—particularly federal student aid—has been to increase the access to higher education for those of limited means. In the last few years, the access goal has been challenged by the argument that it should be replaced by the goal of merit (defined in terms of academic grades and test scores). Nearly three-fourths of the nation's 3,200 colleges and universities now offer some type of merit-based scholarship.[1] The need versus merit debate is the wrong debate. The real issue is how access can be supplemented by merit defined in terms of service—the concept of aiding those students who serve society.

Access for those of limited means must remain the top priority. Measured by the share of each age cohort attending college, access has remained at a plateau for the last decade. Attendance rates for all 18- to 24-year-olds actually dropped slightly, from 35 percent to 33 percent, from 1969 to 1981.[2] For some minority groups, participation also has declined slightly over the last decade. (See Chapter VII.)

The use of merit, as measured by grades and test scores, to select students to receive aid suffers on two counts. It is counterproductive with

69

regard to providing access to all independent of need because of the close correlation between socioeconomic status and test scores. Furthermore, grades and test scores, except in the broadest sense, bear little or no relationship to success outside of school.[3] Not only is the willingness to be of service (and a past record of active involvement) a better guide to success in life, it is more equitably distributed among all groups.

The whole concept of federal student aid was recently challenged by the argument that students should pay a larger share of their costs. This also is the wrong argument. Americans already pay a far larger share than is expected of students elsewhere. Two principles have served as the pillars of national policy for a long time: opportunity for access to anyone with motivation and ability, including the motivation to work for part of their costs; and higher education as an avenue for social mobility. Beyond that, preserving and broadening the opportunity for college is a central force of American social policy. This policy is based, not on sentiment or tradition, but on the fundamental convictions that equality of opportunity is essential if the social, economic, and civic conditions of the nation are to be sustained and strengthened.

Perhaps the most important point is that the form of financial aid a student receives shapes the nature of the student's educational experience and personal development. Almost 75 percent of all college students receive some form of aid. The design of student aid programs should reflect the educational values society seeks. It is possible not only to provide access, and access that enhances student choice as to the type of institution, but to encourage through student aid the understanding that each citizen has an obligation to the society as a whole.

Because a variety of federal student aid programs have been in operation for several years, much can be learned about values that are developed by different approaches. Studies of the GI Bill, for example, indicate that grants provided to those who have completed military service encourage a student to improve academic performance upon entry or return to campus, encourage a greater sense of purpose when the student enters higher education, and clarify career objectives.[4]

Those programs that require students to work—the college work/study program or internship programs—on the whole tend to build character,

70

encourage a sense of responsibility, encourage self-confidence, create a sense that the student is a useful member of society, expand a student's expectations about himself, increase the capacity for cooperation, and add to a student's knowledge of the world of jobs.[5] As of now, approximately 40 percent of all full-time college students work at some sort of job for an average of 20 hours a week. Surprisingly, the percentage is roughly the same for students in all family income categories up to about $50,000 a year.[6]

Grants, such as the Pell grants, provide essential underpinning for the whole student aid system, although they have a relatively neutral effect on grades and values. They clearly help equalize access, and in so doing make the other forms of student aid workable. Even when grants are of a relatively modest amount they encourage students to enroll and to persist.[7]

Loans tend to bring about the highest rate of attrition of any form of student aid, and appear to have a significant effect on student career choices.[8] Unlike other forms of aid, they diminish the very sense of social contract proposed in this report.

While it is essential to preserve the current array of student aid programs, the balance would be better if service and work were expanded.[9] The current rate of growth in certain forms of student aid has upset the traditional balance. Loans have been expanding most rapidly, grants the next most rapidly. Work/study has been level for a long time (though recently increased significantly), and the traditional GI Bill program is being eliminated.[10]

A BACKWARD GLANCE: THE EVOLUTION OF FEDERAL STUDENT FINANCIAL AID PROGRAMS

While there was a small number of federal fellowships before World War II, most notably the Public Health fellowships, major federal support of students began with the GI Bill. Although it was not intended to be the first of any series of programs to aid students, the GI Bill's success opened the door for further federal efforts. The first post–GI Bill programs sought to expand the number of the brightest students preparing to enter fields that served pressing national purposes, such as defense. The earliest examples were fellowships for doctoral students in the sciences. As the number of programs grew, new rationales for student assistance evolved—from supporting only the brightest, to supporting the brightest of limited means, to helping those least able to pay. Until recently, the largest share of federal support of students was in programs to provide equity of access for needy students.

STUDENT AID SINCE 1977

After the initial surge of the first (World War II) and then the second (Korean War) GI Bills, federal programs of student aid began a long growth during the 1960s and early 1970s (Chart 5). Since 1977, both the level and form of federal student aid has changed dramatically. As Chart 6 shows, in current dollar terms student aid continued to rise during the Carter years, then began to decline. In constant dollars, student aid dropped after 1976, rising only slightly until 1979 when the Middle Income Student Assistance Act went into effect. Although the level of funding in 1984 was about the same as the level of funding in 1979 in current dollars, in real terms (constant dollars) student aid is back to where it was in 1973.

One major cause of the sharp drop during the 1980s has been the decision to eliminate two large programs that often go unnoticed because they are administered outside the Department of Education—the GI Bill and the educational benefits for dependents under the Social Security program. Between them they represented $3.6 billion in 1980. By 1989, they will have been completely eliminated.[11] Despite the fact that they were often overlooked by educators, these programs have represented real dollars in the pockets of students and an approach to student aid quite different from the more visible programs.

THE GROWING ROLE OF LOANS

Another critical change is the shift in the importance of loans. The figures in Table 6 represent only the current cost to the federal government of the loans under the Guaranteed Student Loan Program (GSLP). If one

CHART 5

FEDERAL EXPENDITURES FOR STUDENT AID, SELECTED FISCAL YEARS: 1938–1977, CURRENT AND CONSTANT (1967) DOLLARS (IN MILLIONS)

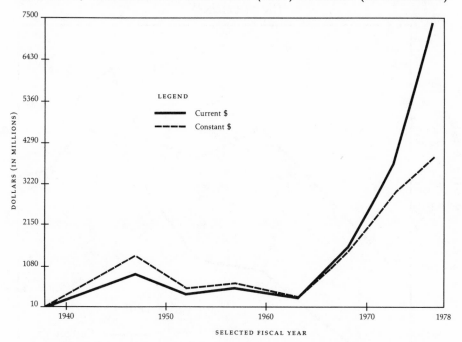

SOURCE: FY 1938 to 1973 from Report of a Special Task Force to the Secretary of Health, Education, and Welfare. *The Second Newman Report: National Policy and Higher Education* (Cambridge, MA: MIT Press, 1973). Later years are from Gillespie and Carlson. *Trends in Student Aid: 1963 to 1983*, Table A–1, p. 30. Constant 1967 dollars were calculated by multiplying current dollar figures by the Consumer Price Index taken from the United States Bureau of the Census. *Statistical Abstract of the United States, 1981*, Washington, D.C., p. 458.

looks at the role that the loans play, as a share of all student aid, a massive shift becomes evident. Chart 7 shows all federal student aid loans in the amount lent to the student, not the cost to the government. In the late 1970s loans became the dominant form of student aid.

For the last three years, as student aid has fallen and costs to the student have continued to rise, the growth in loans has accelerated. In 1983 over 3.5 million students borrowed an average of $2,525 per year under the

CHART 6

FEDERAL EXPENDITURES FOR STUDENT AID, SELECTED ACADEMIC
YEARS: 1970–1984, CURRENT AND CONSTANT (1982) DOLLARS
(IN MILLIONS)

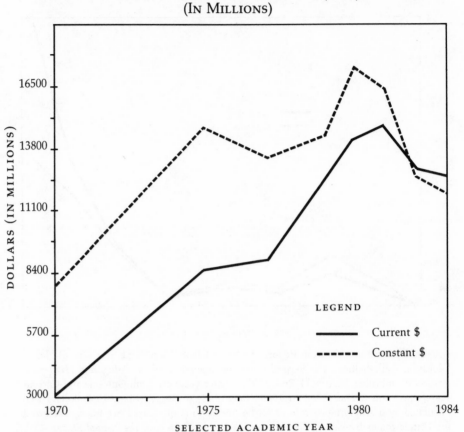

SOURCE: Donald A. Gillespie and Nancy Carlson. *Trends in Student Aid*, Table A–1, p.
30, and Table A–2, p. 33.

guaranteed loan program.[12] Students attending professional schools in
particular have become dependent on loans. In 1981, medical school graduates, on average, had borrowed more than $25,000. Nearly one-third of
1984 medical graduates left school with more than $30,000 in debt.[13]
Graduate and professional school students represented 25 percent of the
borrowers, but over 30 percent of the total borrowed.

TABLE 6

EXPENDITURES FOR STUDENT ASSISTANCE, SELECTED FEDERAL PROGRAMS, FY 1973–1980 (MILLIONS OF DOLLARS)

YEAR	PELL	VETERAN'S EDUCATION	SOCIAL SECURITY	CWS	GSL	NDSL	SEOG	TOTAL	TOTAL IN 1972 DOLLARS
1973	—	2,016[a]	638[a]	270[b]	292[c]	286[d]	189[e]	3,691	3,502
1974	49[a]	2,309[a]	618[a]	270[b]	399[c]	286[d]	200[e]	4,131	3,685
1975[f]	342	4,180	1,093	420	580	321	201	7,137	5,788
1976[f]	1,326	4,301	1,233	390	808	332	284	8,674	6,576
1977[f]	1,529	2,598	1,370	390	357	311	284	6,839	4,857
1978[f]	2,160	2,316	1,450	435	480	326	334	7,501	4,990
1979[f]	2,431	1,784	1,587	550	958	329	417	8,056	4,927
1980[f]	1,718	1,714	1,883	550	1,609	301	447	8,222	4,630
1981[f]	2,604	1,351	1,996	550	2,535	201	370	9,607	4,926
1982[f]	2,419	1,356	733	528	3,074	193	355	8,658	4,126
1983[f]	2,419	1,056	220	590	3,100	193	355	7,933	3,643
1984[f]	2,800	836	35	555	2,255	181	375	7,037	3,077
1985[g]	3,575	800[h]	N/A	593	3,079	190	413	8,650	3,617

LEGEND: Pell was called Basic Educational Opportunity Grants (BEOG) before 1980.
CWS is the College Work-Study Program.
GSL is the Guaranteed Student Loan Program.
NDSL is the National Direct Student Loan Program.
SEOG is the Supplemental Educational Opportunity Grants Program.
This list does not include all federal programs of student financial assistance.

SOURCE: [a] Chester Finn. *Scholars, Dollars and Bureaucrats* (Washington, D.C.: The Brookings Institution, 1978), Table 3–6, p. 68.
[b] United States Department of Education, Office of Student Financial Assistance. *OSFA Program Book*, Washington, D.C., July 1981, p. 73.
[c] *OSFA*, p. 37.
[d] *OSFA*, pp. 54–55.
[e] *OSFA*, p. 19.
[f] Donald A. Gillespie and Nancy Carlson. *Trends in Student Aid: 1963 to 1983* (Washington, D.C.: The Washington Office of the College Board, December 1983), Table A–1, p. 30, and Table A–3, p. 34; and *Trends in Student Aid: 1980 to 1984*, Table 1, p. 5 and Table 3, p. 7.
[g] *Education Week*, November 7, 1984, p. 15. Figures are estimates.
[h] Figures supplied by Veteran's Administration.
Constant 1972 dollars calculated from Price Index Deflation Series obtained from National Science Foundation and applicable to federal obligations.

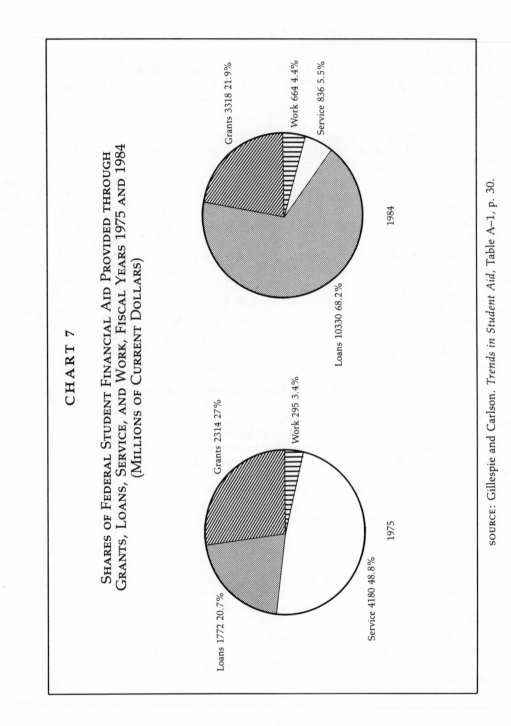

CHART 7

SHARES OF FEDERAL STUDENT FINANCIAL AID PROVIDED THROUGH GRANTS, LOANS, SERVICE, AND WORK, FISCAL YEARS 1975 AND 1984
(MILLIONS OF CURRENT DOLLARS)

Grants 3318 21.9%

Work 664 4.4%

Service 836 5.5%

Loans 10330 68.2%

1984

Grants 2314 27%

Work 295 3.4%

Loans 1772 20.7%

Service 4180 48.8%

1975

SOURCE: Gillespie and Carlson. *Trends in Student Aid*, Table A–1, p. 30.

The next few years are almost certain to see the continuation of the rapid growth of loans.[14] It is now clear that such growth is not in the country's best interest. Loans were conceived as a supplement to other forms of student aid, a means of filling a gap or funding a student over a difficult period. In this mode they serve an important purpose. Excessive dependence on loans (and for many students it is already excessive) has a number of disadvantages:

- Sizable outstanding loans affect the career choices of students. Getting a well-paying job right after graduation becomes a necessity. Graduate school looks less attractive. Sizable loan balances inhibit the willingness of graduates to take further risks. A student who leaves college with a large debt burden may well feel he has already assumed all of the risk that he possibly could. Higher education must help students understand the responsibility that each has toward society. A new doctor or lawyer graduating with a debt of $20,000 or $30,000 is likely to mistakenly believe the reverse.[15] Even marriage may be affected by the issue of "negative dowry."

- The rate of persistence and completion of a degree for students with heavy loans is lower than for students who receive other forms of student aid.[16]

- Disadvantaged students find large loans onerous. Minority students, in particular, are less likely to use loans and therefore less likely to enter or stay in college.[17]

- The accelerated growth in loans means that the costs to the federal government are being postponed to future years because the subsidy cost continues for the life of the loan. Over half of the borrowers to date are still in college. Ten years ago, approximately one-tenth of the yearly cost of the Guaranteed Student Loan Program paid for the loan subsidies of students who had already graduated. Today it is over two-thirds of the cost, and growing steadily. There is a danger that the cost of paying for past students, already well in excess of a billion dollars a year and mounting rapidly, will compete with the funds needed for future students.[18]

- Loans are socially inefficient. While in the short run the government leverages its funds by encouraging the use of private capital, in the long run the total of costs to the student, his parents, the college, and the government is far higher. Growing student indebtedness will mean fewer opportunities for young graduates to buy homes or cars.[19]

- Excessive loans inadvertently undercut traditional values. Working one's way through college is a cherished American concept that conflicts head on with "Go now, pay later."

We are moving toward a system of higher education in which the burden of college cost is being shifted more and more to the student and his or her family—but in the form of future costs. The tradition of this country has been that the colleges and universities are the gateway to a student's future, that a determined and hard-working graduate from a poor family starts out on an equal footing with all other graduates. Today, not only is that student less likely to graduate, but if he does, he is more likely to start out owing tens of thousands of dollars. This is hardly starting even.

This does not argue that all student aid should be given in a single form. There is an advantage to a diversity of programs, both in meeting the tailored needs of some students and in fashioning "packages" of student aid. Multiple student aid programs, including federal, state, and institutional programs, also help insure the differential in student aid depending on cost. This is essential to preserve public and private higher education as well as the range of diversity *within* each of these. That diversity enables American higher education to match the diversity of students enrolled.

Student loans, when kept in moderation, are an important part of the balance. A number of people argue that any criticism of the amount of loans may be used as an argument for their elimination and the overall reduction of student aid. It is important that the sum of student aid programs be expanded, not contracted. However, to continue the shift toward loans and to fail to consider expanding other student aid programs out of fear of misinterpretation or exploitation is surely wrong.

78

RESTRUCTURING STUDENT AID

How, then, can student aid programs be altered to maximize their beneficial effects: increased access, improved persistence, and the development of appropriate values including the concept of service? A variety of programs should be emphasized, moving away from the trend toward just loans. Some existing programs should be expanded, and others diminished in order to alter the balance of student aid and its consequent impact. There must be a base of programs that ensure equity in the access to higher education. *The Pell grants and the current work/study programs should be the cornerstone of the student aid programs. They have proven effective in expanding access, encouraging retention, helping provide equity among students of differing backgrounds. They should be expanded in order to insure access to those of limited income. Loan programs are needed to provide a degree of flexibility.*

THE IDEAL OF SERVICE

For all of the cynicism about political life in this country, for all of the worry about the TV-created passiveness and self-interest of young people, there remains deep in the American psyche a belief in the ideal of service to country as a proper step to adulthood. It is like a quietly burning ember, waiting to be fanned into a visible flame.

Repeatedly over the postwar period, and earlier during the 1930s, a variety of federal programs attempted to respond to that belief. They include the Civilian Conservation Corps, the National Youth Administration, the Peace Corps, the Young Adult Conservation Corps, the National Health Service Corps, the Teacher Corps, the University Year for Action, and various forms of student aid linked to military service. Almost all have proven effective at the three tasks expected of these programs—getting something done for society that needs doing, providing opportunities for personal growth for young men and women, and—most important—burnishing the ideal of service in the youth of the country. Some of these programs have been phased out or cut back.

Many of these programs persist. Some are admittedly complex to manage. All cost money. Because their constituency is ill-defined and their value distant, they are frequent targets of budget cutting. The determination remains, however, and recently the public's interest has grown stronger as the country again turns its attention to the ways by which young men and women reach adulthood. New bills have been introduced into the Congress for a voluntary national youth service and for an American conservation corps. States, such as New York and Minnesota, have proposals pending. Cities, such as San Francisco and New York, have begun new programs.

All young men and women should be encouraged to serve the country. Because this report is aimed at higher education, we have focused on a concept by which those who aspire to college may gain that opportunity— the concept of a social contract, providing student aid in return for service. College graduates are particularly important in this regard, for it is from among them that the country's leadership emerges. The opportunity to serve, however, should be available to all.

One possible approach to voluntary youth service is the concept of national service for all young Americans, but although service in some form for essentially all young men and women is desirable, a voluntary program would be more effective than any compulsory system.[20] Another approach would be for colleges and universities to prescribe some form of service as a graduation requirement.[21] This has much to recommend it, and colleges and universities should consider how to achieve this objective without trivializing the service performed.[22] Such an approach would be even more effective in the high school. The school system in Atlanta has already moved to implement such a program.

Both high schools and higher education can move immediately to create more public service opportunities on a volunteer basis. Many institutions such as Berea, Berry, Brown, Cornell, Georgetown, Hampshire, Minnesota, Stanford, Vanderbilt, and Yale have already done so.[23] States and cities can do so as well.[24]

To effectively reach a large share of American youth, a voluntary approach requires many programs. Differing students have differing needs.[25] It is not a question of whether a federal program will supersede a city or university program. It is rather a question of whether there will be enough different programs to make a significant impact. The following proposals are intended as models. They are focused on federal initiative, but are to complement the programs of the institutions and the states. In fact, the states could well employ some of these same models.[26]

PUBLIC SERVICE TEACHING FELLOWS

When it comes to encouraging service to country in a form that provides students with work experience blended with the traditional academic experience, this country already has one successful example, the ROTC (Reserve Officer Training Corps) program. This program can serve as a model for fields other than the military—to encourage better students to enter the teaching profession, to help the disadvantaged enter professional fields, to provide the opportunity for young men and women to undertake important social tasks, to meet many societal needs. One advantage of this type of a program in a field such as teaching is that it can be used to draw into the schools a stream of new, bright, and able people who are prepared to give two, three or four years of service but who might not be prepared to make a lifetime commitment.[27] Equally important, it can help students understand the concept of service to country.

Specifically a program based on the public service model—a Public Service Fellows Program for teaching—should be created to meet the shortage of math and science teachers as well as teachers willing to work in central urban areas.

Over the last few years, the urgency of attracting able men and women to the teaching profession has become a major concern. The recent Carnegie Foundation report, *High School*, described that urgency and outlined a number of ways to overcome it. The time for talk is over. Action is needed. The Public Service Teaching Fellows program suggested here emphasizes selectivity: students would be admitted to the program by the appropriate body after completing either the freshman or the sophomore year; would accept an obligation after graduation of a minimum of two or three years of teaching and would assume additional responsibilities while in college. In return, the student would receive a grant of

81

$3,000 per year toward higher education.[28] The institution the student attends would receive a supplementary grant of $1,000 a year to help cover the costs of on-site training. Should the student decide after graduation, or after a year of teaching, not to continue in the teaching profession, then the remainder of the grant would turn into a loan at market interest rates.

The other obligations of the student would include activities much similar to the weekend and summer camp activities of the ROTC. One Saturday a month during the school year the student would be required to attend special training sessions to prepare for summer programs. During two summers, the student would be responsible, in return for a small stipend, to undertake the education of a class of students who have fallen behind the national average in reading and math in order to bring these students up to or beyond the national average. The Public Service Teaching Fellows could join under many circumstances in the outreach programs in TRIO, such as Upward Bound in their form described in Chapter VII.

The concept of Public Service Teaching Fellows has several critical advantages over the commonly suggested alternative. That alternative is a loan that would be forgiven in return for service in the profession following graduation.[29] The first advantage of the Public Service Teaching Program is that not everyone is eligible, only those selected. This encourages those most needed in the profession. Participating students also are likely to be attracted from diverse backgrounds. Historically, ROTC has been an avenue for social mobility for those of lower family income but higher motivation.[30] The second advantage is that the students begin "service" immediately, not at some indefinite point in the future. This should help to insure a serious interest. The third is that actual experience is coupled directly with academic class work. The fourth is that the program requires the student to meet certain academic requirements while leaving room for flexibility in the student's major. The program also provides flexibility by allowing the student to participate for the full four years, for three years, or even for two years.

An important feature is that the program asks for a personal commitment of a limited time. This means that young men and women can take on difficult tasks, such as teaching in the urban schools, knowing that they are not being asked to make a lifelong career choice. Experience indicates that they will take these commitments seriously, work hard at them, and volunteer for the riskier assignments.[31] The program also offers easy adaptability from the point of view of the schools. It can be readily expanded or contracted, and the schools have a flow-through of able young people, helping to create an atmosphere of excitement in the schools. No doubt the ablest would be encouraged to stay in teaching.

There are problems to be solved. The cost of a program of 10,000 fellowships a year would be approximately $40 million dollars.[32] There is the additional problem of matching the graduates with the job market. Unlike the military, there is no single agency in education that both sets the number of graduates and provides the actual hiring.[33] None of these problems is insurmountable.

Programs, such as the one suggested, reaffirm the tradition that young men and women spend a portion of their lives in service to their country.[34] Most important, we believe that Public Service Fellowships can be a model for many programs, not just teaching and the military.[35] For example, there is a program at the City University of New York that helps police and firefighters forced to retire at an early age to train for the nursing profession. Massachusetts and Florida have programs designed to attract able people to police work. Georgetown University is negotiating with the Washington, D.C. police force for a similar program to educate young men and women as police officers. Potential fields for such programs might include the encouragement of medical students to practice in inner city or rural areas or of law school graduates to work as public service lawyers.[36]

A GI BILL FOR COMMUNITY SERVICE; RESTORATION OF THE TRADITIONAL GI BILL

The GI Bill has often been considered the most effective student aid program that this country has developed. When proposed in 1943, it represented a major social innovation, a program that provided educational benefits for everyone that served the country in the military, subject only to admission to an approved educational institution. The concept, however, has suffered from the perception that it can be applied only to the military. *Two parallel steps are proposed: restoration of the traditional GI Bill for the military to replace the present version, the Veterans' Educational Assistance Program (VEAP); and a program based on the basic elements of the GI Bill, providing student aid in return for community service on the part of young men and women.*[37]

The program would encourage young men and women between the ages of 18 and 25 to devote one to two years of their lives to a public service undertaking in the military or in civilian programs. The civilian public service jobs would be in either the public or private sector. Certification of the job would be by a federal agency. In return for this service the federal government would provide student aid on a month-for-month matching basis. Fourteen months of student aid, for example, would accrue for 14 months of service. In addition, the scale of the benefits might be varied to match the need to attract young men and women to certain tasks. Service in the infantry might have higher benefits, service in a conservation corps lower.[38]

A number of the major universities have programs that are similar in concept, though small in size, based on private funding.[39] Two recent proposals for federal student aid that embody some variation of this principle have been put before Congress. Congressman Leon Panetta introduced the Voluntary Youth Service Act of 1984, and Senator John Glenn introduced the Student Aid Volunteer Earnings Act (S.A.V.E.) into the 98th Congress.[40] Congressman Panetta's proposal calls for the federal government to give grants to state and local voluntary youth service programs on a 50/50 matching basis. Under the terms of the federal grants, states may provide post–service benefits, including education loans or grants, in addition to in-service remuneration. Senator Glenn's proposal would have student volunteers contribute one-quarter of their salary to an educational trust fund, which would be augmented by federal matching funds equivalent to double their personal contribution upon completion of their service.

Many differing proposals are needed, but the principle—the exchange of service to country in return for subsequent educational benefits—is the important issue. Educational benefits can help the military attract

84

better recruits and public service organizations attract more young workers.[41] Most important, this form of student aid provides a tangible and useful way to demonstrate pride in the country, and strengthens the ideal of public service.[42]

EXPAND THE EFFECTIVENESS OF THE COLLEGE WORK/STUDY PROGRAM

The college work/study program has received generally high marks for its effectiveness. However, since 1980 it has declined in terms of constant dollars. (See Table 7.) Work/study has two important advantages beyond its basic value of helping students pay for their college education. It encourages the development of those values students need in our society, and it allows for the opportunity to create public service roles for students, both on and off campus.[43]

The work/study program should be expanded three ways. *First, the share of all full-time students working, presently about 40 percent, should be expanded to more of those receiving aid, toward the range of 60–70 percent of all students. Second, the significance of the jobs students perform needs to be increased. Third, colleges and universities should be*

TABLE 7

AID AWARDED IN COLLEGE WORK/STUDY

YEAR	CURRENT DOLLARS ($ MILLION)	CONSTANT 1982 DOLLARS
1970	227	552
1970	295	513
1980	658	734
1984	641 (est.)	611 (est.)

SOURCE: Donald A. Gillespie and Nancy Carlson. *Trends in Student Aid: 1963 to 1983,* pp. 30 and 33.

85

encouraged to use at least 20 percent of their work/study funds for public service on and off campus.[44]

There can be dangers in work programs. Too much work—in excess of 20 hours a week—appears to detract from the student's academic effort and weaken students' educational aspirations. On the other hand, all students need the self-confidence that comes from excelling at some aspect of life. Many have a natural capacity to excel at work or managerial responsibilities and less ability at the academic. For almost all students, some blend of academic experience and work experience is the most potent combination.

Much also depends on whether the work experience is constructive. Both on-campus jobs and cooperative education jobs clearly help persistence. Work experience that engages the mind, requires a sense of responsibility, and has real work aspects (the necessity to find a job and to be fired if there is poor performance) is the most valuable.[45] There is a tendency for universities and colleges to assign students to menial or undemanding jobs both because of a deep-seated assumption that they are not yet ready intellectually or personally to play a more responsible role, and because it is simply easier to administer the program that way. There is a good deal of evidence that undergraduate students are not only effective when they assist in the teaching process (as tutors, teaching assistants, or writing fellows) or in the research process (as research assistants or in their own research projects), but when they undertake a wide variety of jobs that require intelligence and responsibility.[46] Several universities have experimented with dining halls completely run by students; others have experimented with housing arrangements that are essentially cooperative. Some have given students the opportunity to teach in adult literacy programs. Students benefit from participating in essentially all jobs, but much more can be gained.

When students participate in such activities, they become colleagues in the educational process rather than objects upon which teaching is practiced. When students take responsibility, they learn to be responsible; far more so than if they are lectured on the importance of being responsible. What is needed is to encourage faculty and administrators to look at the evidence, to examine the large number of successful examples, and to use their imagination in the employment of undergraduates, rather than to pass out the work/study money in the easiest and quickest way.

One question that is frequently raised is whether there are enough "good" jobs or even enough jobs to support such a large number of students working. Our examination of this convinces us that there are more than enough. A number of colleges—Berea, Berry, Warren Wilson, and Tuskegee, to name only a few—make work a basic part of their learning ethic. Essentially all students participate.[47] In addition, more of the funding should be allocated to public service activities, both on and off campus. Several colleges and universities, Cornell is an example, already have such programs.[48] *Therefore, the college work/study program should be expanded in its present form; and a modest-sized system of competitive grants should be added for the employment of undergraduate students that would encourage creation of more active and responsible jobs. These grants should be added to the existing program of formula funding and should function much along the lines of the FIPSE Program.*

In summary, *public service programs such as those proposed above should be increased; Pell grants should be increased; work/study should be expanded in both volume and in the scope of the jobs provided; and loans should be reduced as a means of financing students.* By 1990, the proportion among differing forms of student aid should be more balanced, with loans representing only a third and service programs one-quarter of the total (see Chart 8).

Federal student aid plays a crucial role in assuring opportunity and social mobility in American society. A reduction of such aid would be a grave error.[49] Student aid, however, is more than a means for helping students finance their college education, as important as that is. It is an integral part of the education process, a means of encouraging the development of critical values in the men and women who will become leaders in the society.

CHART 8

SHARES OF FEDERAL STUDENT FINANCIAL AID PROVIDED THROUGH GRANTS, LOANS, SERVICE, AND WORK, FISCAL YEARS 1975, 1984, AND 1990

(MILLIONS OF CURRENT DOLLARS)

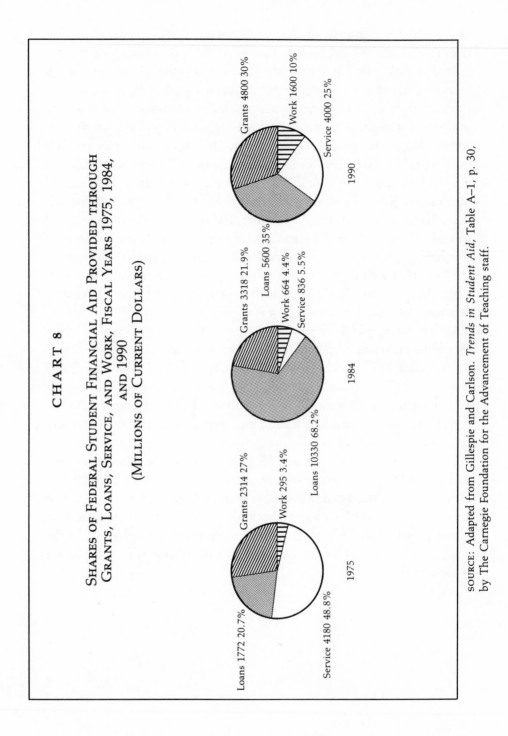

Grants 2314 27%

Work 295 3.4%

Loans 1772 20.7%

Service 4180 48.8%

1975

Grants 3318 21.9%

Work 664 4.4%

Service 836 5.5%

Loans 10330 68.2%

1984

Grants 4800 30%

Work 1600 10%

Loans 5600 35%

Service 4000 25%

1990

SOURCE: Adapted from Gillespie and Carlson. *Trends in Student Aid*, Table A–1, p. 30, by The Carnegie Foundation for the Advancement of Teaching staff.

CHAPTER VII

Participation of Minorities in the Professional Life of the Country

I F ONE CONSIDERS the forces with which this country must contend over the next decade (see Chapters II and III), it is clear that all segments of society must be drawn into the fullest possible participation. Yet for significant parts of the minority communities, after a short burst of progress in the 1970s, there has been little or no recent progress in entering into programs of higher education that lead to the professional and managerial life of the nation.[1] Whether one addresses this as an issue of social equity or of social efficiency, new and more effective approaches must be found.[2]

BEYOND THE OPEN DOOR

The term "minorities" encompasses growing diversity. Each group has different rates of growth, geographic areas of concentration, cultural and family customs, and institutional supports. The historically black colleges play a unique role in the black community. Hispanics, on the other hand, have developed close associations with certain community colleges. Even within the term "Hispanic," there are considerable differences between Cubans in Miami, Puerto Ricans in New York, and Chicanos in Los Angeles.

Over the last decade, from 1975 to 1984, the enrollment share of blacks and Hispanics in higher education barely changed at all.[3] The absence of change contrasted sharply with the preceding decade; when the United States belatedly turned its attention to civil rights, their enrollment in-

89

crease was startling. As the public turned to other issues, minority participation reached a plateau and, despite the growth in minority populations, even declined in some fields. Black enrollment, for example, has fallen despite the rise in the share of all 18-year-olds that are black. The Hispanic share of enrollment grew very slightly, but less than the growth in the share of all Hispanic 14- to 24-year-olds in the population, so Hispanics are proportionally less involved in higher education than before. For both blacks and Hispanics, the share of high school graduates going on to college has fallen.

The number of bachelor's degrees earned by members of black and Hispanic minorities also is falling. Minorities are more likely to attend two-year public institutions than are their white counterparts.[4] Blacks and Hispanics who enroll at urban community colleges are less likely than white students to transfer to four-year programs.[5] In all programs, save some of the effective programs for minorities noted below, attrition rates for both groups are higher. Native American enrollments, though far smaller, follow similar patterns.

These shares of enrollment overall and at four-year and two-year colleges, and of degrees earned and years completed, contrast strikingly with the steadily increasing share of blacks and Hispanics and particularly of those in the college-age years in the total population. Data on Hispanics is sparse, but the situation with respect to blacks is well documented. In 1970, black youth aged 18–24 comprised 11.9 percent of all youth in the U.S. This rose to 14 percent by 1982. Hispanic youth are estimated to constitute 7.5 percent of all youth in that age group.[6]

The problem this creates is clear. Traditionally, the large majority of the country's leaders, the managers and professionals—engineers, architects, lawyers, teachers, legislators, faculty members, etc.—have come from white middle class families. It is precisely these families that have had the sharpest drop in the number of children over the past twenty years. Over the next decade it is likely that the number of white 18-year-olds—who have historically formed the overwhelming majority of entrants to the professional class—will decline by roughly 35 percent from the 1980 peak while the number of black and Hispanic 18-year-olds—who tend to enter higher education at lower rates—will be expanding steadily.

90

TABLE 8

ENROLLMENT IN 4-YEAR INSTITUTIONS BY RACE/ETHNICITY

	NUMBER IN THOUSANDS				PERCENTAGE			
	1976	1978	1980	1982	1976	1978	1980	1982
White	5984	6013	6259	6289	84.4	83.7	82.9	82.4
Total Minority	930	973	1048	1070	13.1	13.5	13.9	14.0
Black	603	611	633	611	8.5	8.5	8.5	8.0
Hispanic	173	190	216	228	2.4	2.6	2.9	3.0
Asian/Pacific Islander	118	137	162	193	1.7	1.9	2.1	2.5
Am. Indian/ Alaskan Native	35	35	37	38	.5	.5	.5	.5

SOURCE: National Center for Education Statistics. *The Condition of Education, 1984 Edition*, Washington, D.C., 1984, Table 2.5, p. 76.

At issue is not just how many members of minorities gain entrance to college, but to which programs. Both blacks and Hispanics are not only underrepresented in college but are even less likely to enter a group of programs that have been identified as key—undergraduate programs at universities or four-year liberal arts colleges, undergraduate programs in engineering and the sciences, graduate programs in business, law, medicine, and those leading to Ph.Ds.[7]

An earlier problem was maldistribution of minorities by field. Blacks in graduate schools, for example, were heavily concentrated in education and sociology. In recent years, there has been progress toward better distribution, particularly with the steady success of drawing blacks into engineering. The problem now is more one of underrepresentation.[8]

During the 1980s and early 1990s the share of individuals under twenty years of age in the American population will decline to below 30 percent for the first time in our nation's history. This will be accompanied by an increase in the percentage of blacks and Hispanics in that age group.[9] Even with intensive efforts to improve minority education, the pool of students qualified for entry to key programs is sure to suffer.

TABLE 9

ENROLLMENT IN INSTITUTIONS OF HIGHER EDUCATION BY TYPE OF INSTITUTION AND RACE/ETHNICITY OF STUDENT—FALL 1982

| | BLACK | | ASIAN/PACIFIC | |
	N	PERCENT	N	PERCENT
All Institutions	1,085,908	100.0	349,915	100.0
4-year Institutions	609,265	56.1	192,355	55.1
2-year Institutions	473,643	43.6	157,560	45.0

| | HISPANIC | | WHITE | |
	N	PERCENT	N	PERCENT
All Institutions	516,504	100.0	9,878,419	100.0
4-year Institutions	227,855	44.1	6,260,670	63.4
2-year Institutions	288,649	55.9	3,617,749	36.6

SOURCE: Unpublished data. U.S. Department of Education. Office of the Assistant Secretary for Education Research and Improvement. National Center for Education Statistics. Taken from "Opening Fall Enrollment Survey, 1982," Table A–20.

TABLE 10

BACHELOR'S DEGREES CONFERRED BY INSTITUTIONS OF HIGHER EDUCATION BY RACE AND ETHNICITY, 1978–79, 1980–81

| | Bachelor's Degrees | | | |
| | 1978–1979 | | 1980–1981 | |
	N	PERCENT	N	PERCENT
Black	60,130	6.6	60,533	6.5
Hispanic	20,029	2.2	21,731	2.3
Am. Indian/ Alaskan Native	15,336	1.7	18,693	2.0

SOURCE: Unpublished data. Department of Education, Office of Civil Rights.

TABLE 11

RATES OF MINORITY PARTICIPATION IN HIGHER EDUCATION, 1980/1981
(IN PERCENTAGES)

	TOTAL POPULATION	TOTAL COLLEGE-AGE*	HIGHER ED. ENROLLMENT	BACHELOR'S DEGREES (1983)	DOCTORAL AND FIRST PROFESSIONAL DEGREES
Blacks	11.7	12.5	9.8	6.5	.7 to 6
Hispanics	6.4	6.8	4.5	2.3	.9 to 3
Asian-Americans	2.0	3.0	3.0	4.8	2 to 16

* Percent of 18- to 24-year-olds.

SOURCE: John B. Lee and Others. *Student Aid and Minority Enrollment in Higher Education*, prepared for American Association of State Colleges and Universities (Washington, D.C.: Applied Systems Institute), Table 1, p. 4, Table 2, p. 9, and Table 3, p. 11; and National Research Council, *Summary Report*, 1981, for Doctoral degrees.

TABLE 12

ENGINEERING DOCTORAL RECIPIENTS (U.S. CITIZENS AND PERMANENT VISAS) BY DEGREE COHORT, RACIAL/ETHNIC GROUP, 1973–1983
(IN PERCENTAGES)

YEAR	TOTAL NUMBERS	WHITE	BLACK	HISPANIC	ASIAN
1973–76	8,934	72.2	.8	.6	13.6
1977–80	6,549	74.4	1.0	1.6	16.8
1981–83	4,409	75.3	1.4	1.8	17.6

SOURCE: Scientific Manpower Commission. *Professional Women and Minorities*, Washington, D.C., August 1984, Table 2.8, p. 34.

CHART 9

Total Enrollment in Medical Colleges for Underrepresented Minorities: Black American, American Indian, Mexican American, and Mainland Puerto Rican, 1969–70 to 1984–85

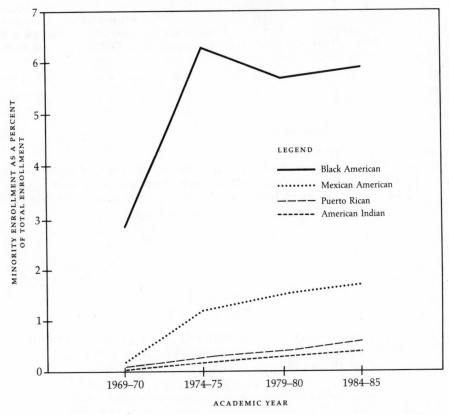

SOURCE: Association of American Medical Colleges. Office of Minority Affairs. *Minority Students in Medical Education: Facts and Figures II* (Washington, D.C.: A.A.M.C., March 1985), p. 11.

94

Our major concern is that these different and important minorities will not be drawn into full participation in society. Higher education has always been the key to social mobility and that role is more essential than ever today. The danger is that we will move toward a society in which the number of good jobs increases but in which almost all are held by whites and Asian Americans, while the rapidly growing share of blacks and Hispanics find themselves trapped in lower level jobs. Such a society will not work.[10]

Asian Americans are quite separate from other minority groups in their pattern of enrollment. Though they make up only 2 percent of the population, they receive 3 percent of M.D. degrees, 4 percent of engineering bachelor's, 7.5 percent of Ph.D. degrees in engineering, and 18 percent of all Doctor of Pharmacy degrees. They are underrepresented, however, in other fields—for example, they receive 1.5 percent of law degrees, and less than 1 percent of the degrees in education and the social sciences.

Family structure and cultural norms have an enormous amount to do with who goes on to college to study what. They contribute to differing rates of completion of high school, deficiencies of math and science skills among some groups, language barriers, and add to the concern over the adequacy of counseling, and the disputes over the suitability of standardized tests. What is needed is an array of imaginative programs. No single simple solution is likely to solve the problems of achieving equal opportunity. The diversity among minorities is a reminder as well that the country has a major task ahead to teach not only language skills but civic understanding and responsibility to many for whom the American concepts are unfamiliar.[11]

CREATING ACCESS TO THE TOP

Over the past fifteen years, great gains in minority enrollments were made primarily through:

> Legal powers of the federal government, and to a lesser extent the states, ending discriminatory practices
>
> Expansion of the number of colleges and universities

Expansion of student aid, and related programs

Active recruiting of minorities by the institutions

Aid for the historically black colleges through a variety of programs.

As important as it is to protect these gains, further progress is not likely to occur from these avenues alone. It is dependent on new efforts at colleges and universities, in communities, and between colleges and schools and businesses that are tailored to the particular needs of each setting. The fact that, to a significant degree, those minority students who have the ability and who are motivated are now going to college, still leaves out millions who have the talent but not necessarily the preparation. It also misses those whose motivation has yet to be kindled. Both of these tasks require individualized approaches and outreach to the elementary and secondary schools.[12]

In recent years, there has been an increase in the number of college and university efforts to reach out to high schools. The recent debate about the quality of elementary and secondary education, fueled by a series of recent reports, has directed more attention to these linkages. Some of the new efforts have focused on upgrading the high school curriculum, others on selection, training, or pay for teachers.[13] While these efforts are both valuable and overdue, there is a danger that the pressure to improve—measured by grades and test scores—could leave disadvantaged students to fend even more for themselves.

An antidote that has proven particularly successful has been those outreach programs that focus on finding, motivating, and preparing disadvantaged youth. A measure of their potential has been the slow but steady increase of black engineering students. This is an exception to the declines in black enrollments noted above, and results from a nationwide effort involving colleges and universities, high schools and junior high schools, and businesses, coordinated in many cases by the National Action Council for Minorities in Engineering. The successful programs tend to include involvement of students as early as junior high school; a focus on academic subjects, including math and science; encouragement of students to think in terms of entering colleges.

Corporate participation often has provided both funding and volunteer

96

manpower. Better counseling that tracks students who develop the necessary motivation into the college programs is required. Often peer tutoring or summer programs are used with effect.

A number of successful programs at universities and colleges recruit and encourage disadvantaged students. They range from the new middle school operated by LaGuardia Community College in New York for urban minorities to that of St. Edwards in Texas for children of migrant workers. Many of the most successful, like the Minority Engineering Program at the California State University at Northridge, reach down to the ninth grade or even to earlier grades.

At the college level, almost all the successful programs include prefreshman summer preparation, an early warning system of potential academic problems, a high degree of faculty/student interaction, and the clear expectation that the students in the program will succeed.

A broader base of financial and moral support is needed to encourage and sustain these programs. Corporate support can and should be increased, but it understandably focuses on fields such as engineering, in which the interest of business is clear. Not only is more funding needed, but the form of support must be such that it can select those programs that will be winners. When the right approach, determined leadership, and modest resources are combined, minority students can be successfully drawn into and will complete academic courses leading to the professional and managerial life of the nation.

The experience of the successful programs is that they have succeeded when and where there is strong personal leadership willing to persist over a long period. Imagination and dedication are impossible to legislate, but they can be encouraged. Support from the college and university administration is essential. The federal government, through the Fund for the Improvement in Post-Secondary Education (FIPSE), has encouraged the establishment of a number of projects that have already proven their worth.[14]

The successful programs around the country have generated an array of models to be emulated or improved upon. (See the Appendix for a representative list of such programs.) Most have struggled to find the financial resources necessary to keep operating.

A new agency should be created, the National Opportunity Fund, modeled in the form of FIPSE, specifically designed to support competitive grants to programs for disadvantaged students. The Fund should support programs within colleges and universities and emphasize programs that link these institutions to high schools.

The funding and function of the TRIO programs should also be included in the Fund.[15] The TRIO program, sponsored by the federal government, contrary to its name, is an amalgam of four major programs designed to complement the federal financial aid programs by addressing the nonfinancial barriers to the enrollment of disadvantaged students.[16] These four programs are:

Talent Search: to identify disadvantaged high school students with academic potential and provide counseling and tutoring in the school.

Upward Bound: to develop better academic skills in disadvantaged junior or senior high school students primarily by exposure to a college environment.

Special Services for Disadvantaged Students: to support disadvantaged college students, including provision of counseling and tutoring, at the college level.

Equal Opportunity Centers: to guide and counsel adults, including high school dropouts and their parents, about meeting postsecondary education preparation requirements.

Of the students served, 41 percent are black, 17 percent are Hispanic, and 4 percent Native American. The students who come through these programs constitute 20 percent of all blacks and Hispanics enrolled in higher education. Over the last four years, these programs have been reduced substantially, but the need is greater than ever. Black and Hispanic TRIO students are several times more likely to attend college than comparable non-TRIO students and, most important, several times more likely to finish when they do attend.[17]

The subject of minority education must return to the head of higher education's agenda.[18]

98

CHAPTER VIII

The Expansion of International Exchange

THE VALUE to the United States of citizens who understand other cultures and languages becomes clearer with each passing decade. It has been propounded, expounded, and documented by several recent studies. A typical observation:

> It is not unusual in a midwestern family these days to see the son engaged in Karate, the wife taking yoga at the YWCA or YMCA, the family eating bean sprouts, running in shoes made in Taiwan and . . . driving a Toyota or Datsun.[1]

A few facts further dramatize the internationalism of our economy, society and polity:[2]

> Roughly 25 percent of the United States' GNP is derived from foreign trade, and the proportion is growing. Banking, the stock markets, the communications industry, even the practice of medicine are becoming international in scope.

> Almost one-third of the United States' corporate profits are generated by international business activities.

> Over one-third of American agricultural land produces food for export.

> The United States spends billions of dollars and countless man-hours on a range of organizations designed to foster international efforts from the World Bank to NATO.

The major argument, however, is neither economic nor military but political. The purpose of fostering international exchange is not to assist a resurgence of American power for military or economic domination, but to enable the United States to exert enlightened world leadership.[3] Yet, how often have we fallen short in that role because our citizens at large and even our leaders or our diplomats did not understand and were not sensitive about the cultures of other countries?[4] To achieve this sensitivity requires more than the study of a foreign language or even a foreign culture, as helpful as this is. It requires immersion in another society through study or work abroad.

Whatever peace and progress the world has experienced since World War II is the responsibility of a generation of European and other leaders educated in the United States, and of United States' leaders with experience learning, living, and working abroad. As this generation passes the mantle of authority to the next generation, there is a danger that the bedrock of cross-cultural experience upon which our alliances were built will be replaced by more parochial and insular loyalties incapable of sustaining solid commitments.[5]

THE ACADEMIC BRIDGE

Traditionally, the college years have been a time for students to become acquainted with other countries.[6] It is a time when young people have reached adulthood but not adult responsibilities. Many of the best known colleges and universities have well-established study abroad programs. About 340,000 students from abroad study here, and that is a ten-fold increase over the number in 1955.[7] Learning about other cultures, meeting students from abroad, or undertaking the personal experience of living in another culture are effective parts of a liberal education.

Universities and colleges serve as a link to the rest of the world. University researchers travel abroad regularly and are often in regular contact with their colleagues overseas; federal programs, including the Fulbright program, foster the continuing interchange of scholars. These programs of study and research are only a part of the total array of international exchanges—scores of youth programs, cultural interchanges, the Peace Corps, Project Hope—built up over the years in recognition that we live in an interdependent world.

100

Effective international student and faculty interchange serve five purposes:

To develop in all students understanding of the international nature of the world

To develop the expertise in international affairs the United States needs to function effectively in the world today

To encourage students from abroad who will become the leaders—intellectual, cultural, industrial, and political—of their countries to study at American colleges and universities

To develop more effective ties between this country and others through the relationships between the academic community here and abroad

To understand the international dimensions and origins of domestic U.S. issues.

To achieve these goals several major federal programs deal directly with international education for faculty and students in higher education. Most notably, they are:[8]

I. *United States Information Agency*
President's International Youth Exchange Initiative (students)
Fulbright: Mutual Educational and Cultural Exchange Act (faculty)
American Scholars
Visiting Scholars
Scholars-in-Residence
Collaborative Research Grants (to start in 1985, for graduate students)
Private Sector Programs (principally students)
Central America Initiative (faculty and students)

II. *Department of Education*
Higher Education Act of 1965, Title IV's National Resource Fellowships (students)
Fulbright-Hays (faculty and students)

Doctoral Dissertation Research Abroad
Faculty Research Abroad
Group Projects Abroad for Non-Western Languages
Teacher Exchange

III. *United States Agency for International Development*
Central America Initiative

THE RETREAT FROM GLOBAL COMMITMENT

Why, with all of these programs, with the various university-based and private programs for American students studying abroad, with foreign students studying here, the sharing of research information, and a number of joint programs, is there so much concern about the state of international education? A rash of recent reports, the National Bipartisan Commission on Central America (the Kissinger Commission) being the latest, have repeatedly argued that this important subject is in a state of neglect.[9]

One reason is that support for international education, both public and private, has been in decline for a decade or more. From 1965 until 1983, the funding for the programs of USIA, including the Fulbright program, declined by 40 percent. Only a determined effort by Congress prevented even further cuts and, in fact, provided an increase in FY 1982. Similarly, many foundations reduced funding after about 1970 as other issues gained attention.[10]

Another reason is that interest in languages and international studies has declined even as the need for them has grown. The share of high school seniors with at least some language skills declined from about one-third before World War II until it reached less than one-sixth a few years ago even though the share of high school graduates going on to college has increased four times. As of 1982, only 14 percent of colleges and universities required study of a foreign language for admission, compared to 34 percent in 1966.[11] (As a result of the ongoing debate about the quality of education in the United States, language study appears to be recovering somewhat.)

A third reason is that programs of study abroad for American students are more common at elite institutions. The estimated number of American students studying overseas is on the order of 50,000, or less than one-half of 1 percent of total U.S. university and college enrollments.[12] A large number of students at Dartmouth, Stanford, and Williams spend some time overseas, but at the less selective colleges and universities it is rare that a student studies abroad.

In addition to the decline in support and the general apathy of the last 15 years, a number of practical problems need attention. International programs are inherently more complicated than domestic programs and, like a spinning top, will slowly wind down unless periodically infused with new energy. Because of the ease of interaction with Europe—of language, custom, travel, and funding—existing programs, both governmental and private, are skewed toward Europe. Moreover, the availability of ready funding has meant growth in programs in Japan, Taiwan, and Korea with little movement in less wealthy countries. It is also in the wealthy countries that the quality of shared research projects attract American faculty. It is there that the quality of the universities makes for the easiest interchange. In 1983, 38 percent of all Fulbright scholars went to Western Europe and 42 percent came from there. If the East Asian countries are included, the share is well over half.[13]

The most critical areas for greater interchange are those that Americans tend to overlook or ignore—Latin America, Africa, Southeast Asia, as well as, surprisingly, Canada, New Zealand, and Australia.[14] In 1983, there were only 99 U.S. Fulbright scholars in all of Latin America and 86 Latin American Fulbright scholars in the U.S. The 99 U.S. scholars represent about .02 percent of all full-time U.S. college and university faculty members.[15]

The United States provides only limited funding, either public or private, for foreign students who come here. Those that come are largely from wealthy nations and well-to-do families. In contrast, the U.S.S.R. and its allies not only fund far more students (102,400 in 1982 compared to 9,000 by USIA and USAID funds), but also focus on students from less well-to-do families, and on the developing nations, particularly those in Africa.[16] The Japanese, as their role on the world stage expands, plan to increase the number of foreign students studying at Japanese universities from 10,000 to 100,000.[17]

A certain proportion of the students who have come to the United States have elected to remain behind here after finishing their education. Whatever other values this has, it adds only a modest amount to meeting the goals noted above. Clearly it is in the national interest to encourage the future leaders of other countries to study here, but it is important to insure that students of promise from all walks of life are included.[18]

A further problem is that the incentive for American faculty to become involved in international exchanges is often marginal. With the difficulty of gaining faculty positions and the pressure toward higher standards for promotion and tenure, particularly the demand to demonstrate research accomplishments, faculty are increasingly reluctant to step out of their hard-won place in the academic pecking order. This is exacerbated by the conditions in those countries where the need for exchanges is the greatest, such as Latin America, where the universities want exchange faculty to focus on teaching and where the quality of research facilities and output is such that it is hard for some faculty to keep up with advances in their field. The discipline most in demand abroad is that of American Studies, but faculty in this area have little disciplinary incentive to study abroad. One result is that few faculty members seek a Fulbright grant unless they already have tenure, yet overseas experience may be more valuable and easier to undertake for younger faculty.

Faculty also find that the financial cost of spending a year abroad is considerable in both financial and immediate career terms. This is hardest in the developing countries, particularly when families are involved, with travel expenses, cultural adjustment, the difficulty of insuring health care, and the like. The increase in two-career families has created a new complication in recent years.[19]

Despite these problems, the need for exchange programs is more important than ever. Faculty are both role models and mentors. Those with personal experience abroad are needed in far larger numbers and from a far wider spectrum of colleges and universities. More than a tiny fraction of American students need the personal and cultural growth experience of studying abroad.[20] With the attention of the country turning once again to the ever more international nature of American life, particularly the attention now devoted to the international aspects of the economy, there is a greater opportunity to build such programs.

INCREASING INVOLVEMENT ABROAD

Much of the interest in the current debate about educational reform has been focused on the need to increase the number of students studying languages and the number of graduate students in area studies programs.[21] An increase in the study of foreign languages and culture and an increase in the number of people expert in each area of the world are themselves important goals. The goals noted above, however, require direct involvement, an immersion in another culture in order to see, feel, and sense differing points of view and their causes.[22] A larger number of individual exchanges of faculty for both teaching and research is essential.[23] It also is in the best interests of the United States that a larger number of students from abroad study here, particularly those who expect to return to their native countries to make their careers and those who represent a more balanced socio-economic mixture of potential leaders.

In addition to the individual exchanges of faculty and students, more needs to be done to develop university-to-university relationships of a lasting nature.[24] Over time, these links provide added and unpredictable forms of interchange, both formal and informal. They help reinforce the permanence of the exchange. However, each takes spadework to develop, and each needs a simple but workable infrastructure to advise and counsel the students and faculty involved.

Finally, more can be done to insure the growth of exchange with those areas of the greatest need—the developing countries of Latin America, Africa, and Asia.

No one program can meet all of the diverse needs of international exchange, particularly since each program must also be country-specific. What serves India well may well have little applicability to Costa Rica. There are already a variety of programs, but we believe that there are important missing pieces and that the scale of exchange, particularly with some areas of the world, is not adequate.

A new segment should be added to the Fulbright program to provide fellowships for an exchange of undergraduate or immediate postgraduate students. Each exchange should be established between two institutions of higher education—one in the United States and one in Latin America, Africa, Asia, or Canada. In a given case, the two institutions would jointly apply for funding for a given number of fellowships to be provided equally to students from each. Students would spend one year at the opposite campus, pay the ordinary fees to their home campus, and receive a fellowship to help offset the added costs, the size of which would vary depending on the country.

Students in some disciplines, engineering or the sciences for example, find it difficult to substitute a year at a foreign university in a tightly structured curriculum. Many American colleges and universities will be reluctant to accept at full credit a year at some universities in less developed countries.[25] These considerations, plus the fact that many students benefit from a break in their studies, argue for the need to make opportunity for study abroad available either during or just after the undergraduate years, even if it adds to the length of time in college.[26]

One other advantage of an institution-to-institution program is that it allows for the creative development of such other programs as a version of the Public Service Teaching Fellows program noted above (see Chapter VI). Immediate postgraduates of that program could spend a year of their service responsibility teaching at a high school in the area of the Latin American university partner, for example.[27] Students need to know that such opportunities are available, and there needs to be a simple infrastructure to support them. Where feasible, recognizing national differences in the practices of student employment, institutions would be encouraged to provide work/study opportunities as well.[28] Not all relationships need be institution-to-institution, but this segment of the total program could augment the currently few but useful linkages of this type.

There are also programs universities and colleges can undertake on their own or with corporate support. Many universities now run major travel and educational programs for their alumni that capitalize on the urge to tourism. *Universities and colleges should create expanded summer programs of organized travel and study, built on the alumni travel/study model, that extend the opportunity for study abroad to a wider share of students.* A few universities have worked with European corporations that have facilities in the U.S. or American corporations that have facilities overseas to create the equivalent of cooperative work/study arrangements. *Universities and colleges should seek more of these corporate sponsored overseas internships of at least a semester in length.*

An additional new segment should be added to the Fulbright program to provide extra funding for larger grants and for more intense recruiting for faculty interchanges for the three areas of Latin America, Africa, and Southeast Asia. More intense outreach and recruiting should also be conducted. These areas are, for reasons noted above, more expensive and difficult for the U.S. faculty involved. In addition, because these countries tend to want exchange faculty who are prepared to teach, the logical sources for candidates are the liberal arts colleges and the state colleges— the very institutions that need more international experience. Within the last few years, the Fulbright Scholar-in-Residence program has added a new form of area fellowships that is intended to address this problem for these three and a few other regions. The recommendation of our panel goes a step further to superimpose specific set-aside funding for grants for faculty and students focused on these three areas without disrupting the existing program.[29]

Specific earmarking and an expansion of the AID funding available for competitive grants to joint projects by an American and an overseas university should be expanded. One function would be to provide the modest infrastructure to support the undergraduate exchange program described above. Such programs cannot function effectively without a small amount of administrative support to provide counseling, and other such services. Other projects might encompass research, such as the comparison of the incidence of heart disease in Louisiana and in Northern Brazil; or public service, such as the development of new training methods for civil servants in Morocco; or even institution building within higher education, such as the building of a new engineering program in a university in Thailand. The proposed expansion of Scholars-in-Residence from Central America, when coupled with this program, will allow Central

American universities to undertake programs of institutional development drawing on their U.S. counterparts. AID, with small amounts of funding devoted to joint projects between American and foreign universities, has often managed to accomplish a great deal, not only in the value of the projects themselves, but in the encouragement of on-going links between two institutions.[30]

Finally, *a specific program should be established to provide for the exchange of high school teachers.* Since one goal is to build into the consciousness of students an awareness of the many differing cultures of the world, the high school teacher is in a role of considerable leverage.[31] Whenever possible, these exchanges should be coupled with the institutional linkages between two universities so as to provide the necessary support. At present, high school teachers pay their own way to teach abroad. They also tend to concentrate in the United Kingdom, France, and West Germany.

The United States now lives in a truly international world. More than ever, we need to listen to and understand those in other countries. The broadening of the student and faculty experience to include other cultures deepens the commitment to liberal values. The outreach to join with students and universities of other countries is in keeping with the most important and honorable American traditions.[32]

SECTION THREE

CHAPTER IX

Progress Report: The University Role in Research and Technology

UNIVERSITIES not only educate the professional and managerial leaders of the United States, but are the home of the scholarship that produces social and technological change. More than half of all basic research is done at universities. Research is not only important to society but to the universities where it has become intertwined with graduate and professional education. The effectiveness of the research universities, therefore, is a central issue of public policy.

As the country faces profound economic and political changes, questions about the effectiveness of higher education as a provider of utilizable knowledge and skilled personnel have come to the surface. Is the United States ahead or behind in research? In technology? Is the research capacity of the country growing or diminishing? Are we choosing the right balance between research and technology, between defense needs and economic development needs, between concentrating resources and competition, and between universities and federal laboratories?

Do we adequately recognize that scholarship in the humanities, in the social sciences, and in every professional field, is as essential to the health of higher education, and the civic health of the nation, as are inquiries in scientific and technological disciplines? What demands do these issues place on the universities, and what risks do they pose for institutional integrity? While this review focuses on science and technology, these proposals are applicable to the whole of research and scholarship.

THE AMERICAN STANDING IN RESEARCH
AND TECHNOLOGY

Forty years ago, this country began its efforts to catch up with European research. Twenty years ago, the United States had surged ahead in virtually every field. Today, we struggle to maintain that leadership in the face of increasingly effective research competition from other nations. In this struggle, the United States, more than the other major developed countries, depends on its universities rather than on government laboratories for basic research; more on competition among researchers or teams of researchers and less on hierarchical management of the research function for leadership.[1] With intensifying international competition, specific questions have been raised as to whether the research capacity of the United States is:

- losing ground to international competitors
- losing vitality and becoming more bureaucratic
- capable of effective translation of research to technology
- forced to move away from traditional patterns of competition and decentralization to more centralized decisions or "targeting" of research
- funded adequately
- supported with the necessary base of instrumentation and libraries.

The ability of the United States to compete economically and politically depends not only on research leadership, but also on leadership in developing technology, and its capacity to turn that technology into imaginative new products. In this country new product development is almost entirely the responsibility of industry, and therefore beyond the scope of this report. The universities' ability to translate research into technology and the effectiveness of the linkages between universities and industry are, however, of major concern for us.

Can the American system continue to lead in *research* through the 1980s and 1990s? Is it effective enough, compared with international

112

competitors, with the research system of 20 years ago, or with the needs of the country?

Our research system, based primarily on the universities, is still the most effective in the world. This is not, however, as much a cause for celebration as it is a reason for renewed determination. The gap between research achievement here and in other developed nations has narrowed. Many aspects of American research, including the infrastructure for its support and the priorities among broad national purposes, need review and action.

Can the American system provide leadership in *technology* through the 1980s and into the 1990s? The Japanese already have wrested leadership from the United States in several fields, and this issue deserves more attention.

ORIGINS OF THE AMERICAN MODEL OF RESEARCH

From the earliest days of American research, the mid-1800s, universities have played a more prominent role in research here than they have in Europe.[2] From the beginning, there also has been an understanding of the linkage between university research and the applications of technology. This point was explicitly recognized in the Land Grant Act of 1862. By the 1930s, American research began to attract international recognition, but the locus of the most advanced research, the great centers where aspiring scientists went for postdoctoral studies, was still in Europe. A group of university scientists and presidents headed by Karl Compton of the Massachusetts Institute of Technology began to argue for a major expansion of research, and for more federal support.

At the close of World War II, scientists prominent in wartime research, led by Vanevar Bush, James Conant, Karl Compton, and others, proposed what became the new American system. Bush's report to President Roosevelt, *Science: The Endless Frontier*[3] was the blueprint. The goal was to defend the country's national interests. The war had driven home in unmistakable terms the nation's danger if it lagged behind in research or remained dependent on European laboratories. In addition, the war had given university scientists and administrators experience in working with their civilian and military counterparts, and inspired ideas on what was needed for developing a permanent system.

Establishment of the Office of Naval Research, the Atomic Energy Commission and the National Science Foundation established the mode:

- Research funding was to be a federal responsibility.

- Although a range of agencies, including government and industrial laboratories, would be involved in research, *basic* research (i.e., the expansion of knowledge for its own sake) was to be conducted primarily in universities.

- Within the universities, research funding was to go to individual researchers or teams rather than institutions. Within the granting agencies, projects would be selected on the basis of peer review of researcher-generated proposals.

- Rather than having a single agency for research support, there would be multiple agencies, each with its own mission, and each competing for the attention of researchers.[4]

The results were remarkable. By the 1960s, the United States had become the leader in virtually every research field; Americans came to dominate the Nobel Prize selections in science fields; graduate and post-graduate students came to the United States in order to study with those scholars at the forefront of their fields.

In 1950, when the National Science Foundation (NSF) was established, federal research support to universities was several million dollars per year and half a dozen agencies supported university research. By 1980, 40 federal agencies were providing such support and the level of financing had reached $4 billion.[5] Not only was the federal government transformed, the universities of the country became great graduate and research centers. In 1940, Stanford's budget for research for the entire university was $5,000. By 1980, it was over $100 million.[6] Entirely new research universities, such as the University of California at San Diego or the State University of New York at Stony Brook were created. MIT, which did not begin graduate education until the 1930s, enrolled as many graduate students as undergraduates. Today, approximately 350 universities undertake serious research and about 100 universities conduct sponsored research costing at least $20 million.[7]

With this record, why should we consider any changes? New forces have entered the equation, including international competition and the growing realization that economic growth is more dependent on advanced technology than had been recognized.

THE AMERICAN STANDING IN RESEARCH

Are we really falling behind other industrialized nations in research? After almost 40 years of achievement, does our system need upgrading, or renewal, or even a complete overhaul? To assess whether this is the case, the National Science Foundation has compiled some objective measures it calls "Science Indicators." These include international comparisons of funding levels, numbers of scientists, Nobel prizes, numbers and quality of journal articles, citations, and patents issued. All of these are useful but flawed or inadequate as an overall measure of research standing.[8] For example, Nobel prizes are few in number and have a long time constant (for example, the 1983 prize in medicine was awarded to Barbara McClintock for work done over 30 years earlier);[9] patents usually rise in number toward the end of the life of a particular field rather than at the beginning.[10]

While they are helpful in describing trends and the relative dimensions of science in the United States, Western Europe, and Japan, the science indicators inadequately define actual research leadership. Such leadership is dependent on such intangibles as leadership of individuals within the research community, the quality of available scientific talent, the morale and ambitions of those involved, the climate of freedom from bureaucratic constraint. No single, or even multiple, objective measure, therefore, seems to answer the overall question of who is leading in research.

For this report, scientists themselves were asked where the leading research was being undertaken in their own fields—in which countries and laboratories, where graduate students and postdoctoral fellows wished to study, and where they actually were studying. Although scientists may value their own or their national colleague's work out of familiarity or pride, the level of knowledge and candor of those interviewed was striking. There also was close agreement among the scientists in different settings.

The scientists themselves "vote with their feet." In interviews both here and abroad, the researchers acknowledge that the United States is the place to be—at the graduate, postdoctoral, and professional levels.[11] This evidence, coupled with the scientists' own perceptions of where the best work is going on, strongly suggests that the U.S. is ahead of the rest of the world in terms of basic research. Several sources, however, cited the following fields in which the United States is behind in research:[12]

AREA	LEADER
1. Deep drilling for research on earth's crust (geophysics)	USSR
2. Arctic research	USSR
3. High energy physics	Europeans[13] European Consortium for Nuclear Research (CERN)
4. Solid state chemistry	Germany and France

In such specialized areas as the physics of surfaces and interfaces and fluid mechanics, other nations (the United Kingdom and the Soviet Union) have advanced. In no significant case, however, was the United States out of serious contention. The general picture is one of continuing American leadership essentially across the board, a gradual narrowing of the gap between researchers in this country and those in Europe and Japan, a great deal of communication across borders among researchers in a given field, and a widespread recognition here and abroad that the flexibility and competitive-cooperative model of university research in this country has given the United States a considerable advantage.

THE EFFECTIVENESS OF UNIVERSITY RESEARCH

Is the American research system as effective as it has been in the past? Is some of the nation's narrowing margin of leadership caused by an

116

erosion of effectiveness? Has federal sponsorship become slowly and inexorably more bureaucratic? Has the number and quality of new researchers been adequate to keep the system vibrant?[14]

Efforts to measure whether the system had become bogged down in red tape produced surprising results. A 1977 study, *The State of Academic Science*, found increasing frustration with government bureaucracy and regulations. "To the academic observer, the university has become bureaucratized virtually overnight."[15] The panel's findings, however, indicate that while the level of regulations has not fallen, the push to regulate has slowed substantially and academic skill in coping with the system has risen. While this does not eliminate the problem of wasted resources—particularly time—it does highlight the flexibility of the current research structure. Most of the researchers interviewed did not consider over-regulation to be a major problem.

A more serious concern is whether the research effort is losing vitality because of fewer new, younger faculty members. The statistics here do not necessarily provide a clear answer. The number of Ph.D. degrees in the sciences increased a few years ago; there are fewer young scientists in faculty positions, more in postdoctoral and research positions.[16] There is concern that young scientists in soft money research positions and without faculty status are less able to break out in new directions. This problem is exacerbated by the difficulty of finding research funding for newly hired faculty, for new ideas and research directions, and for interdisciplinary research. These issues must be addressed.

THE INTERNATIONAL COMPETITION IN TECHNOLOGY

Historically, this country's greatest strength has been not in research, but in technology. By technology we mean synthesizing from available knowledge and from applied research a way to do something—to synthesize a useful chemical compound, to develop a scheme whereby a robot can "see" an object, or to pack more functions onto a silicon chip so that more complex yet less expensive integrated circuits can be manufactured.

The measurement of international standing in applied research—or the translation of research to technology—is far more complicated than the

117

measurement of leadership in basic research. Most basic research is sorted into disciplines and subdisciplines and therefore can more readily be compared. American researchers are primarily located in universities. Through publications, conferences, computer networks, and visiting scholar arrangements, they are regularly in touch with each other's work.

Translating research into technology is more complex, diverse, and less open. Universities play a crucial though less dominant role. In such academic disciplines as agriculture or medicine, universities not only have a long tradition of involvement in technology, but extensive organizations—such as the agricultural extension agents or hospital-based clinical faculty—to carry out this function. Government and industrial laboratories are deeply involved in those areas of technology where the military and commercial advantage is obvious. In some fields, medical technology, for example, information is shared widely, but in others, semiconductor technology or genetic engineering, much is not.

In addition, a country's standing in the development of technology is often confused with its standing in the third phase—the development of new products. A country may lead in the development of a given technology, such as robotics or semiconductors, but find that aggressive, better-managed firms in another country have excelled at exploiting that technology. Despite these difficulties, we have attempted to measure the United States' position in translating research into technology.

The entrepreneurship of American industry and universities has traditionally allowed this country to exploit new research rapidly wherever it is done, both that done in the United States and in Europe. In fact, much of the American wartime technology as well as American industrial progress in the 1950s and 1960s was an outgrowth of European research. The success of this entrepreneurial tradition was so widely assumed that technology policy has become an issue only recently. There has been a conscious national research policy since 1945, but technology policy was not even an issue until the 1960s, and it did not become a matter of national debate until the 1980s.[17]

American research and technology were particularly effective in the defense field—perhaps because one federal agency was responsible for funding research, funding technology, and funding the development of

118

new products. The influence of the user, in this case the Defense Department, could be felt directly all along the chain of research and technology.

Largely the translation of research to technology was a matter of serendipity, a serendipity that was encouraged and nurtured but was more assumed than planned. The Soviet Union, our major competitor in defense, could not match this somewhat casual system. Until recently, we also had no serious economic competitor.

Today, however, although America still holds an edge over Europe in the capacity to create new technologies, we are seriously challenged in the field of economic development. The new factor in the equation is Japan. While significantly behind the United States in research, Japan has managed to do to this country what it has been doing for several decades to Europe—capitalize on research done here to create new technologies. Because of the relative openness of this country and the far greater understanding of the English language in Japan compared to the knowledge of the Japanese language in the United States, the flow of information is out of balance. In some areas, the question of leadership is a subject of controversy. In 1983, the Office of Technology Assessment released a study of the world electronics industry that found the United States holding a virtually unassailable lead in the computer industry and dominating semiconductor technology. Still, in a January 1984 issue of *Computerworld*, the president of an American computer company argued, "Japan will continue its dominance in many areas of the semiconductor market."[18]

Fields in which there is an intense American-Japanese struggle over technological leadership include:

Advanced ceramics

Large-scale integrated circuits

Supercomputing

Artificial intelligence

Optical fibers

Machine tool technology

119

Video recording

Robotics

Computer-assisted design.[19]

There are, as one might expect, fields European countries tend to dominate, such as:

Nuclear generation of power

Flat glass technology

Paper making technology

Textile manufacturing technology.

Still, for now, it is primarily a two-horse race—a fact that has alarmed European policy makers and business executives who fear being crushed in the technology trade war between the United States and Japan.[20] Although the United States remains ahead in the translation of research into technology, the Japanese challenge is formidable, and already is successful in many critical areas.

There is a third task beyond both improving research and translating that research into technology—translating technology into new products. This task is almost exclusively a function of industry, and is beyond the scope of this study. However, successful effort in this area depends directly on the first two tasks as well as on such factors as the quality of industrial leadership, interest in new product development, tax policy, and the availability of capital. This third task appears to be the area of greatest vulnerability for the United States.

The whole of American research and technology is working well. Its great strength lies in flexible, diverse, and decentralized management that allows it to be both competitive—releasing the creative energies of researchers—and cooperative—with rapid sharing of knowledge and shared use of larger facilities. Compared to other developed nations, it is more of a bottom up, or researcher-driven and developer-driven approach to the choice of research projects. It is a centrally coordinated rather than a centrally managed system—overall coordination and focusing is provided by the selection of the areas to be researched by the granting agencies,

120

by the use of some large and focused projects such as the synfuel projects funded by the Department of Energy, and by the more centrally directed roles of the federal laboratories and the Federally Funded Research and Development Centers.

The United States cannot assume its continued leadership in either research or the translation of research to technology. Leadership involves constant striving. But while working at staying out front, the United States must improve its capacity to make full use of the fruits of research—both here and abroad—to exploit its technological potential, to apply it to practical problems in industry, the environment, and society. To pursue this strategy several key issues must be addressed—the balance of resources devoted to technology, the willingness of universities to be more involved in the development of new technologies, the funding of research supporting economic development, the desirability of improving the flow of new talent and the funding of new ideas, the need to modernize the support system upon which the research rests, and the imperative of guaranteeing the free flow of information.

CHAPTER X

Research Funding: A New Balance For Effectiveness

FEDERAL SPENDING on research and development has increased threefold in the last decade. However, much of this increase is attributable to inflation and not to real expenditure growth (see Chart 10), leaving federal support of research in 1982 roughly comparable to what it was in 1972. Traditionally, most attention has been focused on the *level* of federal support. More attention needs to be paid to the *allocation* of this support. Specifically:

- Is the division of federal funds between basic and applied research, and between civilian and defense research, the right division in light of the problems identified in Chapters II and IX?

- Should the means for allocating federal research be changed from primary dependence on decentralized decisions and competition among researchers to greater centralization and targeting?

- Are resources being distributed to the most effective research performers?

In considering these issues, it is useful to review the background and scope of federal support for research.

THE RECENT SHIFTS IN FEDERAL SUPPORT

In 1972, federal support for research and development by all performers totaled $17 billion. The bulk of this amount, 68 percent, was for support of development projects, and 32 percent was for support of research. Of the research funding, about 40 percent went for basic research and the other 60 percent went for applied research. By 1984, the total level of federal obligations had not quite tripled to $47 billion, though most of this growth was inflationary. In real dollar terms, there was only a slight upward trend, which became more pronounced after 1981. The division between research and development was almost unchanged: 31 percent to research and 69 percent to development. But within research there was a marked shift toward basic research (45 percent) and away from applied research (55 percent).[1]

Not only the amount but the nature of federal support for research and development changed direction after 1981. There has been a growth in both current and constant dollar support. Despite pressures on the federal budget caused by the large deficits, the administration chose to continue this trend with an increase of 18 percent in 1985 for a total research and development budget of $54 billion.[2]

The bulk of this buildup comes from the expansion of defense expenditures, both defense-related research and defense-related development, especially weapons development. Between 1980 and 1984, because of the high cost of weapons systems work, the share devoted to development has increased from 63 percent to 69 percent.

The mix also changed in nondefense research and development, as shown in Chart 12. Nondefense basic research as a share of total nondefense research has grown noticeably since 1980. The sharp decline in nondefense development is largely attributable to the phasing down or cancellation of the alternative fuel projects in the energy field.

Chart 13 illustrates the disproportionate share of federal support going to defense research at the expense of nondefense research activities.[3] From 1980 to 1984 there was a 65 percent increase in national defense-related research. The National Science Foundation lists 15 nondefense budget items. Of these, only one, general science, received a modest 7 percent constant dollar growth rate in the same four-year period.

THE ROLE OF UNIVERSITIES

To whom does the federal government turn when it funds basic research? The universities dominate, receiving almost half of all federal dollars for

124

CHART 10

FEDERAL OBLIGATIONS AND DEVELOPMENT TO ALL PERFORMERS, 1972–1984

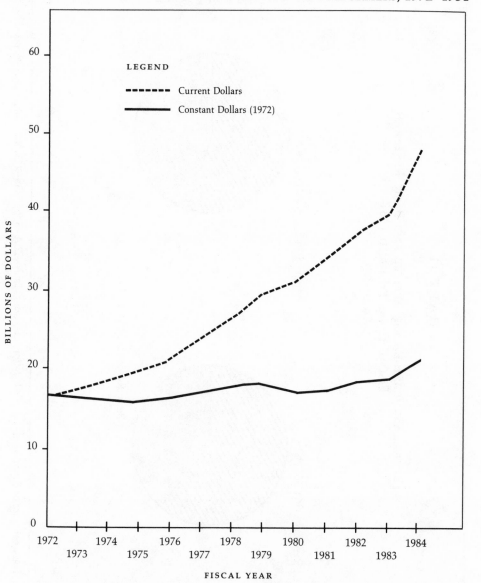

LEGEND

- - - - - - Current Dollars
———— Constant Dollars (1972)

BILLIONS OF DOLLARS

FISCAL YEAR

SOURCE: National Science Foundation. *Federal Funds for Research and Development, Detailed Historical Tables: Fiscal Year 1955–1984*, Tables 4A–B, pp. 73–86. Constant (1972) dollars calculated from price index deflation series used by the Division of Science Resources Studies.

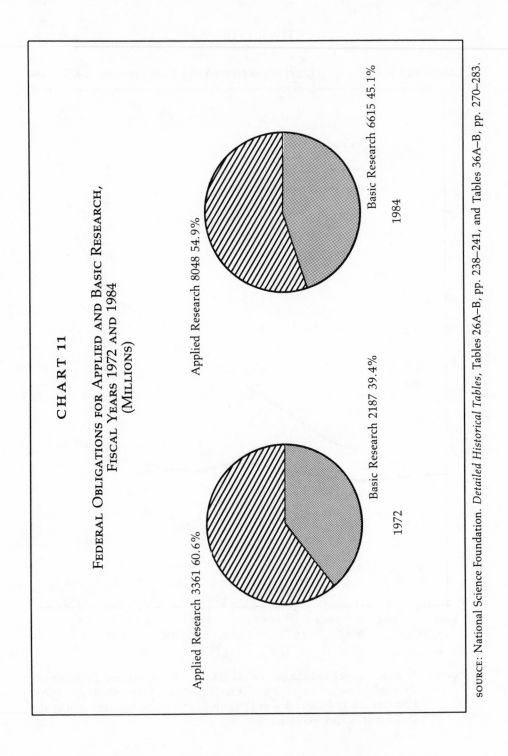

CHART 11

FEDERAL OBLIGATIONS FOR APPLIED AND BASIC RESEARCH,
FISCAL YEARS 1972 AND 1984
(MILLIONS)

Applied Research 3361 60.6%

Basic Research 2187 39.4%

1972

Applied Research 8048 54.9%

Basic Research 6615 45.1%

1984

SOURCE: National Science Foundation. *Detailed Historical Tables*, Tables 26A–B, pp. 238–241, and Tables 36A–B, pp. 270–283.

CHART 12

FEDERAL RESEARCH AND DEVELOPMENT OBLIGATIONS FOR NON-DEFENSE IN CONSTANT 1983 DOLLARS, SELECTED YEARS: 1978 TO 1985

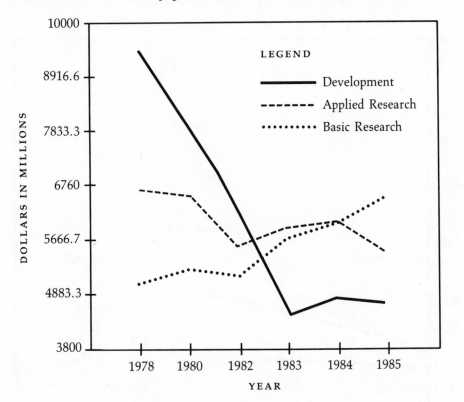

SOURCE: George A. Keyworth. "Four Years of Reagan Science Policy: Notable Shifts in Priorities" *Science*, April 6, 1984, reprint.

basic research.[4] A widespread assumption has been that the universities should be the primary performer of basic research; that applied research is the proper domain of the users—industry and government laboratories—with the universities providing a modest assist; and that, except in unusual cases, development should be beyond the responsibility of the universities.

127

CHART 13

FEDERAL R&D BUDGET AUTHORITY FOR DEFENSE AND NON-DEFENSE ACTIVITIES

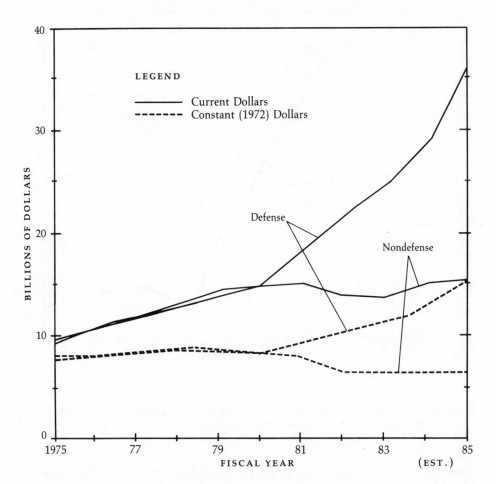

Since 1981, R&D funds for defense-related activities have more than doubled. Defense receives substantial support since it is the principal area in which the federal government is the ultimate user of the products of its R&D efforts.

SOURCE: Division of Science Resources Studies, National Science Foundation.

128

Actually, universities do a good deal of the applied research (or the development of new technology). They received $1.90 billion in research and development support in 1972 from the federal government and this amount rose to $5 billion in 1984. (See Chart 14.) Of this amount, 53 percent went for basic research and 33 percent went for applied research. Since 1972, federal support in constant dollars has been approximately level (rising from 1976 to 1980, falling during 1981 and 1982, then rising again). The share going to basic research, however, climbed to 63 percent, whereas the share to applied research fell to 26 percent. (See Chart 15.) Most of the shift occurred in the past four years.[5]

In the last few years, then, funding for research and development has increased in real terms. Basic research has grown. A growing share of research and development expenditure (including that devoted to basic research) is focused on defense. The universities continue to be the major performers of basic research, but the share of their efforts devoted to applied research has declined. In light of increased world competition and the need to maximize the performance of American research and development, is this disposition of support appropriate?

CENTRALIZATION VERSUS COMPETITION: THE DEBATE OVER TARGETING

A key question is whether the United States should move away from dependence on the decentralized and competitive mode of fund allocation we have used or toward more targeted and centrally managed research.[6] Should the United States create a set of intellectual zaibatsu in critical fields?

The American system of research and technology is already extraordinarily diverse, more so than its international competitors. Much of the research effort is already "targeted," particularly in applied research. Basic research is more spontaneous, save where large facilities are involved. The federal budget summary lists seven categories of research organizations:

- Intramural (federal agencies)
- Universities

CHART 14

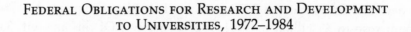

FEDERAL OBLIGATIONS FOR RESEARCH AND DEVELOPMENT
TO UNIVERSITIES, 1972–1984

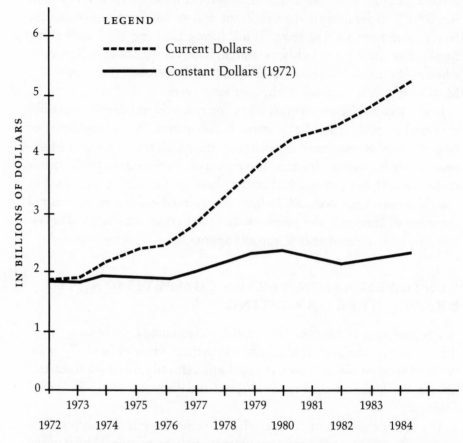

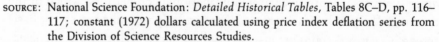

SOURCE: National Science Foundation: *Detailed Historical Tables*, Tables 8C–D, pp. 116–117; constant (1972) dollars calculated using price index deflation series from the Division of Science Resources Studies.

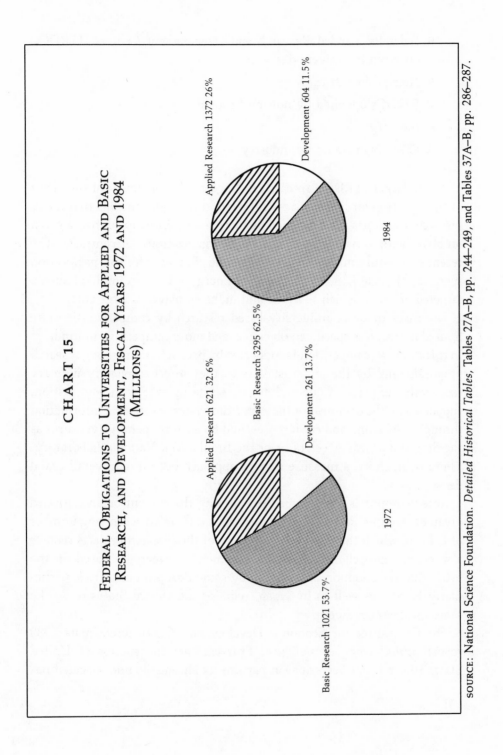

CHART 15

FEDERAL OBLIGATIONS TO UNIVERSITIES FOR APPLIED AND BASIC RESEARCH, AND DEVELOPMENT, FISCAL YEARS 1972 AND 1984
(MILLIONS)

Applied Research 1372 26%

Development 604 11.5%

Applied Research 621 32.6%

Basic Research 3295 62.5%

Development 261 13.7%

1984

Basic Research 1021 53.7%

Development 261 13.7%

1972

SOURCE: National Science Foundation. *Detailed Historical Tables*, Tables 27A–B, pp. 244–249, and Tables 37A–B, pp. 286–287.

- Federally Funded Research and Development Centers (FFRDCs) operated by universities
- Non-profit institutes
- FFRDCs operated by non-profit institutes
- Industry
- FFRDCs operated by industry

At the larger FFRDCs, research is "targeted," as is much of the effort of the government laboratories. Targeted in this sense means that many researchers' efforts are combined in a large-scale effort to address a given problem, with decisions as to goals and organizations set centrally. The recent successful completion of a large-scale pilot plant for coal gasification sponsored by the U.S. Department of Energy was an example of such a targeted effort in which FFRDCs and industry played a large role.

The main mode of university-based research by comparison is more limited in size, less specific in objective, and more competitive in funding. In this country, competition is supported by peer selection among research proposals (and by the antitrust laws as they affect university-industry cooperative efforts).[7] Cooperation exists side by side with competition, supported by the openness of the American system of sharing information through publishing and conferences, and by such cooperative ventures as the Stanford Linear Accelerator or the Brookhaven National Laboratory. There is, in short, a measure of each approach but not an overall grand design.

Recent proposals have argued for altering the current balance toward greater targeting. Part of the argument is that there are a growing number of fields in which the size and complexity of the research projects require a targeted approach. Much of the argument, however, is based on the belief that the adoption of targeting by some European countries, particularly France, as well as by Japan, requires the United States to do the same to remain competitive.[8]

The Committee for Economic Development (CED) noted in its 1980 report *Stimulating Technological Progress* that the success of United States research has been due, in part, to its pluralistic, non-targeted nature.[9] *The State of Academic Science* (1977) sounded a similar theme. "(One) of the factors contributing to the apprehension include(s) a tendency toward less diversity in funding sources and toward conservatism in the choice of research topics."[10]

A related issue is whether the federal government should revise its antitrust laws to permit formation of university/industry research consortia. Among such consortia established recently, the most celebrated is the Microelectronics and Computer Technology Corporation (MCC), a consortium of several universities and corporations with headquarters in Austin, Texas.

To resolve these questions, one must know about the record of university laboratories that receive allocated versus competitive funding, whether universities are more effective than other institutions at basic research and whether targeting has, in fact, helped the Japanese and French.

It is doubtful that a major shift toward more targeting is desirable. While this nation's ability to review the effectiveness of Japanese and European applied research efforts has been limited, one might question whether their progress in certain technologies was as related to their targeting as has been implied. Nor do problems in those fields where the United States has fallen behind seem to be because of the American approach.

The rapidly changing nature of research requires that the method of decision making have certain characteristics: the ability to shift priorities, funding, and talented personnel from less pressing or outdated projects to those of greater importance; openness to new ideas; and, above all, decisions based on the quality of proposal and effort. The peer review grant system employed for federal research grants to universities has come closer to this ideal than any other system in the world. It regularly terminates research projects of lower need or quality. On a number of occasions, it has lead to closing large-scale facilities no longer judged essential, such as the Pennsylvania-Princeton Particle Accelerator. The new National Science Foundation's university-industry centers in specific fields add an additional range of semi-targeted efforts. A major worry is that the current enthusiasm for targeting will obscure the main advantages

133

of peer review competition—its avoidance of political decision making and entrenched bureaucracy, problems that have plagued other countries as well as many federal laboratories here.

An additional policy issue flows from recent successful lobbying efforts of some universities to gain federal funding for new facilities. No matter how important or well justified such facilities are, the shift of any federal funding for support of research away from merit as determined by such mechanisms as peer review and toward political decision making is inimical to research quality. If unchecked, it will lead to an increase in lobbying and, ultimately, an increase in the type of political involvement that has hampered research quality in other countries.[11]

The current balance between "targeted" and "competitive" research is appropriate and should be maintained. In addition, all federal support of any nature for university research should be based on careful measures of merit with primary dependence on peer review.

BALANCING THE NEEDS OF DEFENSE, HEALTH, AND ECONOMIC DEVELOPMENT

A second major issue is the balance of resources to support research among the broad fields of defense, health sciences, and economic development. Does the share of funding reflect the appropriate balance of national needs for the next decade?

The striking fact is that the share of basic research devoted to health sciences, just over 50 percent, is approximately double what it is in most other developed countries. Health science research has had, even before the postwar period, strong support in the United States. In some years, Congress voted *more* funding for the National Institutes of Health than had been requested.[12] Today, the National Institutes of Health funds research both here and in the laboratories of other countries. Not only is the concept of research to reduce sickness in keeping with the best of American traditions, but the results have been impressive. To a significant degree, the U.S. is providing the health sciences research for the world.[13]

Clearly, other countries expect to continue to reap the fruits of improved health sciences from the American effort. The devotion of such a large

134

share of our university research resources raises the question of whether the United States is diverting scarce manpower and dollars from research essential to critical industrial projects necessary to keep the United States competitive.[14] The result is an awkward policy choice between economic development and health. In the last few years, the current administration has slowed the growth of research funding for the life sciences and proposes to slow it further in the 1985 budget—below the anticipated rate of inflation.

Another difference is the high share of research dollars that supports defense, again the highest share, approached only by Russia and Great Britain. Historically, both researchers and defense officials have argued that defense research expenditures provide a byproduct of technological leadership in economic development. In the 1950s and 1960s many commercial advantages—jet aircraft, reliable transistors, and computers, to name only a few—accrued to the United States because of this. (The same argument can be made for the commercial benefits of some research in the health sciences, as evidenced by the current worldwide race to exploit biotechnology.)[15]

In recent years, many thoughtful observers have begun to question whether the commercial fallout from defense research is still occurring on a similar scale.[16] As the sophistication of defense needs has increased, the fallout of benefits appears to have diminished. In a world of more intense industrial competition based increasingly on advanced technology, countries such as Germany, Japan, Taiwan, or Singapore appear to gain an advantage by concentrating their research and technology dollars in areas that are expected to have commercial significance.

The most fundamental policy decisions are involved. To some degree, one can argue that both the defense and health needs of the country would be better served by greater emphasis on those aspects of research and particularly the translation of research to technology that lead to jobs. While research into health science will continue to yield new concepts of great value for both the United States and the world, the reduction of poverty in this country would probably do as much as anything to reduce the incidence of disease. A strong economy and a strong balance of trade would similarly have a major impact on the United States' role in the

135

world. A sound case can be made that both in terms of defense and the health of the country, the greatest gains can be made if the economy is stronger.

The share of all basic research funds devoted to economic development should be increased. For health sciences the share of funds should be held at its present level and for defense the share should be decreased.

FUNDING FEDERAL OR UNIVERSITY LABORATORIES

A major policy issue is where the federal government should place its resources in order to gain the greatest effectiveness. For the last three years, basic research funding for federal laboratories has been growing at a faster rate than that for universities, raising the question of whether this is a conscious policy choice. From 1980 to 1983, the federal funding for basic research grew 9.7 percent for intramural recipients (i.e., federal labs), and only 7.4 percent for universities and colleges.[17] (See Chart 16.)

A strong political constituency supports the federal laboratory system. The 700 federal laboratories currently house over, $25 billion in tools and instruments and employ over 206,000 people. In many locales this makes the federal laboratories the largest employer in the area.[18] Nonetheless, report after report has questioned the effectiveness of their performance.[19] For example, "In any case, they (the federal laboratories) have not contributed significantly to industrial innovation in general."[20] Inflexibility is a special problem with government research facilities. It has proven difficult to reduce staff and activity levels in response to changes in government spending priorities. Too often, needed budget cuts are implemented by reducing support of university research rather than government research institutions. As another report argues, "A second problem with government research is quality."[21] In an attempt to measure the effectiveness of the different approaches, federal laboratories and university laboratories, researchers were asked where the leading research is being done in their own fields. Researchers at both government laboratories and universities and in a variety of fields almost always named university laboratories.

It should be noted that some federal laboratories serve purposes that

136

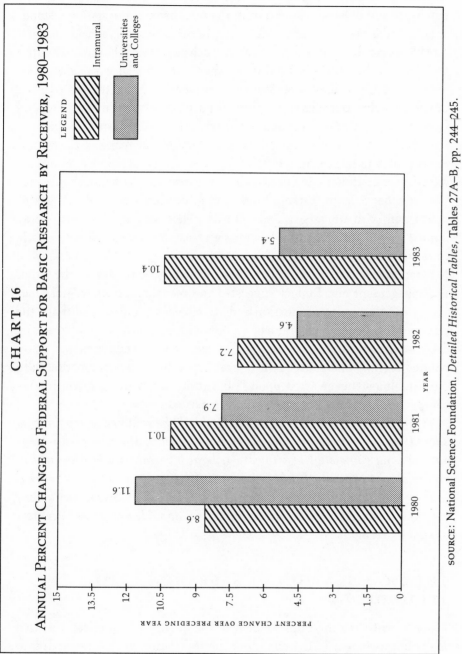

CHART 16
ANNUAL PERCENT CHANGE OF FEDERAL SUPPORT FOR BASIC RESEARCH BY RECEIVER, 1980–1983

LEGEND

Intramural

Universities and Colleges

SOURCE: National Science Foundation. *Detailed Historical Tables*, Tables 27A–B, pp. 244–245.

may not be appropriate for university laboratories—for example, in certain aspects of defense research or in the establishment of national standards.[22] There are also some federal laboratories that are considered first rate by researchers from all walks alike, such as certain laboratories within the National Institutes of Health and the Center for Disease Control.[23]

Many of the federal laboratories, however, are uncertain as to their mission, having outlived their original purpose. Over the years, federal laboratories (with the exception of the few stars of the system) have been criticized for confusion over mission; a climate that makes attraction of top researchers difficult; ineffectiveness in scientific decision making, including poorly functioning peer review; the intrusion of political influence into judgments as to funding levels and project choices; and the lack of interaction with university and industry scientists. There is also some limited evidence that federal laboratory research may cost more per scientist than university research.[24]

A recent report of a review panel established at the request of the Office of Management and Budget suggested the reevaluation of federal laboratory funding based on mission and effectiveness, and argued that "the size of each Federal laboratory . . . should be allowed to increase or decrease (to zero, if necessary)."[25] Such recommendations for more pointed reviews and consequent budget action have occurred periodically but are almost never acted upon.[26] In a time when the demand for resources and personnel is high, action is needed.

While the basic structure of diversity should be retained, a rebalancing should occur so that funding flows more toward the university laboratories and somewhat less toward federal laboratories. Particularly in those laboratories which have proven ineffective over the years in generating high-quality research, or in those that have unclear or dubious missions, the need to reduce or eliminate questionable programs or centers should be recognized.

THE TRANSLATION OF RESEARCH INTO TECHNOLOGY

More urgent than the improvement in the quality of American research is the improvement in the quality of the translation of that research into technology. The increasing demand for technological leadership, not just in economic competition and defense, but in health care, in addressing problems of the environment, in insuring adequate energy supplies, and in a host of other areas has brought to the forefront the question of the capacity to develop and utilize technology from any and every source.[27]

The demand for greater university involvement in applied research goes far beyond the need to develop new technologies to include such urgent problems as the involvement of higher education in the improvement of the elementary and secondary schools.

Do universities have the will to lead in the development of technology, or would they prefer to continue to focus primarily on basic research? In general, universities can and should—and in some fields do—play a major role in the translation of research into technology, that is, in performing applied research, but they should refrain from involvement in product development. However, many within the universities, both administrators and faculty, see the development of technology as less appropriate to the university than basic research. Faculty involved in applied projects are often discriminated against in terms of tenure or promotion. How and where the borderline between appropriate and inappropriate university activity should be drawn needs to be clarified.

There are three subjects that deserve attention:

> The general recognition that applied research and such applied fields as engineering are part of the mainstream of modern life and not subservient in prestige or value to the traditional sciences
>
> Efforts to improve university/industry linkages
>
> The role of the National Science Foundation program in applied research and particularly in engineering.

A change of climate within universities is called for to upgrade the role of applied research or the development of technology. What is needed, in short, is less ideological separation between basic science on the one hand and applied science and engineering on the other and more overlap in granting procedures, research programs, and in curricula.

This raises issues that trouble many academics. One is the awkward issue of drawing a line between the appropriate and the inappropriate.

There is a danger that closer linkages to practical problems and to industry could undermine both the objectivity of the university's pursuit of scholarship and the openness of exchange of scholarly information in a quest for usefulness and profit. Some of the recent large grants to universities from corporations have generated keen debate on campus over these points.[28] While the large majority of university/industry, university/government, or university/school relations has proven both safe and effective, a few appear to compromise the university's rights of open inquiry and control over appointments.

A few also led the university close to the borderline of engaging in product development. To cross the boundary would not only distract the university from its tasks of teaching and advancing knowledge, but, if past experience is a guide, it would place the university in a job for which it is ill-suited. The reason that university research is more effective than industrial research is the same reason that the obverse is true. These are different tasks requiring differing organizations.

Yet, it is clear that universities have successfully developed the organizational capacity for the translation of research into technology in a number of fields: most notably agriculture and the health sciences. Some universities such as Carnegie-Mellon, Michigan, Stanford, Utah, Delaware, Illinois, and Wisconsin have developed a considerable skill in the generation of new technologies across the spectrum of academic disciplines with no loss of either quality or autonomy. To meet the urgent needs for applied skills and new technologies, the universities are needed. To engage more fully in applied activity without damaging the integrity of the university requires learning new ground rules on the part of the university and the corporation alike.

UNIVERSITY/INDUSTRY PARTNERSHIPS

One element of the system that is ripe for improvement is the linkage between university and industry. To excel in the current world economy, industry needs the stimulation of close contact with faculty, graduate students, and the most advanced technology. But the flow must also go in the opposite direction. Universities need the linkage in order to stimulate the development of technology and even to focus basic research in needed areas (without the requirement of central direction of research projects by government). Contact with users also provides a stream of technology and often new resources that enhance the university's capacity for basic research and for graduate and undergraduate education.

Some university experience with industry linkages has a long history. In the postwar period, several universities, most notably the Massachusetts Institute of Technology and Stanford, began to develop industrial affiliate programs designed to build both formal and informal relationships between faculty members and their industrial counterparts. A few universities, led by the University of Wisconsin and later Stanford, began formal programs for patenting and licensing technology—a move that not only helps provide resources needed for university research but helps insure that new technologies will be used by industry. The record of these pioneer efforts is clear: the standing of these universities as centers of scientific research has not been jeopardized.

Since 1980, as the country has focused on high technology, there has been a rapid spread of such efforts. Almost every major research university now has an active patent program; Stanford's generated an income to the University of $3 million in 1983–84. Major efforts at developing new forms of linkage have been undertaken by a range of universities—Rensselaer Polytechnic Institute, Carnegie-Mellon, the University of Utah, the University of Texas, and the University of Michigan, to name only a handful. Several universities—Wisconsin, Delaware, and Illinois—have an internal fund to support efforts to help move the fruits of research into more applied technologies.

In the past, the debates about higher education and the new programs to meet national needs have been led by the federal government. In this case, the states have been more aggressive in taking the lead. In a number of cases, Massachusetts, Michigan, Virginia, Colorado, North Carolina, Arizona, or Indiana, the state government assumed the initiative in establishing a university/industry consortium designed to spur economic development based on technology. Eighteen states have established some form of a research park to aid this process.[29]

The federal government has responded with some new programs of its

141

own. Over the last several years, the National Science Foundation has moved to assist this process.[30] One of the most important steps has been a series of National Science Foundation grants to aid the establishment of university/industry research centers. The first, the Polymer Processing Center at the Massachusetts Institute of Technology, was actually created ten years ago. In the last three years, the number has grown rapidly, so that in 1984 there were twelve such centers.

List of University/Industry Cooperative Research Centers

University of Massachusetts Center for U-Mass/Industry Research in Polymers

Ohio State University Center for Welding Research

Case Western Reserve University Center for Applied Polymer Research

Rensselaer Polytechnic Institute Center for Interactive Computer Graphics

North Carolina State University Cooperative Research Center for Communications and Signal Processing

Rutgers University Ceramics Cooperative Research Center

Iowa State University Building Energy Utilization Laboratories

University of Rhode Island/Industry Cooperative Center for Robotics

Georgia Institute of Technology Material Handling Research Center

Pennsylvania State University Center for Dielectric Studies

Texas A & M University Center for Hydrogen Technology

Worcester Polytechnic University Center for the Management of Advanced Automation Technology

The National Science Foundation goal is to provide five-year funding with the expectation that effective centers will, by that time, generate sufficient industrial support to assure their continuation. Currently, industrial support provides over half of the funding of these centers. There are, as well, a number of such centers that have been established without National Science Foundation grants—the Center for Integrated Systems at Stanford, the Microelectronics and Computer Technology Corporation in Austin, and a series of "centers of excellence" now being founded at universities by a consortium of semiconductor manufacturers. In fact, the 1984–1985 *Research Center Directory* lists some 7,500 nonprofit research organizations, a majority of which are university related.

There is a question as to which or how many of these differing forms of linkages will prove effective. Several studies are already underway.[31]

The National Science Foundation should support the implementation of existing studies which address effectiveness of the various research approaches and fund sufficient further study to determine the most efficient and the safest mechanisms.

The National Science Foundation should continue to fund new university/industry research centers, concentrating, as has been the case, on funding for the first five years. The National Science Foundation should also encourage competing approaches—not only differing types of linkages, but competing types in the same fields, for example, multiple research centers in polymers, or in computer graphics.

The National Science Foundation and the mission agencies should also expand substantially their support of university-based applied research.

There has been considerable discussion about whether a separate National Science Foundation for engineering is needed. One National Science Foundation will serve the need better than two and the advantage of multiple funding through the various existing agencies, already well demonstrated in the funding of basic university research, can be applied toward this goal too.

There has also been considerable concern expressed that the funding of university research will suffer if the National Science Foundation, or the federal agencies as a whole, turn their attention to applied technology.[32] This is a valid concern. It has taken a long time to establish the importance of basic research in the collective mind of American policy. Now, however, it is established and has been funded for several decades, and the urgency of the national need for more effective development of technology is so great that it would be folly to fail to address that need in order to insure no loss of research funding.

There has also been concern expressed that a new emphasis on technology could change the nature of the research university. This is not only possible but likely; a new form of university, the research and technology university, is already emerging in response to escalating needs of society. Should the universities fail to respond, some other organizational answer will emerge as it has in other countries. The result would most likely be damaging to the university's ability to conduct research and teaching. It would also be damaging to open sharing of the applied sciences that now characterizes most of our society.

In the immediate aftermath of World War II, when the idea of federal support for university research was proposed, there was considerable opposition from the academic community on the grounds that the nature of the university would be altered. It was, and the research university emerged. The success of that transformation should not be a reason to accept this next change without careful consideration of its effects. The successful experience of the first research and technology universities and the urgent national need should, however, propel us forward.

CHAPTER XI

Investments To Insure Continuing Leadership

T HE CURRENT QUALITY of American university research is high. As a result, the United States remains the research leader in almost every field. This is hardly a reason for resting on our "laureates." We should, instead, be gearing up to meet the increasing demand for research and technology—both as a result of the intensifying international competition as well as of the need to meet the seemingly endless demands of American society for the knowledge to create a better, safer, and fairer life. Continuing leadership requires continuing investment.

A part of the investment required is to insure that university researchers are equipped with the most advanced instruments and information. A generation ago, "advanced" meant an instrument acquired within a decade or less and information of only a year or two in age. Today, instruments remain advanced for only a matter of a few years, and the half-life of information in many fields is measured in months.

To enhance innovation in research, investment is required. In the sciences, particularly, universities find themselves operating larger and more sophisticated facilities. To cite one of the more dramatic cases, Lawrence built and operated his cyclotron at Berkeley by himself with the aid of a few graduate students. Today, the linear accelerator at Stanford is a multibillion dollar facility with a staff in excess of a thousand. While few cases have required that degree of change, there is an inexorable trend toward complexity and cost. The danger is that the growing demands of these projects will freeze out new researchers, researchers at the smaller universities, wholly new ideas, and interdisciplinary approaches so essential to progress. Without such flexible elements, the centers of American

145

university research will, in time, become the twenty-first century's steam engines. There are three particular areas which need help.

IMPROVED INSTRUMENTATION

As instrumentation has become more sophisticated and institutional budgets more constrained, the problem of affording the necessary expenditures has been complicated by the spread of technology across the campus. The problems in the research laboratories are visible enough to have attracted attention.[1] The National Science Foundation has indicated its concern about the level of university instrumentation and has begun an effort to include more instrumentation funding in project grants.[2] However, the scope of the problem appears significantly larger than can be met by this program.[3] University budgets must also bear the increasing costs of maintenance accompanying the growing sophistication of the instrumentation.

Yet, sophisticated instrumentation is becoming a routine way of life in field after field. Beyond the revolution of word processing and microcomputing are fields as diverse as journalism or film making. Equally important, the opportunity to work with advanced equipment is needed not just for graduate students but also for undergraduates in every field. The involvement of undergraduates with the latest techniques helps generate creativity and awareness of the importance of new ideas, and in turn affects the creativity of their teachers. A critical part of the diffusion of knowledge occurs with the diffusion of university and college graduates throughout society. But many, if not most, undergraduate programs are still in the quill pen and eyeshade stage in relation to today's technology.

At some level, the increase in cost and sophistication of tools requires a different mode of administration. There already are models for the most expensive installations, such as the large particle accelerators or the operation of an oceanographic research vessel. In both cases, consortia are established to allow the sharing of such equipment by a wide variety of universities and principal investigators. Because of the added complexity of coordination, such an arrangement is of value only when the costs are high. The most difficult area concerns not the most expensive instru-

146

mentation, such as a linear accelerator or a research vessel, but rather the intermediate range. In this range, instrumentation is too expensive to be operated by a single university yet the costs of acquisition are not so high and the level of use is not so low that elaborate sharing mechanisms are in order. A new mode of sharing is therefore needed for this intermediate ground.

A method of financing the ongoing purchase of instrumentation is needed to overcome several problems. What is needed is a mode for continuing support. A one-time blitz to correct the current crisis will result in temporary help but promises a return of the problem in aggravated form in a decade or less. Also needed is a means to insure that instrumentation for undergraduate teaching is widely dispersed and that access for students and faculty to expensive centers of advanced instrumentation is maintained. Without this, the gulf between the haves and the have-nots will widen further. As a part of preventing this problem, greater college and university outreach to the high schools must take place.

The magnitude of the need is a subject of speculation and controversy. There is agreement about one thing—the cost is high, more than the colleges and universities can muster from their own resources. The National Science Foundation has estimated the cost of modernization at roughly $1.3 billion. The Association of American Universities estimates that over $1 billion a year for the next three years is needed just to re-equip the top 100 research universities. None of this takes into account the added cost of personnel and maintenance.[4]

THE CURRENT STATE OF FEDERAL SUPPORT

Most federally funded instrumentation has been obtained as a part of a project grant. This type of support has been essential for equipping university laboratories. As effective as project grants are in funding research, they have significant disadvantages in funding instrumentation:

1. Project grants usually do not fund equipment that is used regularly by more than one investigator or principally by students.

147

2. Project grants tend to favor established scientists with a proven record of success to the detriment of young investigators.

3. Project grants may discourage scientists from changing their field of research.

4. Project grants lead to gaps in funding that can undermine research capacity built on earlier stages of work.

5. Project grants fail to fund the replacement and renovation of worn or obsolete equipment and facilities.

The holes left by project grants in earlier decades were filled by federal grants for research and development plant (construction, institutional development and instrumentation). In 1966, 11 percent of federal obligations for academic science were in this form. By 1977, this type of funding had dropped to 1 percent.[5]

The National Institutes of Health, alone among the granting agencies, has continued a program of general institutional support—the Biomedical Research Support Grants (BRSGs). They are intended to support pilot research, new investigators, and new research opportunities, unexpected research requirements, new laboratories and equipment, and shared facilities. While intended to be 15 percent of all National Institutes of Health research grant appropriations, by the 1980s BRSGs were under 2 percent. In 1982, the awards, distributed to 516 institutions, amounted to just over $44 million.[6]

The National Science Foundation off and on has had an Institutional Improvement for Science Program, but actual funding has proved difficult. The request for FY 1985, however, was up sharply to $237 million. In addition, in 1978, the National Science Foundation established a Regional Instrumentation Program to provide regional access to high cost, state-of-the-art instrumentation. Fourteen centers were established at a total cost of $20 million.

The National Science Foundation has also recently begun a $20 million initiative to give researchers access to supercomputers.[7] The Defense Department established a five-year effort at $30 million per year to upgrade research instrumentation in those laboratories that carry out defense-related research. In the first year, 1983, 2500 applications were received amounting to requests for more than $645 million.[8]

148

The Department of Energy has also established a small program. FY 1984 was budgeted at $4 million and the FY 1985 request was $6 million. Taken together, the Reagan administration requests for FY 1985 were $800 million, a clear recognition of the problem.[9] But these programs fund individual projects, not laboratories, and do not fund equipment that may cost several hundreds of thousands of dollars.[10]

While the mission agencies, such as the Department of Defense and the Department of Education should continue to carry on programs to help equip the laboratories that serve their needs, the primary responsibility should be assigned to the National Institutes of Health and the National Science Foundation. Each should establish programs of multi-area competitive research grants for instrumentation. Some part of the grants should be set aside for instrumentation for developing institutions (not, however, for the encouragement of new Ph.D. programs, but rather for the improvement of instrumentation necessary for teaching undergraduate students). Funding agencies should also allow universities to set aside a fixed percent, up to 10 percent, of research overhead expenses to be placed in a fund for future instrumentation needs. The university would use its discretion on what and when to buy new equipment or facilities. An additional part should be set aside for a series of competitive "infrastructure grants" to provide universities with instruments in the intermediate range on the condition that the university has operated for the five previous years in a way that is open to scholars from the surrounding region. The estimated costs would be approximately $400 million per year for each program above and beyond the current levels of project grants so that some continuing level of instrumentation would be funded as now, as a part of project grants.

THE INFORMATION REVOLUTION
AND RESEARCH LIBRARIES

Research in every field depends on the availability of the latest knowledge (data, analysis, ideas). As research has accelerated, the available knowledge has grown at an incredible rate—the well-documented "knowledge explosion."[11] The expansion in the numbers of research universities has meant a parallel expansion in the numbers and quality of research li-

149

braries. Two major problems now face research libraries—the costs of providing for their users a huge and growing array of books, scholarly journals, government documents, and other works;[12] and the confusion brought about by the advent of widespread electronic as opposed to printed information.[13] Both demand fundamentally new ways of thinking about the function of the library.

What is now plain is even the wealthiest research libraries cannot hope to acquire and maintain all of the scholarly materials now available. As Robert Rosenzweig put it, "It is now commonly accepted that such completeness is unattainable for a single library (only the Library of Congress comes close to having such an aspiration) and that cooperation among libraries is essential to provide scholars and others with the products of the 'knowledge explosion' of the past few decades."[14] The problem has moved beyond even this level, as profound as that is, and a fundamental and wrenching shift lies ahead for research libraries.

Much of the pressure for change that is already recognized comes from the sheer explosion of scholarly publications. Just in scientific and technical works, the number of books published each year in the United States has grown from 3,000 in 1960 to 15,000 in 1980; the number of serial titles rose from 20,000 to over 50,000.[15] Other forms of scholarly material— government documents, video and audio materials, and the like—grow steadily. With greater international competition and cooperation, there is a growing need to track scholarship abroad, and in ever more countries.

In recent years, research libraries have undertaken major programs to take advantage of the new capacities of data processing. Automated cataloging, search, and exchange programs are now available.[16] A variety of consortia have been developed to share library materials, technology, and common tasks (such as preparing cataloging information).

Despite this progress, with the continuing expansion of knowledge, the costs of maintaining a research library in the form it is now known continue to accelerate at a rate impossible for universities to sustain. With the growing sophistication of electronic transmission and retrieval mechanisms, it no longer makes sense for every research library to attempt to maintain 15,000 to 20,000 or more differing journals, the majority of which are used only infrequently. Even though the use of most journals is infrequent, access is critical.

150

Historically, the difficulty that has prevented a national effort of such sharing, as in the proposals for a national periodicals center, has been the need to insure the survival of the journals and to avoid the danger, should the federal government undertake to subsidize the journals, of undue interference in a sensitive area of the academic world.

The original proposal was made for a single national periodicals center.[17] *Instead, the establishment of four regional periodicals centers, run as consortia by the major research libraries of each area, is recommended. Each would provide overnight an immediate delivery service, often electronic, of articles and other materials. Presumably, most universities would, at least for now, continue to keep the most popular journals available on campus.*

As needed as this step is, it does not address the need for a deeper change. In a growing range of circumstances, data (or information of all sorts) no longer appear in the old familiar forms. Many government reports—some Census reports, the Chemical Information System of the Environmental Protection Agency, and the gene splicing bank at National Institutes of Health—are available in computer data banks. More and more scientific research involves major computing. Researchers active in these projects often communicate electronically on a daily basis.[18]

In a number of fields, the journal article no longer serves the town crier function, announcing new information. Instead, it has become a memorandum of record, documenting what has long since become information in regular use. Scientist after scientist report that they are moving slowly away from regular use of the library.

The trend toward electronic information is hardly confined to scholarly research. It has become everyday practice in a range of fields, from the brokerage business to the military.[19] This does not imply a decline in the need for access to research material, but just the opposite. It does pose three crucial problems:

- In the traditional method of providing access to materials, the research library acquires the material outright and then makes it available to scholars essentially free of charge. The large bulk of research library costs are for the acquisition, cataloging, and maintenance of this material. Now, a number of data bases are available

151

to libraries, but when the library gains access there is most often a charge which is passed on to the user. The result is to discriminate in favor of acquired as opposed to accessed material, and to discriminate in favor of the haves as opposed to the have-nots.[20]

- Library personnel, while now fully competent to handle the library automation that has taken place, have neither the education nor the emotional commitment to prepare for the shift in outlook required to change from owning, cataloging, and lending, to becoming electronic data sleuths ready to link a student or faculty member to someone else's data bank. Moreover, the time has come for information specialists to learn more about the needs of libraries.[21]

- The old hard copy system of library materials provides important services such as indexing to scholars. While there are some newly available indices to certain electronic data bases, most notably those that are available commercially, the large majority are simply hidden from sight. One great loss is that information used in one field, or even a sub-field, is not available to researchers in other fields who are not aware of its existence. Another service is the control of quality through such steps as the refereeing of journal articles. A third service is the provision of an accessible, orderly historical record. For many of the electronic data in the most critical research areas, none of these is available.

The basic problem is that the research community, and much of the rest of the society, is moving beyond the capacity of the research library. It is time to shift from the main emphasis on acquisition to an emphasis on access. Perhaps it is time to stop calling these centers "libraries."[22] Time is important. The problems of access, indexing, cost structures, and quality could easily get out of hand.

It is not clear how to achieve an evolution to a new system, or even how a new system would function. One thing is clear, however: the federal government will surely be involved. It has a major stake in the existence of an efficient system with rapid exchange of the latest information so that American research and American industry can gain a competitive edge. And only the federal government is likely to have the resources and clout necessary for the transition.[23]

A working group from the key academic, library, and governmental organizations should be formed and charged with the task of proposing the model for the next generation of scholarship information systems.[24]

NEW RESEARCHERS AND NEW IDEAS

In discussions with researchers, the most common cause of concern has been, as competition among researchers for limited funds has intensified, the fear that young new researchers or researchers trying to enter a new field, or researchers pioneering a new field or new interdisciplinary area, will be unable to find the funding they need to make a start. They worry as well that there are not enough U.S. citizens entering graduate study in certain fields. It is just these people who open new avenues of research, or enough new faculty entering the fields of teaching and research, although their success is essential to insuring the flexibility and vitality of the whole. Therefore, special provisions need to be made to encourage the continuous infusion of new talent.

ATTRACTING AMERICANS TO KEY GRADUATE PROGRAMS

Taken as a whole, the graduate schools of this country enroll enough Ph.D. candidates for the needs of the future. In 1983, total graduate enrollment was 1.37 million, and 32,000 received their Ph.D. degrees. In certain key fields, however, primarily engineering and computer science, there is a serious shortage.

Within these two fields graduate enrollments have been rising since 1975, and Ph.D. degrees have been up since 1980 after a ten-year drop. The share of foreign graduate students in these fields has been rising as well until, by last year, it had reached 50 percent (see Chapter IV). While many of the foreign nationals stay in the United States and a percentage take faculty positions, there are distinct advantages in a better balance of U.S. citizens in these programs.[25]

153

Increasing the numbers of graduate students is a problem with which there has been a good deal of experience. The method that has proven both practical and effective has been to make graduate fellowships available. In recent years, graduate education has become more expensive, and available graduate student financial aid has declined.[26]

Levels of grant-in-aid support for graduate students has fallen dramatically from the boom period of the early 1970s. The result has been to force graduate students into borrowing heavily to finance their graduate education.[27] (See Chapter VI.) The eligibility requirements for Guaranteed Student Loans (GSL) have been tightened, particularly for independent students, which include most Ph.D. candidates. The cost of National Direct Student Loans has increased. There were in 1982 an estimated 50,000 graduate students supported by NDSL. These debt burdens clearly deter prospective graduate students from pursuing a risky, long-term venture as a graduate student. The certainties of professional life look all the more attractive to a bright and capable baccalaureate concerned with paying off his accumulated educational debt and worried about adding to it. The situation is exacerbated by the administration's proposed zero funding for several programs of graduate support, including the Graduate and Professional Study Grant Program (of particular importance to women and minority students) and the Public Service Fellowships (designed to encourage careers in the public sector).[28]

In fields such as engineering and computer science, the critical period for the availability of fellowship aid is the first year or years of the student's graduate experience. This both allows universities to recruit able students and helps the potential student see the possibility of support. After the student has moved into graduate study there are usually research assistantships and other research positions available. These opportunities will be increasingly available as the amount of research in these two fields rises.[29]

The National Science Foundation has proposed a FY 1985 budget of $21 million for a series of 1,550 awards which would provide student stipends, $9,000, plus a cost-of-education grant to the university of $4,000. *The National Science Foundation program for support of graduate students should be funded for a period of five years, and the grants should be concentrated on the first three years of the student's graduate experience.*[30]

SEEDS FOR THE FUTURE

Within certain of the federal granting agencies and within certain universities there are already mechanisms that set aside a modest amount of funding for new researchers.[31] The National Science Foundation, for example, has a new program called the Presidential Young Investigator Awards. Universities nominate the young investigators, a panel selects the grantees, and an NSF award is made contingent on the university raising a matching amount from industry. Two hundred such awards were extended the first year, 1984, with half of that going into engineering. The awards are intended to induce young scientists into universities. The awards are substantial, approaching $100,000 a year for five years.[32]

While the concept of these awards seems excellent, their administration has proven somewhat cumbersome. Once the initial shakedown period has been completed, however, these will be valuable. Insuring flexibility and diversity requires many avenues if bright ideas and people outside the mainstream of their profession are to be encouraged. And, as the Carnegie Institution of Washington has argued after considerable experience in making such grants, small amounts of money in these circumstances can be effective.[33]

Other federal agencies—Defense, Energy, Agriculture, Humanities, Arts, NASA, and NIH—should establish programs similar to the Young Investigator Awards. The same problem exists in all fields, not just the sciences.

An additional sum of 3 percent of the overhead recovery of each university should be accumulated up to a maximum of $500,000 and set aside by each university for the purposes of funding new researchers just getting started or those researchers beginning a new field of research and unable as yet to attract funds. Each grant to a researcher would be limited

155

to a maximum of $30,000 with a maximum of two consecutive grants for any project.

Foundations and corporations also should concentrate some resources on small grants to assist new researchers as a needed antidote to the tendency to support known people in established fields.

NOTES

PROLOGUE

1. Cooperation is as important to solving these problems as competition. Scientists have begun to look for the biological basis of cooperation. "[C]ooperating is not only a nice thing to do, it is *the* thing if you are looking for ways to get through long stretches of evolutionary time in the presence of numberless other creatures with which you are obliged to interact." Lewis Thomas. "Scientific Frontiers and National Frontiers: A Look Ahead" *Foreign Affairs*, Spring 1984, 989.
2. The recent growth in the federal deficit during Reagan's first term greatly restricts domestic spending. As of 1984, 72 percent of the budget was allocated for "uncontrollable" purposes, such as interest payments and entitlement programs. Interest on the debt rose by $20 billion in 1984. Michael O'Keefe. "Incumbent and Challenger: The Future for Higher Education," MS, August 8, 1984, 35.

CHAPTER I.

1. The last major debate on national higher education policy surrounded the 1972 amendments to the Higher Education Act. Lawrence E. Gladieux and Thomas R. Wolanin. *Congress and the Colleges* (Lexington, MA: Lexington Books, 1976).
2. For an early statement from the Reagan administration on the need to shift priorities in research and development funding to reflect changes in the economy, see George A. Keyworth, II. "The Role of Science in a New Era of Competition" *Science*, vol. 217, August 13, 1982, 606–609. Growing interest in these topics is shown in the Fall 1983 issue of *Educational Record*, vol. 64, no. 4, which was devoted to education and the economy. In particular, Anthony P. Carnevale. "Higher Education's Role in the American Economy," 6–16; and Linda S. Wilson. "The Role of University-based Research in Generating Human Capital for the Economy," 40–45. Also, Charles E. Smith. "Sputnik II—Where Are You When We Need You?" *Change*, vol. 15, no. 7, October 1983, 7–10. Stanford University's Institute on Educational Finance and Governance has studied these issues. Henry M. Levin and Russell Rumberger. *The Educational Implications of High Technology*, Project Report No. 83–A4 (Palo Alto, CA: Stanford University, February 1983); Russell W. Rumberger. *The Structure of Work and the Under-utilization of College-Educated Workers*, Program Report No. 82–B7, December 1982; and Rumberger. *Education, Unemployment and Productivity*, Project Report No. 83–A14, May 1983. A good review of several monographs on

this subject is by Ernest A Lynton. "The Economic Impact of Higher Education" *Journal of Higher Education*, November/December 1983, 693–708.

3. "Although the Reagan administration has failed to realize its goal of reducing the higher education budget significantly, program dollar levels are of less importance than are the facts of the attempted reductions, along with other actions to tighten eligibility standards for participation in student aid programs and to increase requirements for family contribution to college costs. Clearly, through its budget recommendations and related actions, the Reagan administration has set a course to reestablish the traditional view that the primary responsibility for the costs of higher education should rest with the student and his family. The administration rejects the two-decade liberal consensus that called for a partnership of family-school-government in financing a student's education but that had, in President Reagan's view, too generously shared government funds in the cost of financing higher education." John T. Wilson. *Academic Science, Higher Education, and the Federal Government, 1950–1983* (Chicago: University of Chicago Press, 1983), 82–83.

4. This point is made by Chester E. Finn, Jr. "Toward A New Consensus" *Change*, September 1981, 16–21 and 60–63; and "Moving Toward A Public Consensus" *Change*, April 1983, 14–22.

5. Charles Saunders. "Reshaping Federal Aid to Higher Education" in Joseph Froomkin (Ed.). *The Crisis in Higher Education*, Proceedings, vol. 35, no. 2 (New York: Academy of Political Science, 1983), 119–134; and the American Association for the Advancement of Sciences' Intersociety Working Group, *R & D in the FY 1984 Budget: A Preliminary Analysis* (Washington, D.C.: AAAS, March 1983) and *AAAS Report IX: Research and Development, FY 1985* (Washington, D.C.: AAAS, 1984).

   In its first two years, the Reagan administration eliminated 145 programs and cut back on dozens more. Fred I. Greenstein and Others. *The Reagan Presidency: An Early Assessment* (Baltimore: The Johns Hopkins University Press, 1983). For reactions from the higher education community, see Charles B. Saunders, Jr. "Sorry this Commitment May be Cancelled—Higher Education and Ronald Reagan" *Change*, January/February 1982, 7–9; and Jack W. Peltason. "Federal Dollars: Providing the Margin of Quality" *Change*, October 1981, 26–27.

6. The American public strongly supports federal aid to higher education. In ranking which items should receive increased funding by the federal government in the years ahead, respondents placed higher education second only to medical care. Defense was placed last. Group Attitudes Corporation. "American Attitudes Toward Higher Education—1983" (New York: Group Attitudes Corporation, October 3, 1983).

   President Reagan has transformed the federal role in education by transferring many of its policy and program responsibilities from Washington to state capitals. Mary Anne Amiot and David L. Clark. "The Impact of the Reagan Administration on Federal Education Policy" *Phi Delta Kappan*, December 1981, 258–262; Amiot and Clark. "The Disassembly of the Federal Educational Role" *Education and Urban Society*, May 1983, 367–387; and Terry Astuto, David Clark, and Paula Rooney. "The Changing Structure of Federal Education Policy in the 1980s" *Phi Delta Kappan*, November 1983, 188–193.

   Perhaps the most dramatic of Reagan's changes in the federal role has been the increased politicalization of science policy and the decline in the influence of scientific elites on federal science policy. The erosion of elitism began with the Daddario-Kennedy Amendment of 1968 and progressed with the tenure of Dr. William McElroy as director of the National Science Foundation under Nixon. It was during this time that the Office of Management and Budget became a powerful force in setting priorities within the National Science Foundation. Politicalization culminated in President Reagan's appointment of Knapp to head the National Science Foundation, and in the forced resignations of the deputy director and three assistant directors, all of whom had been appointed by Carter. John T. Wilson. *Academic Science, Higher Education, and the Federal Government, 1950–1983* (Chicago: University of Chicago Press, 1983), 32–38, 89, passim. "From the fiscal 1982 budget to the pronouncements of administration strategy for science budgets in fiscal 1984, it is obvious, in the words of former National Science Board Chairman Walker, that control of natural science policies, including academic science policy, has shifted from the scientific community to the bureaucracy." *Ibid.*, 103.

7. "At the level beyond the high school, plans cannot be made by the state alone, nor by private institutions alone, nor by Washington alone. But no nationwide policy can be successfully formulated if any of the three is excluded." James Bryant Conant. *Shaping Educational Policy* (New York: McGraw-Hill, 1964), 110.

8. Vanevar Bush and Others. *Science: The Endless Frontier* (Washington, D.C.: Government Printing Office, 1945). One exception is early federal support in the field of agriculture. Alice Rivlin. *The Role of the Federal Government in Financing Higher Education* (Washington, D.C.: The Brookings Institution, 1961).

9. National Science Foundation. *Detailed Historical Tables, FY 1967–1983*, Washington, D.C., 1984, Tables 62 A–B.

10. See Chart 1, Federal Support for Higher Education, in this chapter.

11. Over the past several decades, the number of federal programs has increased; presently there are about 400. They can be classified into six categories, according to their objectives:

    1) To support research in areas of national interest
    2) To provide equal access for low-income students
    3) To strengthen certain types of schools and certain types of programs within schools
    4) To train the work force and to increase employment
    5) To provide benefits to certain classes, for example, veterans and the handicapped
    6) To encourage gifts to colleges and universities. Chester Finn. *Scholars, Dollars, and Bureaucrats* (Washington, D.C.: Brookings Institution, 1978, 8).

The federal government employs three different mechanisms for financing higher education: 1) income transfers (an example is a student aid grant or loan subsidy), 2) fee-for-service payments (such as a research grant given to a university in return for performance of a specific research project), and 3) tax exemptions (the most significant of which have been the tax exemptions for private gifts to colleges and universities and the parental exemptions for children still in college—essentially another form of student aid).

The diversity of programs, mechanisms, and objectives means that the federal

159

government is not a monolithic entity. This administrative structure is complex and seemingly unmanageable. But it has the advantage of adaptability to differing circumstances and of responsiveness to changing needs. New programs can be added and old ones can be eliminated without necessitating a redesign of the entire complex. There is room for maneuver and experimentation. See Table N–1, page 161.

12. James Bryant Conant called the federal government's use of pump-priming and selective incentives "educational reform through philanthropic bribery." Conant. *Shaping Educational Policy* (New York: McGraw-Hill, 1964), 118. The federal government uses the promise of funds as an inducement to "good" behavior.

13. The least effective block grants are those for agricultural research and former grants to the NIE (National Institute of Education) centers under Title III. A law enacted in 1984 that authorizes new funds for the National Science Foundation to support its science education programs, calls for use of block grants, in contravention of the National Science Foundation's traditional use of competitive grants. John Walsh. "Science Education Law Poses Problems for NSF" *Science*, September 28, 1984, 1453–1455.

14. An exception is the large accelerator projects in high energy physics.

15. In 1976 the Committee on Science and Technology in the United States House of Representatives (94th Congress, Second Session) held six days of hearings into the National Science Foundation's peer review procedures. A principal finding of that report was "no method superior to peer review has been found for judging the scientific competence of proposers." House of Representatives. *NSF Peer Review*, vol. 1, Washington, D.C., 1976.

16. Several universities hired a lobbying firm, Schlossberg-Cassidy, to help them gain appropriations for special projects or research facilities and by-pass the peer review process. "How to Win Buildings and Influence Congress" *Science*, December 16, 1983, 1211–1213; "New York Primate Lab Seeks Help from Congress" *Science*, August 3, 1984, 488; Kim McDonald. "U.S. Science Officials Ask Congress to Stop Bypassing Peer Review of Research Grants" *Chronicle of Higher Education*, October 3, 1984, 13–14; and "Northwestern Seeks a Federal Lab" *Science*, September 28, 1984, 1454. Business interference with government-supported science deemed threatening to business interests is also on the rise. Eliot Marshall. "Legal Threat Halts CDC Meeting on Lead" *Science*, February 17, 1984, 672.

17. The higher education community has generally lauded the Reagan administration's deregulation of higher education. Sheldon Steinbach. "Reagan, Regulations, and Relief" *Change*, March 1981, 30–34; Sheldon Steinbach. "Deregulation and Higher Education: The View of a Year Later" *Business Officer*, May 1982, 15–17; and Jack Peltason. "Federal Dollars: Providing the Margin of Quality" *Change*, October 1981, 26–27.

The Heritage Foundation came out with a full-scale plan to deregulate federal higher education policy. Ron Docksai. *Mandate for Leadership* (Washington, D.C.: The Heritage Foundation, 1981). Reagan is said to have been greatly influenced by their recommendations.

The administration has been selective by tightening regulations in certain programs,

TABLE N-1

FEDERAL OUTLAYS FOR POSTSECONDARY STUDENT AID AND ACADEMIC RESEARCH AND DEVELOPMENT
FY 1936, FY 1947, FY 1957, FY 1967, FY 1978, FY 1984

MILLIONS OF CURRENT DOLLARS

	1936[a]		1947[a]		1957[a]		1967[b]		1978		1984	
	AMOUNT	PERCENT	AMOUNT	PERCENT	AMOUNT	PERCENT	AMOUNT	PERCENT	AMOUNT	PERCENT	AMOUNT	PERCENT
Student Aid	10.54	63.0	1,000	87	463	67	1,455	50	7,828[c]	70	7,453[c]	59
Academic Research and Development	6.20	37.0	150	13	224[d]	33	1,454[d]	50	3,375[d]	30	5,271[d]	41
Total	16.74	100.0	1,150	100	687	100	2,909	100	11,203	100	12,724	100
Total in Constant 1972 Dollars[e]	62.58		2,321		1,058		3,679		7,748		5,823	

[a] *The Second Newman Report: National Policy and Higher Education,* Table A, p. 165. These figures are estimates based upon obligations.

[b] *Special Analyses, Budget of the United States Government, Fiscal Year 1970,* p. 123.

[c] Donald A. Gillespie and Nancy Carlson. *Trends in Student Aid: 1963 to 1983,* Table A–1, p. 30, Table A–3, p. 34 and *Update: 1980 to 1984,* Table 1, p. 5, Table 3, p. 7. Figures are based on federal fiscal year appropriations for all Title IV aid and on academic year aid awarded for specially directed forms of aid.

[d] National Science Foundation. *Detailed Historical Tables, 1955–1984,* Table 80, pp. 114–117. Figures represent federal *obligations.* Funds for FFRDCs administered by universities are excluded.

[e] *Economic Report of the President,* Washington, D.C., February 1984. Table B–3, pp. 224–225. Constant 1972 dollars calculated using implicit price deflators for gross national product. 1936 is estimated. 1984 is the fourth quarter of 1983. There is some error due to mismatch between calendar year and federal fiscal year.

for example student aid. Robin Jenkins. "Student Financial Aid Deregulation: Rhetoric or Reality?" *Business Officer*, May 1982, 18–19.

CHAPTER II.

1. For a summary of state efforts, see the National Governors' Association Final Report on *Technology and Growth: State Initiatives in Technological Innovation*, Washington, D.C., October, 1983.
2. Department of Commerce, Bureau of Budget Analysis.
3. The Brookings Institution reports that the United States international trade *surplus* in products of high-technology industries grew from $12 billion in 1972 to $40 billion in 1979.
4. In private conversation, Commerce Secretary Malcolm Baldridge has noted: It has been estimated that for every billion dollars' worth of increased imports 25,000 United States jobs are eliminated.
5. To cite only one example, the commercial bank funds on deposit—in dollars—in Europe are substantially larger than in the United States. How can we then make sense of our monetary policy unless we think in international terms? And how can we remain in a leading financial role unless we stay at the forefront of the rapidly changing electronic techniques for the management of money? Even the stock market is changing. The New York Stock Exchange, long the dominant force in the trading of American stocks, is experiencing new competition. "It now operates in a world of pressing competition. International financial activity is expanding and markets the world over are trading new products at a dizzying pace." Leslie Wayne. "The Big Board's Fight to Stay on Top" *New York Times*, October 14, 1984, C1.
6. The pressure is felt on many fronts. "You look over your shoulder," Mr. Davis of Stanley Works (the nation's largest producer of hardware and hand tools) says, "and there are a dozen little Japans out there." Laurie McGinley. "Cautious Approach" *Wall Street Journal*, October 26, 1984, 1.
7. Organization for Economic Cooperation and Development (OECD). *Economic Outlook* (Paris: OECD, semiannual, 1984).
8. International Monetary Fund. *World Economic Outlook* (Washington, D.C.: IMF, 1983, 1984); and World Bank. *World Development Report* (Washington, D.C.: World Bank, 1984).
9. John Kenneth Galbraith. *The New Industrial State* (New York: New American Library, 1968). Jean Jacques Servan-Schreiber. *The American Challenge* (London: H. Hamilton, 1968).
10. Art Pine. "Trade Threat" *Wall Street Journal*, April 13, 1984, 1.
11. Kent Calder and Ray Hofheinz, Jr. *The Eastasian Edge* (New York: Basic Books, 1982).
12. Yissum Research and Development Company was established in 1964 as a wholly owned subsidiary of the Hebrew University of Jerusalem. The company is primarily concerned with the promotion, protection and commercialization of Hebrew University research results.

The Chinese government has consciously set out to establish their own Silicon Valley in Haiding (a suburb of Beijing). The area has a high concentration of research institutes, scientists and engineers. China is seeking technology transfers from foreign joint ventures (e.g., Otis Elevator and Computerland).

The dollar volume of imports from newly industrialized economies illustrates their presence in the U.S. market.

TABLE N-2

U.S. IMPORTS FROM NEWLY INDUSTRIALIZED COUNTRIES
(BILLIONS OF DOLLARS)

COUNTRY	1983	1982	1981
Mexico	$16.8	$15.6	$13.8
Taiwan	11.2	8.9	8.0
Korea	7.1	5.6	5.1
Hong Kong	6.4	5.5	5.4
Brazil	4.9	4.3	4.5
Singapore	2.9	2.2	2.1

Source: United States Commerce Department.

13. For example, during the first half of 1983, United States imports of computer products rose by 84 percent. Most of this increase was from the nations of the Pacific Rim, with the less developed countries doing the best. The increase in computer imports from Singapore was nearly 700 percent; from Taiwan, 186 percent; Hong Kong, 157 percent; and from Japan, 134 percent.

14. For a discussion of this point see Chapter IX.

15. The phenomenal growth of the Silicon Valley highlights this point. It is now the nation's ninth-largest manufacturing center. The local economy is the fastest-growing (and wealthiest) in the United States. From 1970 to 1980, according to Census data, San Jose rose from being the 29th to being the 18th largest city in the United States, making it the fastest growing city in the United States.

16. By 1977, according to the Bureau of Labor Statistics, more than one out of every five manufacturing workers worked in the so-called sunset industries—textiles, apparel, iron, steel, and automobiles. The United States' performance even in these "smoke-stack" jobs is superior (at least in terms of number of jobs) to other nations. But no less a smokestack state than New Jersey is in the process of shifting out of manu-facturing and into service-based industries. It has the highest per capita concentration of scientists and engineers of any state. New Jersey Department of Higher Education. *Towards the Year 2000*, Special Report Series, Volume 5: Report Number 2, Trenton, NJ, January 1985.

17. Prior to 1980, countries such as Korea and Mexico were noted for producing apparel and shoes. In the past few years they have taken a leap into industrialization.

18. An interesting example of both elements has been occurring in the textile industry.

163

By intensive efforts at automation and improved products American textile manufacturers have begun a slow recovery in an international market which many had long since written off. Vinad Aggarwal and Stephen Haggard. "The Politics of Protection in the U.S. Textile and Apparel Industries," in John Zysman and Laura Tyson (Eds.). *American Industry in International Competition* (Ithaca, N.Y.: Cornell University Press, 1983), 249–312; "Imports are Still Ripping into the Textile Industry" *Businessweek*, September 5, 1983, 56–57; and Peter T. Kilborn. "Another Surprise: A Boom in Jobs" *New York Times*, December 11, 1983, D1.

19. For a summary of state efforts see Herb Brody. "The High Tech Sweepstakes" *High Technology*, January, 1985, 16–28. As more and more states seek to recreate these conditions, the question being raised is how many Silicon Valleys the country can support. The answer appears to depend only on the ability of each area to create a successful climate of entrepreneurship. Success in broadening the number of areas of progressive, entrepreneurial growth is central to the capacity of the United States economy to continue to generate jobs.

20. Congressmen Ed Zschau, Chairman, and Don Ritter, Vice-Chairman of the Republican Task Force on High Technology Initiatives in the House of Representatives have said, "America's biggest challenge is to create enough new and satisfying jobs to employ our growing work force and to increase the standard of living of all Americans. The key to meeting this challenge is industrial competitiveness—developing and producing goods and services with quality and prices that make them attractive to consumers here and abroad." "Encourage Innovation Instead of Industrial Lemons" *Wall Street Journal*, August 1, 1984, 24.

21. Charles L. Schultze. "Industrial Policy: A Dissent" *The Brookings Review*, Fall 1983, 3–12.

In other aspects as well, the United States' performance stands out. The Department of Labor compares various economies in terms of how large a percentage of the working-age population is employed. At nearly 59 percent in April of 1984, the United States' rate exceeded those in West Germany (51 percent), France (53 percent), Britain (56 percent) and Italy (46 percent) and is very close to Japan (61 percent). Further, of all the countries listed, only the United States has shown an increase in this measure from the early 1970s.

22. United States Department of Commerce, Bureau of the Census, 1980, Public Use Tapes, unpublished.

23. The amount workers were paid also rose over the same period. In constant (1981) dollars the median wage of the American male worker rose from $9,700 to $13,800, or an improvement of 40 percent. Family income rose principally due to the increase in the number of family members working.

24. The growth in the labor force reflects the larger population. The United States population over these three decades increased from 152 million to 228 million or by 50 percent. Further, a larger share of the population wants to work. While the number of jobs grew 67 percent, the number of people seeking work grew 72 percent.

Between 1949 and 1980, the number of men in the work force increased by just over 40 percent, but the number of women increased by over 170 percent. In 1950, of all women between 18 and 35, only about a third were working. Today it is approaching two-thirds.

In 1950, about 2.5 million young people turned 18 and entered the labor force (or entered college or the military and then the labor force). By 1980, when the postwar baby boom had reached its peak, 4 million turned 18. The result—1.5 times more people seeking jobs each year.

The number of legal immigrants grew from 250,000 per year in the 1950s to 460,000 in 1979 and a one-time peak of 808,000 in 1980. A significant unknown is the number of illegal immigrants that have entered the country over this time. Some entered the country, worked for a while, and left. The estimates of the numbers that are still here range from 2 million to 10 or 12 million. What is unique is how open the United States has been to immigration despite the added burden it places on the economy. Not all immigrants (e.g., children and the elderly) are seeking work or holding jobs. James Fallows. "Immigration: How It's Affecting Us" *The Atlantic Monthly*, November 1983. Edward N. Fullerton, Jr. and John Tschetter. "The 1995 Labor Force: A Second Look" *Monthly Labor Review*, November 1983, 5.

25. There is uncertainty about who will want to work and for how long. Life spans are stretching toward 80, the retirement age has already moved to 70. There are some signs that despite this, white males are retiring earlier. Will a new, part-time, older work force develop? It appears that a significant pattern of part-time or even underground work for this age group has already developed.

26. United Nations. *United Nations' Yearbook of Industrial Statistics* (New York: United Nations, Economic Analysis, 1983); OECD, 1984, op. cit.; and Robert Lawrence. *Can America Compete?* (Washington, D.C.: The Brookings Institution, 1984).

27.

TABLE N–3

TOTAL U.S. FARMWORKERS (THOUSANDS)

1950	7,160
1960	5,176
1970	3,126
1980	2,704

Source: U.S. Department of Labor, Bureau of Labor Statistics.

28. Diebold, Inc., historically a producer of bank safes and security systems, decided to compete in the automatic teller market. In the early 1970s it was dominated by Docutel Corp. with entry threatened by such electronic giants as IBM and NCR. By 1983 Diebold had a 47 percent market share. "Almost every other teller machine operating in the U.S. is a Diebold" (Lilson Report, industry newsletter, 1983).

29. Government employment declined between 1979 and 1982 according to the Bureau of Labor Statistics.

30. Edward N. Fullerton, Jr. and John Tschetter. "The 1995 Labor Force: A Second Look" *Monthly Labor Review*, November 1983, 5.

31. Barry Bluestone and Bennett Harrison in *The Deindustrialization of America* (New York: Basic Books, 1982) claim that "the new technology has also permitted a substantial amount of 'deskilling' " (p. 117). Bob Kuttner's article, "The Declining Middle" *The Atlantic*, July 1983 (based on the work of Henry Levin at Stanford) and a similar article, "The Mass Market is Splitting Apart" *Fortune*, November 1983, both sketch a world of polar extremes in income and lost skilled jobs.

   Counter to these claims is a growing body of evidence that, as Robert J. Samuelson put it in the "Middle-Class Media Myth" *National Journal*, December 31, 1983, "[T]here is virtually no evidence that this future (deskilled, polarized) is actually unfolding" (p. 2673).

32. A study conducted by Aetna Life Insurance demonstrated that jobs in their firm were becoming more skilled. A Bureau of Labor Statistics projection of the labor force to 1995 found it to be larger (total employment up 25 percent) but not vastly different. ITT Educational Services surveyed 322 American companies and found that nearly half are still replacing workers with outdated skills. This means more firms are *retraining* obsolete workers than replacing them. Hewlett-Packard, for example, is spending $1 million to move 350 workers to new jobs. Dresser Industries in Dallas offers more than 500 training and development courses.

   A report by Robert T. Lund and John A. Hanson. *Connected Machines, Disconnected Jobs: Technology and Work in the Next Decade* (Cambridge, MA: The Center for Policy Alternatives, Massachusetts Institute of Technology, 1983) reveals substantial job attrition on a plant-by-plant basis. However, automation with newly emerging technologies was seen as requiring new and more generalized skills. The potential clearly exists for a bimodal distribution of skill requirements in a firm, yet "few managers had given much thought to the issue of career paths available in their firm" (p. 65).

33. Nell Eurich. *Corporate Classrooms: The Learning Business*, The Carnegie Foundation for the Advancement of Teaching (Princeton, NJ: Princeton University Press, 1985).

34. A study by Cathy Henderson and Cecilia Ottinger. *Employment Prospects for College Graduates*, Policy Brief (Washington, D.C.: American Council on Education, November 1984) confirms that the job outlook for college graduates remains encouraging.

35. United States economic growth is particularly evident when compared to other developed economies. Data provided by the Organization for Economic Cooperation and Development (whose 24 members including the United States account for 70 percent of world output) highlight United States performance:

TABLE N–4

UNITED STATES GDP* AS PERCENT OF OECD TOTAL GDP

1975	38 percent
1982	40 percent
1983	42 percent
1984	47 percent (projection)

* Gross Domestic Product

36. "Indian Development Trends" *Science*, August 3, 1984, 465+; "Economic Benefits from Research: An Example from Agriculture" *Science*, September 14, 1979, 1101+; and "Rice" *Scientific American*, January, 1984, 81+.

37. For example, Brazil in soybeans, Canada in wheat, India in wheat, Indonesia in rice.

38. The disparity among the nation's expenditures on health and health-related science as a proportion of *basic* research becomes dramatically more pronounced. Definitional differences of basic research vs. development and health vs. welfare make inter-country statistical comparisons more difficult. However, Organization for Economic Cooperation and Development (OECD) records indicate that the United States spends over twice the proportion of any other industrialized country.

TABLE N–5

PERCENT HEALTH RELATED RESEARCH TO BASIC RESEARCH

COUNTRY	RESEARCH, 1980
U. S.	12.1
Germany	9.3
Japan	6.1
France	4.9
U. K.	1.8

The differences are even more pronounced if the focus is on *federally* funded basic research. In the United States, the budget for the National Institutes of Health is roughly three times that of the National Science Foundation. Compare that with France, where the budget of the National Institute for Health and Medical Research is a mere 20 percent of the budget of the National Center for Scientific Research. In the United Kingdom, the Medical Research Council budget is only 40 percent of the Science Research Council. In Germany there is no separate agency with responsibility for basic research in health. National Research Council. *Outlook for Science and Technology: The Next Five Years* (San Francisco: W. H. Freeman, 1982).

39. Brazil is currently assessing its stance on protectionism and the development of technology. They nurture their computer industry via a complex network of regulations administered by a single government bureau. Any foreign firm who wishes to manufacture computers in Brazil must obtain government approval while the lucrative and booming micro- and minicomputer markets are strictly reserved for Brazilian companies.

CHAPTER III.

1. Carved in the stone above the mantlepiece of the Board Room at the New York Public Library are Jefferson's words: We "look to the diffusion of light and education as the resource most to be relied on for ameliorating the condition, promoting the virtue and advancing the happiness of man."

2. Some, for example gains in education of minorities, have been mitigated, but the issue is hardly resolved. See Chapter VII.

3. David Mathews. "The Liberal Arts and the Civic Arts" *Liberal Education*, Special Issue, vol. 68, no. 4, Winter 1982, 270.

4. "The public school appears to be the most important and effective instrument of political socialization in the United States. It reinforces other community institutions and contributes a cognitive dimension to political involvement. As an agent of socialization it operates through classroom instruction and ceremonies." Robert D. Hess and Judith V. Torney. *The Development of Political Attitudes in Children* (Garden City, NY: Anchor Books, 1968), 120–121.

5. Thomas Jefferson. *Jefferson's Letters*, compiled by Whitman Willson (Eau Claire, WI: E.M. Hale, 1940), 338–339. From letter to William Charles Jarvis, September 28, 1820. Quoted in Ernest L. Boyer and Fred M. Hechinger. *Higher Learning in the Nation's Service* (Washington, D.C.: The Carnegie Foundation for the Advancement of Teaching, 1981), 43.

6. Mark Curtis, President of the Association of American Colleges, shares this belief. "Redefining the Baccalaureate Degree—An Interview with Mark Curtis" *Antaeus Report*, Winter 1984, 2–5.

7. Derek Bok. *Beyond the Ivory Tower* (Cambridge, MA: Harvard University Press, 1983), 116; and Joseph Veroff. *The Inner American: A Self-Portrait From 1957–1976* (New York: Basic Books, 1981), 156. "It is time to accept the persisting tension between family and public values and to design creative ways of living with both." Mary Jo Bane. *Here to Stay* (New York: Basic Books, 1976), 143.

8. "Most scholars of political socialization agree that the family is one of the most pervasive agents of political socialization. This is to be expected, for the child is usually exposed to familial influence for a long period of time. Studies have demonstrated . . . that the child tends to assimilate the party preference of the parent and to look to the parent as a source of political advice. However, as the child grows older . . . the parents' influence appears to decline." Herbert Hirsch. *Poverty and Politicization: Political Socialization in an American Sub-Culture* (New York: Free Press, 1971), 33. See also Jon D. Miller, Robert W. Scuhner and Alan M. Voelker. *Citizenship in an Age of Science* (New York: Pergamon Press, 1980).

9. Sanford M. Dornbusch and Catherine Gray. "The New Families" in S. M. Dornbusch and M. S. Strober (Eds.). *Feminism, Children, and the New Families* (New York: Guilford Press, 1985, forthcoming). The problems seem to stem more from the process of breaking up rather than as a consequence of having broken up. Seven studies recently released by the National Institute of Mental Health suggest that the long-term ill-effects are more pronounced for children from dissonant homes than for children whose parents divorced. Marilyn Adams. "Kids and Divorce: No Long-term Harm" *USA Today*, Thursday, December 20, 1984, 1.

To some degree, day care centers can substitute for the weakening family, but only if staff ratios are reasonable, groups of children are not too large, the care-givers are well trained and attentive, and the children are not too young. All too often care is less than optimal, especially for disadvantaged children who need it most. Glenn

Collins. "Experts Debate Impact of Day Care on Children and on Society" *New York Times*, Tuesday, September 4, 1984, B11.

10. Peter A. Morrison. "Current Demographic Trends and Federal Policy: An Overview," A RAND Note Prepared for The National Institute of Child Health and Human Development, August 1983, p. 2; and Bureau of the Census. *Current Population Reports; Population Characteristics; Household and Family Characteristics: March 1983*, Series, no. 388, Table E. "Two-Parent and One-Parent Families as Proportions of All Families with Children Present, by Race: 1983, 1980, and 1970," 7.

   Forty-one percent of all female students who drop out of high school do so because of pregnancy and/or marriage. The Alan Guttmacher Institute reports that nationwide there are over one million teen-age mothers with 1.3 million children. They tend to be trapped in a cycle of poverty. The League of Women Voters suggests that women and their children make up 80 percent of all poverty victims. This is not a problem confined to any particular ethnic group. In 1979, 63 percent of the over 200,000 women under age 18 who gave birth were white. But the problem is greater for blacks than for others. Margaret C. Dunkle and Susan M. Bailey. "Schools Must Ease the Impact of Teen-Age Pregnancy and Parenthood" *Education Week*, October 24, 1984, 24 and 18.

   The trend for educated women to marry later and bear children later, due to improved job opportunities, means that a split is widening between poor mothers and better-off mothers. Spencer Rich. "U.S. Childbearing Patterns are Changing, Study Says" *Washington Post*, November 14, 1984, A2.

11. Douglas S. Massey. "Patterns and Effects of the Hispanic Immigration to the United States," Report to The National Commission for Employment Policy, Washington, D.C., March 1982. A growing number of Hispanics think of themselves as Hispanics first, Americans second. Reported in *Education Week*, September 19, 1984, 8.

12. Larry T. McGehee, letter to Robert Payton, July 31, 1984. An excellent study documenting the non-objectivity of television news coverage can be found in David L. Altheide. *Creating Reality* (Beverly Hills, CA: SAGE, 1976).

13. One set of frightening indicators shows a tripling, and for some a sextupling, in the rate of youth homicide, suicide, and illegitimate births since the 1960s. See graph in *Developing Character: Transmitting Knowledge*, A Thanksgiving Day Statement by A Group of 27 Americans (Posen, IL: Thanksgiving Statement Group, November 21, 1984), 4.

   Suicide was the tenth leading cause of death for the nation as a whole, but the third leading cause for those aged 15–24, comprising 10.7 percent of all deaths for that age group in 1981. Accidents and homicide were first and second. John L. McIntosh. *Suicide Among Children, Adolescents, and Students, 1980–1984: A Comprehensive Bibliography*, Public Administration Series: Bibliography (Monticello, IL: Vance Bibliographies, December 1984), 2.

   Although minorities generally have lower rates of suicide than do whites, with the exception of native Americans, these rates have been on the rise in recent years. Moreover, the rates are highest for young males in these groups. John L. McIntosh. *Suicide Among United States Racial/Ethnic Minorities, 1980–1984: A Comprehen-*

sive Bibliography, Public Administration Series: Bibliography (Monticello, IL: Vance Bibliographies, December 1984), 2.

14. Amitai Etzioni. *An Immodest Agenda: Rebuilding America Before the Twenty-First Century* (New York: McGraw-Hill Book Company, 1983), 26. Chapters I and II.

15. Everett C. Ladd, Jr. "Public Opinion: Questions at the Quinquennial" *Public Opinion*, April/May 1983, 24.

16. Ernest L. Boyer and Fred M. Hechinger. *Higher Learning in the Nation's Service* (Washington, D.C.: The Carnegie Foundation for the Advancement of Teaching, 1981), Chapter V.

17. Everett Carl Ladd, Jr., and Seymour Martin Lipset. "Anatomy of a Decade" *Public Opinion*, December/January 1980, and December/January 1984, 2–9.

18. Recent surveys have yielded these results: Those that agreed on the general question that "the lot of the average man is getting worse" increased 10 percent, from 58 percent in the early seventies to 68 percent in the early eighties. Those who agreed that "it's hardly fair to bring a child into the world with the way things look for the future" increased by five percent, from 37 percent in the early seventies to 42 percent in the early eighties. (*Public Opinion*, December/January 1984, 32.) One sign of diminishing confidence in the future is the growth in popularity of apocalyptic speculation. Michael Barkun. "Divided Apocalypse: Thinking About the End in Contemporary America" *Soundings*, Fall 1983, 257–280.

19. Seymour Martin Lipset and William Schneider. *The Confidence Gap: Business, Labor and Government in the Public Mind* (New York: Free Press, 1983), 340.

   Age and education have been found to be the two most powerful predictors of whether a person votes. Raymond E. Wolfinger and Steven J. Rosenstone. *Who Votes?* (New Haven: Yale University Press, 1980).

   Education also accounts for differences in political knowledge, political interest, and political opinions, even for youths. National Assessment of Educational Progress. *Education for Citizenship: A Bicentennial Survey*, Citizenship/Social Studies Report No. 07–CS–O1 (Denver, CO: NAEP, November 1976).

   Education has even been shown to have a positive effect on attentiveness to science and issues in science policy. John D. Miller. "The Future of Public Participation in Science Policy," Chapter 9 of *The American People and Science Policy* (New York: Pergamon Press, 1983), 105–124.

20. Norman Nie, Sidney Verba and John Petrocik. *The Changing American Voter* (Cambridge, MA: Harvard University Press, 1979).

21. Committee for the Study of the American Electorate. "Non-Voter Study '84–'85," Washington, D.C., 1984.

22. Jack L. Walker. "The Origins and Maintenance of Interest Groups in America" *The American Political Science Review*, June 1983, 390–405; Thomas L. Gais, Mark A. Peterson, Jack L. Walker. "Interest Groups, Iron Triangles and Representative Institutions in American National Government" *British Journal of Political Science*, vol. 14, 161–185; and Jack L. Walker. "Three Modes of Political Mobilization," Paper prepared for the Annual Meeting of the American Political Science Association, August 30–September 2, 1984.

   The 1984 presidential election betrayed signs of growing racial polarization. Blacks voted for Mondale by an 88-to-12 margin. Whites supported Reagan by a 62-to-37 margin. "Turnout is Up First Time in 20 Years" *Providence Journal-Bulletin*, November 10, 1984.

Politically, blacks' position has improved enormously. From 1,469 elected black officials nationwide in 1970, there were nearly quadruple that number, 5,606, in 1983. At the same time, although black voter registration has fallen from 60.8 percent to 59.1 percent, non-black voter registration has fallen even further, from 68.9 percent to 64.6 percent. Mireille Grangenois and Jay T. Harris. "Blacks Become Political Force to be Reckoned With" *USA Today*, February 28, 1984, 9A.

23. David Mathews has commented that "Citizen groups are less than what they might be because the only model of citizenship available to them is that of a consumer, and that does not challenge them with any higher model of behavior; their better instincts and their public mindedness are not called forth."

Quoted in "A Symposium on Public Life and Civic Literacy" *Antaeus Report*, Fall 1983, 3.

24. Voluntary reform efforts have roots as old as the first Colonial settlements. Their role was espoused by Cotton Mather and John Winthrop and observed with fascination by de Tocqueville and Emerson. But the present situation is different. Interests are being organized in a manner inimicable to the public interest.

Americans are very charitable people according to statistics. "Some 40 million individuals make contributions in support of some 300,000 not-for-profit organizations which serve, directly or indirectly, all of the United States and much of the rest of the world. Another 500,000 business corporations and foundations also contribute, and the total of private philanthropy from all sources and for all purposes—at least as defined by the Internal Revenue Service—came to more than $53 billion in 1981." Religion received almost half of that. This is still only a fraction of what the government spends on social welfare. Robert L. Payton. "Philanthropic Values," paper prepared for the Wilson Center Colloquium, October 2–3, 1982, 28 and 30. This does not include the 84 million full-time and part-time volunteers (86 percent of all adults) that contribute 8.4 billion hours of work to American society each year, work that is equivalent to 4.9 million full-time employees, or about $63 billion worth of uncompensated services. That represents almost 6 percent of national income. Robert Payton. "Philanthropy As A Right" in Adlai E. Stevenson and Others (Eds.). *The Citizen and His Government*, The Andrew R. Cecil Lectures on Moral Values in a Free Society, vol. V, 129–130 (Austin, TX: University of Texas Press, 1984).

25. Brian O'Connell (Ed.). *America's Voluntary Spirit, A Book of Readings* (New York: The Foundation Center, 1983).

26. But the responses are not always in the public interest. In February 1984, the Lead Industries Association acting through its law firm threatened legal recourse if the Center for Disease Control did not cancel their scheduled scientific meeting on "Preventing Lead Poisoning in Children." The lead manufacturers' complaint, which succeeded in its purpose, was that they were not represented on an advisory committee to oversee the meeting. Eliot Marshall. "Legal Threat Halts CDC meeting on Lead" *Science*, February 17, 1984, 672.

27. "John W. Gardner maintains that American political processes suffer from a paralysis

of polarization. His oft-quoted analogy compares contemporary politics to a game of checkers in which special interest groups put their fingers on various checkers in turn and say, 'Go ahead and play, just don't touch this one'." John W. Gardner, as cited by David Mathews in "The Liberal Arts and the Civic Arts," 269.

In 1974 there were 608 Political Action Committees (PACs) who spent $12.5 million in national elections. By 1982 there were 3,371 PACs who spent some $83 million. "For better or for worse, a new political organization—the political action committee—has entered America electoral politics without the extensive mechanisms that have long held political parties accountable to their publics." Frank J. Sorauf. "Accountability in Political Action Committees" *Political Science Quarterly*, Winter 1984–85, 593 and 613.

28. American Council on Education. *The American Freshman: National Norms for Fall*, (Los Angeles: Cooperative Institutional Research Program, University of California, 1975–1984, annually). Other questions, the responses to which also indicate a further decline in a sense of civic responsibility, were: "Influencing Political Structure," "Influencing Social Values," "Being Involved in Environmental Cleanup," "Promoting Racial Understanding," and "Keeping Up with Political Affairs." For further evidence see Dennis Wall. "Student Response in the 80's: Style Vs. Substance" *AAHE Bulletin*, November 1983, 3–5; and Ernest L. Boyer and Fred Hechinger. *Higher Learning in the Nation's Service* (Washington, D.C.: The Carnegie Foundation for the Advancement of Teaching, 1981), 44–46.

A recent trend for Americans to view higher education as a means to specific ends rather than as a means for broadening one's outlook is further evidence of the privatization of concerns. Group Attitudes Corporation. "American Attitudes toward Higher Education—1983" (New York: Group Attitudes Corporation, October 3, 1983).

29. Jon D. Miller. "The American College Student: An Educational and Social Portrait," paper presented to the 1984 annual meeting of the American Educational Research Association, April 25, 1984.

30. James Billington, director of the Woodrow Wilson International Center for Scholars, argues that the increasing specialization of the academic curriculum contributes to the decay of students' civic view. Alvin P. Sanoff. "Universities have Fallen Down on the Job of Teaching Values, A Conversation with James Billington" *U.S. News and World Report*, October 1, 1984, 60–70.

Professional specialization is affecting moral attitudes in other spheres as well. Associate Justice of the Supreme Court Sandra Day O'Connor has said:

> "Too many lawyers are insensitive to their greater ethical and social responsibilities . . . because legal education has nurtured inattention to them. I'd like to think that if there were a consistent and diligent focus in the law schools in general on the lawyers' moral and social responsibility, there would be more concern with such concepts." Quoted in "Verbatim: Ethics and the Law" *New York Times*, News of the Week in Review, October 28, 1984, 1.

172

Robert Payton sees the professionalization of philanthrophy as weakening public charity.

> "Although charity and philanthropy reflect the enduring aspirations of western civilization and are commonly cited as among the most admirable traits of American society, their further evolution may be in question.
>
> "Policy makers are farther removed from the recipients of charity and philanthropy than was the case in simpler and smaller societies." Organizational values replace personal ones and neutral terms like "grantmaking" and "contributions" replace religion, charity, and philanthropy. Robert L. Payton. "Philanthropic Values," paper prepared for the Wilson Center Colloquium, unpublished MS, October 2 and 3, 1982, 4–5.

31. The Carnegie Council's Surveys of Institutional Adaptations to the 1970s. Unpublished survey conducted in 1978.

   Dennis Wall has observed the contrast between present and past conservatism. "Students are back to the traditional pursuits. But the '80s are not the '50s. Students are not confident about their futures. 'Success' is the goal, but there is an edge to the striving, a desperation to 'make it'. . . . Professions are chosen not for the satisfaction they bring but for their marketability. Fear of un- or underemployment is a major motivator." Dennis Wall. "Student Response in the '80s: Style vs. Substance" *AAHE Bulletin*, November 1984, 3.

32. Daniel Yankelovich, as quoted in Karlyn Keene. "American Values: Change and Stability" *Public Opinion*, December/January 1984, 2–3; and "Values: Generations Apart," 21.

33. This does not argue that it is the highest priority. As Aristotle said in his letter to Alexander. "For it is far more honorable and kingly to have the mind well ordered than to see the bodily force well arrayed." "Aristotle's Rhetoric to Alexander" (attributed to Aristotle) in Aristotle, *Problems II, Book XXII–XXXVIII and Rhetorica Ad Alexandrium*, translated by W. S. Hett and H. Rackham (Cambridge, MA: The Loeb Classical Library, Harvard University Press, 1957).

34. Some schools have begun teaching classes on honesty, generosity, courage, and tolerance as a means to combat vandalism and disciplinary problems. Thus far, the effort seems to be paying off. Jay Mathews. "Teaching Values in U.S. Schools" *Washington Post*, November 21, 1984, A1 and A4; and Lucia Solorzano. "Rights, Wrongs; Now Schools Teach Them" *U.S. News and World Report*, May 13, 1985, 51.

35. Preamble of the Charter of the University of Georgia, 1785.

CHAPTER IV.

1. Marvin Stone. "Editorial: A Scary Shortage" *U.S. News and World Report*, March 15, 1982, 88. Also, Val Fitch. "We are in Danger of Losing Our Scientific Leadership" *U.S. News and World Report*, June 21, 1982, 56.

2. American Council on Education. The Business-Higher Education Forum. *Engineering Manpower and Education: Foundation for Future Competitiveness* (Washington, D.C.: American Council on Education, October 1982); also, National Academy of Engineering Panel on the Machine-Tool Industry, E. Ray McClure, Chairman. *Report to National Science Foundation* (Washington, D.C., 1983).

3. National Research Council. *International Competition in Advanced Technology: Decisions for America* (Washington, D.C.: National Academy Press, 1983), 48.

4. W. Edmund Lear. "The State of Engineering Education" *Journal of Metals*, February 1983, 48–51.

5. American Association of Engineering Societies, American Society of Mechanical Engineers, American Society for Engineering Education. *Data Related to the Crisis in Engineering Education* (New York: AAES, March 1981), Table 2.1.

6. W. Edmund Lear. "The State of Engineering Education."

7. *Engineers Joint Council, Engineering Manpower Bulletin #50* (New York: Engineers Joint Council, November 1979); and Engineering Manpower Commission, *Engineering and Technology Degrees 1983*.

8. American Council on Education. *The American Freshman: National Norms for Fall 1974, 1982* (Los Angeles: Cooperative Institutional Research Program, University of California, 1974, 1982). "Women, Minorities Making Gains in Professional Workforce" *Higher Education Daily*, September 19, 1984, last page.

9. National Science Foundation. *Science and Engineering Doctorates: 1960–82* (Washington, D.C.: National Science Foundation, 1983), Tables 1 and 3.

10. In 1981 the proportion of blacks receiving a bachelor's in engineering was 3.3, the proportion of Hispanics was 2.0. National Center for Education Statistics. *Digest of Education Statistics 1983–1984*, Washington, D.C., December 1983, Table 101, 20. In 1983, black enrollment in engineering was down by 5.7 percent. Patrick J. Sheridan. "Engineering Enrollments, Fall 1983" *Engineering Education*, October 1984, 46.

11. Scientific Manpower Commission. *Professional Women and Minorities: A Manpower Data Resource Service*, Washington, D.C., 1984, Table 1–26, 25.

12. National Science Foundation. *Science and Engineering Doctorates: 1960–1982*, Washington, D.C., 1983, Table 3, 58–60.

13. National Science Foundation. *Projections of Science and Engineering Doctorate Supply and Utilization*, Washington, D.C., 1979; National Science Foundation and Department of Education. *Science and Engineering for the 1980s and Beyond*, Washington, D.C., October 1980; American Council on Education, Business-Higher Education Forum. *Engineering Manpower and Education: Foundation for Future Competitiveness*, Washington, D.C., October 1982; and National Science Foundation. *Projected Response of the Science, Engineering and Technical Labor Market to Defense and Nondefense Needs: 1982–87*, Special Report, Washington, D.C., 1984.

14. National Science Foundation and Department of Education. *Science and Engineering Education for the 1980s and Beyond* (Washington, D.C.: Government Printing Office, October, 1980).

15. Massachusetts Institute of Technology. *1984 Registrar's Report, Massachusetts Institute of Technology, for the Academic Year 1983–1984* (Cambridge, MA: Office of

the Registrar, Massachusetts Institute of Technology, 1984); and *Reports to the President: 1982–1983* (Cambridge, MA: Massachusetts Institute of Technology, 1983), 139. Conversations and communications with Dr. Margaret L. A. MacVicar of Massachusetts Institute of Technology.

16. Paul Doigan. "Engineering Enrollment, Fall 1984" *Engineering Education*, October 1983, 18–20; and "Schools Ride the Enrollment Wave, Trying to Match Supply with Demand" *Engineering Education News*, October 1984, 1–3.

17. Science, engineering and technician employment outpaced the growth in total work force in private industry between 1979 and 1982, growing 6.3 percent per year versus 0.4 percent per year. Mechanical, electrical, chemical, and aeronautical engineers fell in numbers whereas civil, industrial, and nuclear engineers grew. National Science Foundation, Division of Resource Studies. *Scientific and Technical Work Force in Trade and Regulated Industries Shows Major Shift in Occupational Composition: 1979–82*, Washington, D.C., May 1984, 1.

18. National Science Foundation. *Science and Engineering Doctorates 1960–82*, Washington, D.C., 1983, Table 1, 17.

19. As Jack Welch, General Electric's Chief Executive Officer, recently told a group of engineering deans, "What we are looking for is bright and risk-oriented, entrepreneurial engineers, ready to take the ball and run with it." "Deans and GE Managers Evaluate Engineering Education" *Engineering Education News*, October 1984, 1–3.

CHAPTER V.

1. Robert Payton sees individual entrepreneurial behavior as the prime mover behind progress even in donating to charity.

    "Increases in scale made possible by taxation presumably expand the government's role (in philanthropy) and diminish the private one. But philanthropy continues to be the source of much—and probably most—social and cultural innovation. Ideas are introduced and tested by social and cultural entrepreneurs supported by philanthropic venture capital, and the successful innovations come to constitute a claim on public funds." Robert Payton. "Philanthropic Values," paper prepared for the Wilson Center Colloquium, October 2–3, 1982, 36.

2. This term is borrowed from Roy W. Heath. *The Reasonable Adventurer: A Study of the Development of 36 Undergraduates at Princeton* (Pittsburgh: University of Pittsburgh Press, 1964).

3. Jerome B. Wiesner. "Education for Creativity in the Sciences" *Daedalus*, Summer 1965, 527–529.

4. *Ibid.* Also, Benjamin S. Bloom of the University of Chicago has completed a study of 120 world-class artists, athletes, and scholars to find out what educational factors help explain their achievements. He discovered that talented people, despite their innate abilities, do not succeed without help and encouragement from the home and teachers.

5. "Even within some specific area of learning, at least two distinguishable tasks confront

the teacher who is trying to promote critical thinking. On the one hand, he is *teaching how*, which issues in procedures or skills; on the other, he is *teaching to*, which issues in dispositions, propensities, or tendencies. And the things that the teacher does to achieve the one might not be sufficient for achieving the other. In short, he is trying to provide the student with both the capacity and the will to use it." John E. McPeck. *Critical Thinking and Education* (New York: St. Martin's Press, 1981), 17–18.

George Prince maintains "that the thinking operations we use to be creative are exactly the same as those we use to learn and understand." George Prince. "Mindspring: Suggesting Answers to Why Productivity is Low" *Chemtech*, May 1976, 293.

Not only must creativity be nurtured as an individual develops, but it must be supported in the actual working environment. One study of researchers found that creativity was just as likely to be punished as to be rewarded. Donald C. Pelz and Frank M. Andrews. Chapter 9, "Creativity" in *Scientists in Organizations* (New York: John Wiley and Sons, 1966), 154–173.

6. Although a competitive environment outside a group will encourage creativity, a cooperative structure within the group is more fruitful for producing creative thinking. George M. Prince. "Synectics: Twenty-Five Years of Research into Creativity and Group Process" *American Society for Training and Development*, 1982, 91–103.

7. Joseph D. Novak. *A Theory of Education* (Ithaca, NY: Cornell University Press, 1977); and Joseph D. Novak. "Metalearning and Metaknowledge: Strategies to Help Students Learn How to Learn," version of a paper presented at the International Seminar on Misconceptions in Science and Mathematics, Cornell University, June 21, 1981.

8. Harriet Zuckerman. *Scientific Elite: Nobel Prize Laureates in the United States* (New York: The Free Press, 1977) supports this suggestion. For an anecdotal example, see Nobel Laureate Paul A. Samuelson's comments in "Economics in A Golden Age: A Personal Memoire" in G. Holton (Ed.). *The Twentieth Century Sciences* (New York: Norton, 1972). The empirical study by Jack Chambers, "College Teachers: Their Effect on Creative Students" *Journal of Educational Psychology*, 1973, 326–334, also presents strong evidence of the importance of teachers who are strongly motivated, creative, and tolerant of dissent in producing students with the same values and characteristics.

9. Jack A. Chambers. "College Teachers: Their Effect on Creativity of Students"; and John E. Dreydahl. "Some Developmental and Environmental Factors in Creativity."

10. Neal Whitman. "Teaching Problem-Solving and Creativity in College Courses" *AAHE Bulletin*, February 1983, 9–13; and Jerry K. Stonewater and Barbara A. Stonewater. "Teaching Problem Solving: Applications from Cognitive Development Research" *AAHE Bulletin*, February 1984, 7–10.

11. Robert Glaser. "Education and Thinking: The Role of Knowledge" *American Psychologist*, February 1984, 93–104; John A. Passmore. *The Philosophy of Teaching* (Cambridge, MA: Harvard University Press, 1980); and John E. McPeck. *Critical Thinking and Education* (New York: St. Martin's Press, 1981).

12. Jack A. Chambers. "College Teachers: Their Effect on Creativity of Students" *Journal*

    of *Educational Psychology*, 1973, 326–334; and Douglas H. Heath. "A College's
    Ethos: A Neglected Key to Effectiveness and Survival" *Education*, Summer 1981,
    89–111.

13. J. W. Getzels and P. W. Jackson. *Creativity and Intelligence* (New York: John Wiley
    and Sons, 1962); J. P. Guilford. "Creativity" *American Psychologist*, 1980, 444–454;
    J. E. Drevdahl. "Factors of Importance for Creativity" *Journal of Clinical Psychology*,
    1956, 21–26; Paul Heist (Ed.). *The Creative College Student: An Unmet Challenge*
    (San Francisco: Jossey-Bass, 1969); D. W. MacKinnon. "Characteristics of the Cre-
    ative Person: Implications for the Teaching-Learning Process" *Current Issues in
    Higher Education* (Washington, D.C.: National Educational Association, 1961), 89–
    92; C. W. Taylor (Ed.). *The Third (1959) University of Utah Research Conference
    on the Identification of Creative Scientific Talent* (Salt Lake City: University of Utah
    Press, 1959); E. P. Torrance and Others. *Assessing the Creative Thinking Abilities
    of Children* (Minneapolis: Bureau of Educational Research, University of Minnesota,
    1960); Michael A. Wallach. "Psychology of Talent in Graduate Education" in Samuel
    Messick and Associates (Eds.). *Individuality in Teachers* (San Francisco: Jossey-Bass,
    1976); Michael A. Wallach. "Tests Tell Us Little About Talent" *American Scientist*,
    January-February 1977, 57–63; Warren W. Willingham and Hunter M. Breland.
    Personal Qualities and College Admissions (New York: College Entrance Examination
    Board, 1982); Cliff W. Wing, Jr. and Michael A. Wallach. *College Admissions and
    the Psychology of Talent* (New York: Holt, Rinehart and Winston, 1971); and Jean
    Zmolek. "Correlation between Creativity and Academic Success," Department of
    Psychology, University of Utah, Salt Lake City, December 1984. Both MacKinnon
    and Torrance set an I.Q. of 120 as the minimum needed for mastery of important
    subject matter, and found that above that level there is no correlation between "crea-
    tivity" and intelligence.

    Intelligence tests measure only cognitive variables. Early studies done at the behest
    of the military found *no* cognitive factors associated with skills of military leadership.
    Alvin Marks, J. P. Guilford, and P. R. Merrifield. *A Study of Military Leadership in
    Relation to Selected Intellectual Factors*, Report No. 21 (Los Angeles: University of
    Southern California Psychology Laboratory, November 1959). The same is true for
    business leadership. Patricia Casserly and Joel T. Campbell. *A Survey of Skills and
    Abilities Needed for Graduate Study in Business*, prepared for Graduate Business
    Admissions Council (Princeton, NJ: Educational Testing Service, October 1973).

14. Joseph D. Novak. "Metalearning and Metaknowledge: Strategies to Help Students Learn
    How to Learn," version of a paper presented at the International Seminar on Mis-
    conceptions in Science and Mathematics, Cornell University, June 21, 1981, 12.

    A new book, Richard Moll's *The Public Ivys* (New York: Viking Press, 1985) argues
    that selective schools are least interested in using test scores to judge applicants. They
    are more interested in whether students have shown a willingness to take risks by
    taking difficult courses.

15. "Above a certain minimum threshold, neither GRE scores nor college grades give
    clear signals about who will be the stars in graduate school or, more importantly,
    who will be the stars in academic careers five or ten years out." Robert E. Klitgaard.

177

The Decline of the Best? Number 65D (Cambridge, MA: Harvard University, Kennedy School of Government, May 1979), 54–59.

It is interesting to note that not only are SAT scores down for students entering college, GRE scores are down for students leaving college. The reasons for this unmistakable trend remain unexplained. Clifford Adelman. *The Standardized Test Scores of College Graduates 1964–1982*, prepared for the Study Group on the Conditions of Excellence in American Higher Education (Washington, D.C.: National Institute of Education, October 1984), 16–36.

16. Many Ph.D. students do not even attain the Ph.D. but become A.B.D. (All But Dissertation). J. W. Getzels of the University of Chicago thinks this is because students have mastered how to find solutions to problems, but not how to find a problem in the first place. Remarks made in personal correspondence, September 19, 1984.

    In their survey of research activity in higher education, Martin Trow and Oliver Fulton found that over half of all academics had not published a research or scholarly paper in the two years preceding the survey. The percentage of faculty who *have* published jumps to almost 80 percent at high-quality universities.

    Martin Trow (Ed.). *Teachers and Students: Aspects of American Higher Education*, Carnegie Commission on Higher Education (New York: McGraw-Hill, 1975), 40–41.

17. J. W. Getzels and M. Csikszentmihaly. *The Creative Vision: A Longitudinal Study of Problem Finding in Art* (New York: Wiley-Interscience, 1976); D. W. MacKinnon. "Identifying and Developing Creativity" in *Selection and Educational Differentiation* (Berkeley: Field Service Center and Center for the Study of Higher Education, University of California, 1960), 75–89; D. W. MacKinnon. "Proceedings of the Conference on The Creative Person" (Berkeley: University of California, Alumni Center, University of California Extension, 1961); and Calvin W. Taylor (Ed.). *Widening Horizons in Creativity* (New York: John Wiley and Sons, 1964).

    Harvard University's Project Zero researchers have discovered that creativity is an extension of the everyday abilities of perception, understanding, and memory. It does not require a flash of inspiration. It is encouraged by a sense of positive self-assessment and confidence. Laurie H. Hutzle. "Creative Confidence" *Frontier*, March 1985, 31–32.

18. John H. Lounsbury reports in his nationwide study of 141 high schools that added emphasis given to critical thinking and active learning is more important than a return to the basics, increased discipline, or longer school hours. Barbara Zigli. "Ninth-Grade Cure: More Learning and Less Teaching" *USA Today*, January 28, 1985, 3D.

    This could best be done by giving students opportunities to participate in programs that allowed them to exercise their creative talents. Use of experiential education programs is one method. Although many experiential education programs are directed toward developing basic skills or career aptitudes, some are designed to stimulate personal growth. This is true of New York City's Executive High School Internship Program, which has been adopted by schools in over 20 states. Michael R. Crowe and Kay A. Adams. *The Current Status of Assessing Experiential Education Programs*, Information Series No. 163 (Columbus, OH: The National Center for Research in Vocational Education, Ohio State University, March 1979), 47–56.

Colleges and universities could then use the record of students' performance in these programs to judge the degree of their creativity and risk taking.

19. Discussion with Professor Sheldon Rothblatt, Chairman of the History Department, University of California, Berkeley.

20. "Good citizenship in a representative democracy is not just a matter of keeping within the law and being a decent person and a kind neighbor. Good citizenship calls for the attainment of a working understanding of our social, political, and economic arrangements, and for the ability to think critically about issues concerning which there may be an honest (or even dishonest) difference of opinion." Edward M. Glaser. "Critical Thinking: Educating for Responsible Citizenship in a Democracy" *National Forum*, Winter 1985, 25.

21. A Carnegie Commission on Higher Education study found that university administrators and faculty thought their institution's goals placed "prepare student for citizenship" as twenty-fifth out of a list of forty-seven goals for higher education. "Develop students' character" came in forty-first. In contrast, "prepare students for useful careers" was ranked tenth. Edward Gross and Paul V. Grambsch. *Changes in University Organization, 1964–1971*, Carnegie Commission on Higher Education (New York: McGraw-Hill, 1974), 46–47.

    However, when asked what goals higher education *should* strive for, the faculty and administrators ranked "prepare student for citizenship" and "develop students' character" fifteenth and sixteenth. "Prepare students for useful careers" fell to thirtieth place. *Ibid.*, 52–53.

    Moreover, this discrepancy between *actual* and *preferred* goals had widened from 1964 to 1971. *Ibid.*, 60–61.

22. Ernest L. Boyer and Fred M. Hechinger. *Higher Learning in the Nation's Service* (Washington, D.C.: The Carnegie Foundation for the Advancement of Teaching, 1981), 56.

23. Derek Bok. *Beyond the Ivory Tower* (Cambridge, MA: Harvard University Press, 1982), 116.

24. Carol Gilligan. "Moral Development"; and William G. Perry. "Cognitive and Ethical Growth: The Making of Meaning," both in Arthur W. Chickering (Ed.). *The Modern American College* (San Francisco: Jossey-Bass, 1981).

25. Kenneth A. Feldman and Thomas M. Newcomb. *The Impact of College on Students*, vol. 1 (San Francisco: Jossey-Bass, 1973).

26. Amitai Etzioni. *An Immodest Agenda* (New York: McGraw-Hill, 1983), 135.

27. Allan Bloom. "Our Listless Universities" *Change*, April 1983, 29.

28. To be released in a forthcoming Carnegie Foundation for the Advancement of Teaching study on undergraduate education.

29. Alexander Astin. *Four Critical Years* (San Francisco: Jossey-Bass, 1978).

30. Harold T. Shapiro. "Is Taking Sides a Good Idea for Universities?" *Science*, July 6, 1984.

31. Those issues that society mandates, such as affirmative action, as well as those few that the academic community feels are universal, such as an aesthetic sense, must be added.

32. Robert W. White. "Humanitarian Concerns," from *The Modern American College*;

Derek Bok. *Beyond the Ivory Tower*, 119, 120; and Frederick Rudolph. "The Effect of Professionalism on the Curriculum" *Change*, May/June 1984, 13–17.

It would seem natural for political science to concentrate upon the teaching of civic values. At one time it did so. Albert Somit and Joseph Tanenhaus. *The Development of American Political Science: From Burgess to Behavioralism* (Boston: Allyn and Bacon, 1967). This is no longer the case: a victim of professionalism and academic departmentalism. Morris Janowitz. *The Reconstruction of Patriotism: Education for Civic Consciousness* (Chicago: University of Chicago Press, 1983).

33. Robert W. White. "Humanitarian Concerns," 169.
34. Derek Bok. *Beyond the Ivory Tower*, 122; Kenneth Eble. "Interview" *AAHE Bulletin*, May 1984, 4.
35. Derek Bok, op. cit., 123. The colleges and universities involved include Barnard, Brown, Cornell, Georgetown, Hampshire, and Stanford.
36. David P. Ausubel. *The Psychology of Meaningful Learning* (New York: Grune and Straton, 1963), and *Educational Psychology: A Cognitive View* (New York: Holt, Rinehart and Winston, 1968), as well as Joseph D. Novak. *A Theory of Education*, and "Metalearning and Metaknowledge."
37. Joseph D. Novak. "Metalearning and Metaknowledge," 6. Nevitt Sanford found in studies done at Vassar and Stanford that involving students in research projects, whether as subjects or objects, had a greater effect on their personality development than any other college experience. Nevitt Sanford. "Whatever Happened to Action Research?" unpublished manuscript, n.d. This point has been re-emphasized by the report of the Study Group on the Conditions of Excellence in American Higher Education. "Involvement in Learning: Realizing the Potential of American Higher Education" reprinted in *Chronicle of Higher Education*, October 24, 1984, 40–41.
38. Jerome B. Wiesner. "Education for Creativity in the Sciences."
39. Fund for the Improvement of Postsecondary Education (FIPSE). "FY 1974 Program Information and Application Procedures," Washington, D.C., Department of Health, Education, and Welfare, October 25, 1973, 6. Glen R. Johnson and James F. McNamara. "Do Disciplines Differ in Their Verbal Interaction Within the College Classroom?" unpublished manuscript, Texas A & M University; Arthur Levine. *When Dreams and Heroes Died* (San Francisco: Jossey-Bass, 1980), 60; Richard C. Richardson, Jr., Elizabeth C. Fisk and Morris A. Okun. *Literacy in the Open Access Classroom* (San Francisco: Jossey-Bass, 1983), 60–62; and Yukie Tokuyama. "A Survey of Instructional Practices" in *The Humanities and Sciences in Two-Year Colleges* (Los Angeles: Center for the Study of Community Colleges and ERIC Clearinghouse for Junior Colleges, University of California, Summer 1980), 81–91.
40. Ernest L. Boyer. *High School: A Report on Secondary Education in America*, report by The Carnegie Foundation for the Advancement of Teaching (New York: Harper & Row, 1983), 148; The Carnegie Foundation Survey of Faculty and Undergraduates, 1984; and earlier surveys partly reported on in Arthur Levine. *When Dreams and Heroes Died*, 77. B. Everard Blanchard. "Curriculum Articulation Between the College of Liberal Arts and the Secondary School: A National Survey, Second Interim Report." (Chicago, IL: DePaul University, School of Education, 1971) reports

that approximately 30 percent of the subject matter studied in high school is repeated in college classrooms, leading to a high degree of boredom.

41. Theodore Sizer. *Horace's Compromise: The Dilemma of the American High School* (Boston: Houghton Mifflin Company, 1984), 54–55.

42. W. J. McKeachie. "Research on Teaching at the College and University Level," Chapter 23, of N. J. Gage (Ed.). *Handbook of Research on Teaching* (Chicago: Rand McNally, 1963), 1118–1171, summarizes studies on the effects of lecturing versus discussion in the college classsroom: "Despite the many findings of no significant differences in effectiveness between lecture and discussion, those studies which have found differences made surprising good sense. In only two studies was one method superior to the other on a measure of knowledge of subject matter; both studies favored the lecture method. In all six experiments finding significant differences favoring discussion over lecture, the measures were other than final examinations testing for knowledge" (p. 1127).

43. Jack A. Chambers. "College Teachers: Their Effect on Creativity of Students" *Journal of Educational Psychology*, 1973, 326–334; and Robert E. Wilson and Others (Eds.). "The Characteristics of Effective College Teachers," Chapter 10 of *College Professors and Their Impact on Students* (New York: John Wiley and Sons, 1975), 100–198.

44. Xenia Coulter and Laurie Johnson. "The Use of the Undergraduate Teaching Assistant at Stony Brook," Report No. 21 (Stony Brook, NY: Research Group for Human Development and Educational Policy, State University of New York-Stony Brook, 1984) make the following observation: "The faculty interviewed who have used undergraduates as TAs [Teaching Assistants] were extremely enthusiastic about the practice. When asked how important they felt the TAs were to their effectiveness as instructors, eight out of ten faculty used words such as 'crucial,' 'essential,' 'indispensable' and 'vital' in their responses . . ." (p. 34).

Hampshire College's charter, *The New College Plan*, written in 1958, states:

> "It will be a major goal of the college to develop and maintain a style of life which will make it habitual for students to work together in groups, and individually, without constant recourse to the faculty."

45. Study Group on the Conditions of Excellence in American Higher Education. *Involvement in Learning: Realizing the Potential of American Higher Education* (Washington, D.C.: Department of Education, October 1984); and Ronald G. Downey "Long-term Outcomes of Participation in Student Government" *Journal of College Student Personnel*, 1984, 245–250. On the important role that extracurricular activities play in the maturation of college students, see William G. Perry, Jr. *Forms of Intellectual and Ethical Development in the College Years* (New York: Holt, Rinehart, and Winston, 1970).

46. G. G. Dye and J. B. Stephens. "Learning Ethics through Public Service Internship—Evaluation of an Experimental Program" *Liberal Education*, October 1978, 341–356; and Janet Eyler and Beth Halteman. "The Impact of a Legislative Internship on Students' Political Skillfulness and Sophistication" *Teaching Political Science*, Fall 1981, 27–34.

In a study of 70 students at Boston College, one group of whom took a service-learning course involving help to disadvantaged people and one group of whom were simply involved in a course on ethics, it was found that students in the service course showed a far greater gain on Rest's Defining Issues Test than did the Control group. This test measures principled moral reasoning. Margaret Gorman and Others. "Service Experience and the Moral Development of College Students," paper (Chestnut Hill, MA: Boston College, 1982).

47. Alexander W. Astin. *Four Critical Years: Effects of College on Beliefs, Attitudes and Knowledge* (San Francisco: Jossey-Bass, 1978); Alexander W. Astin. *The College Environment* (Washington, D.C.: American Council on Education, 1968); and Alexander W. Astin. "The Impact of Dormitory Living on Students" *Educational Record*, Summer 1973, 204–210.

48. The educational effects of work/study are dealt with in Chapter VI of this report. For the effects of internships, see Bernard C. Hennessy. *Political Internships: Theory, Practice, Evaluation* (University Park, PA: Pennsylvania State University, 1970); and Thomas P. Murphy. *Government Management Internship and Executive Development* (Lexington, MA: D. C. Heath, 1973). Not all internships have pronounced effects. They must present appropriate challenges to the student intern. Michelle Whitham with Albert Erdynast. "Applications of Developmental Theory to the Design and Conduct of Quality Field Experience Programs: Exercises for Educators," PANEL Resource Paper #8 (Washington, D.C.: National Society for Internship and Experiential Education, 1982), 7–12. They must also actively involve the student in value-forming experiences, such as community change. Richard A. Couto. "Catalysts for Change" *Synergist*, Fall 1980, 41–44.

"Indeed, despite their many attributes, internships cannot, nor should they, serve as substitutes for the traditional classroom learning experience. What they can do, it seems, is to supplement one's classroom education by providing what is essentially a kind of laboratory experience that may, if all goes well, enable the student to obtain both a deeper and broader understanding of the phenomena that concern them." Allan Rosenbaum. *Public Service Internships and Education in Public Affairs: Administrative Issues and Problems* (Washington, D.C.: National Center for Public Service Internship Programs, April 1976), 4–5.

49. One reason for the unwillingness on the part of graduate students to take risks is the increasing burden of student loans. See discussion in Chapter VI.

50. A 1978 survey of 103 experiential courses at Michigan State University in East Lansing discovered that the greatest challenge to the faculty member conducting the course was overcoming the traditional attitudes of docility, compliance, and dependence and getting the students to take greater initiative in their own learning. John S. Duley. "Nurturing Service-Learners" *Synergist*, Winter 1981, 12–15.

51. Team teaching, active class involvement (which, contrary to the conventional wisdom is not restricted to classes of 15 or 20), peer tutoring, collaborative course planning, and so forth.

52. For example, the Writing Fellows Program at Brown University, the Undergraduate Teaching Assistants Program at SUNY-Stony Brook, the Undergraduate Research

Opportunities Program at Massachusetts Institute of Technology, the Undergraduate Research Program at the University of Delaware, the Stanford University Undergraduate Research Opportunities Program, the Interdisciplinary Course Development Project at SUNY-Oswego, and at Ohio University. Several colleges regularly use the active learning mode. Hampshire College is one. It encourages students to design their own majors, has no departmental boundaries, and has many courses that are team taught.

53. Joseph Katz, evaluating the Brown University Writing Fellows Program as part of a larger curriculum report to FIPSE, has written, "At some point during the interview, I had to remind myself that I was sitting with a group of undergraduate students because their level of pedagogical sophistication was such as I might have expected from a group of experienced teachers. It seems that the task of teaching others had matured these students considerably." The panel met with the Director of this program, Professor Tori Herring-Smith and the 1983–84 fellows.

54. The program was initiated with a grant from the National Endowment for the Humanities. For comments on its effectiveness see Clifton Fadiman and James Howard. *Empty Pages* (New York: Fearson Pitman Publishers, 1979), 138–140; and Clark Bouton and Russell Y. Garth (Eds.). *Learning in Groups* (San Francisco: Jossey-Bass, 1983), 27–28. For an account of the philosophy behind this program, Elaine P. Maimon. "Talking to Strangers" *College Composition and Communication*, December 1979, 364–369; and Elaine P. Maimon. "Writing Across the Curriculum: Past, Present and Future" in C. W. Griffith (Ed.). *New Directions for Teaching and Learning: Teaching Writing in All Disciplines*, December 1982, 67–73.

55. Kenneth A. Bruffee. "The Brooklyn Plan: Attaining Intellectual Growth Through Peer-Group Tutoring" *Liberal Education*, December 1978, 447–468.

56. The program at the Massachusetts Institute of Technology has expanded to embrace a wide range of academic disciplines. Margaret MacVicar and Norma McGovern. "Not Only Engineering: MIT Undergraduate Research Opportunities Programs," commissioned by the Society for Research into Higher Education, Ltd. at the University of Surrey, Guilford, England, for its 1984 Annual Conference, "Education for the Professions," January 1984, 257–269. Many universities and colleges provide opportunities for undergraduates to do research, although they may have no explicit program. Princeton University requires every senior to complete a research project before graduation. Hampshire College requires every science major to design and complete an experiment.

57. Utah State University's first effort in NASA's "Getaway Special" was on the space shuttle Columbia in 1982. The second project was in 1984. Five more are planned. "In general, a far better education is obtained by a student involved in a Getaway Special experiment than by one who pursues a straight academic program." David Yodel and Others. "The First Getaway Special—How It Was Done" *Space World*, May 1983, 15. Students reported that the program increased their problem-solving abilities, taught them how to work in a team, improved their appreciation of academic subjects, and facilitated access to better employment opportunities. L. R. Megill. "Results of the Utah State University Involvement in the Getaway Shuttle Program,"

paper presented at the 1984 Getaway Special Experimenters' Symposium, NASA/Goddard Space Flight Center, Greenbelt, MD, August 1, 1984.

58. Gerard S. Gryski, Gerald W. Johnson and Laurence J. O'Toole, Jr. "Undergraduate Internships: An Empirical Review," paper presented at the annual meeting of the American Society for Public Administration, Denver, April 10, 1984.

Several liberal arts institutions, such as Bennington College, Colgate University, Oberlin College, Skidmore College, and Wheaton College, encourage students to spend January away from campus in internships. Usually there is no pay, but there is academic credit, and most students claim to derive some benefit from the experience. Thomas J. Meyer. "January Internships Give Many Students a Feel for World Beyond the Campus" *Chronicle of Higher Education*, January 23, 1985, 19–20.

59. After seven years of studying the learning outcomes of Alverno College's ability-based liberal arts curriculum, Marcia Mentkowski and Austin Doherty. *Careering After College: Establishing the Validity of Abilities Learned in College for Later Success* (Milwaukee, Wisconsin: Alverno College, 1983), argue that students' career and professional values can be used to get students to adopt liberal learning values. Bridging that transition helps increase learning and job performance after graduation.

60. See Chapter VI for more on this point.

CHAPTER VI.

1. About 70 percent of all financial aid is currently provided through federal need-based programs. Gary L. Jones, the former Undersecretary of Education, has called for a $500 million trust fund, financed privately, to give merit scholarships to 20,000 students annually. Not all no-need scholarships are based on academic merit. No-need financial aid includes athletic scholarships, the GI Bill, and low-tuition colleges. Fred Hechinger. "The No-Need Scholarship Rekindles a Heated Debate" *New York Times*, Higher Education Winter Survey, January 6, 1985, 17.

Two recent surveys document the prevalance of granting merit-based scholarships. One survey of 367 institutions conducted by Betsy Porter and Suzanne McCulloch of the University of Pittsburgh, found that over 80 percent of their respondents offered financial awards to students whose families could otherwise afford to pay the full cost of their education. Lawrence Biemiller. "Over 80 Pct. of Colleges in Survey Say They Give 'No Need' Scholarships" *Chronicle of Higher Education*, October 10, 1984. A larger survey of 2,310 institutions found that about 75 percent of the colleges and universities offered no-need scholarships. The percentage was higher for 4-year than 2-year schools, and for public than private schools. College Scholarship Service of the College Board and National Association of Student Financial Aid Administrators. "A Survey of Undergraduate Need Analysis Policies, Practices, and Procedures," Winter 1984, Table 15, 16.

In the summer of 1983, Assistant Secretary for Post–Secondary Education Edward M. Elmendorf held six public hearings around the country at which he aired administration proposals to give more scholarships to academically talented students. For the most part, college officials responded lukewarmly to the idea. Janet S. Hook.

"Student Aid Based on Merit Eyed by U.S." *Chronicle of Higher Education*, August 31, 1983, 1 and 13.

It is possible to combine reward for merit with a subsidy based on need. This is what the Moorehead Scholarships do, by linking job opportunity with entry to an honors program.

2. American Council on Education. *Rates of College Participation, 1969, 1974, 1981,* Policy Brief, April 1984, Table 1.

3. Research by Henry Freeman at the University of Michigan's Center for the Study of Higher Education suggests that merit based awards are ineffective devices for recruiting the better student who has no financial need. They are only effective in attracting needy students. "Michigan University Researcher Questions Lure of Merit Aid" *Higher Education Daily*, July 16, 1984, 5. Other studies confirm the importance of non-monetary factors in influencing the college choices of high ability, high-income students. Rex Jackson and Randall G. Chapman. *The Influence of No-Need Financial Aid Awards on the College Choices of High Ability Students* (Washington, D.C.: The College Board, October 1984); and Richard R. Spies. *The Effects of Rising Costs on College Choice* (New York: College Entrance Examination Board, 1978).

On the weak relationship between test scores and post–school performance for business executives see Daniel Goleman. "Successful Executives Rely on Own Kind of Intelligence" *New York Times*, Science Times Section, July 31, 1984. On the weak effect of GRE scores and college grades on performance in graduate school see the studies cited in Robert E. Klitgaard. *The Decline of the Best?* Discussion Paper Series (Cambridge, MA: Kennedy School of Government, Harvard University, December 1978), 54–59.

4. The most comprehensive study of these issues was completed over 30 years ago and has not been up-dated. Norman Frederiksen and W. B. Schrader. *Adjustment to College: A Study of 10,000 Veteran and Nonveteran Students in Sixteen American Colleges* (Princeton, NJ: Educational Testing Service, 1951). Also, Keith W. Olson. *The GI Bill Veterans and the Colleges* (Lexington, KY: The University Press of Kentucky, 1974).

5. Judith F. Hammes and Emil J. Haller. "Making Ends Meet: Some of the Consequences of Part-time Work for College Students" *Journal of College Student Personnel*, 1983, 529–535. A survey of selective and non-selective cooperative education programs by Paul Dube of Northeastern University and Alice Korngold of Pace University has shown work experience to have a positive effect on the post–graduate earnings and persistence of students. Work experience increased students' confidence, motivation, and career direction, in that order. (Information provided through personal correspondence with Paul Dube and Alice Korngold.)

One caveat is in order, however. There is reason to question the positive educational benefits of work experience for traditional students *before* attending college. Work in high school may diminish educational and occupational aspirations. Jeylan T. Mortimer and Michael D. Finch. "The Effects of Part-Time Work on Adolescent Self-Concept and Achievement," in Kathryn Borman and Jane Reiman (Eds.). *Becoming a Worker* (Norwood, NJ: Aflex, 1985, forthcoming); and Ellen Greenberger. "Chil-

185

dren, Families and Work" in N. D. Reppucci, L. A. Weithorn, E. P. Mulvey, and J. Monahan (Eds.). *Mental Health, Law, and Children* (Beverly Hills, CA: SAGE, 1983). But the evidence is not uniform: Denise Gottfedson. *Youth Employment, Crime, and Schooling: A Longitudinal Study of a National Sample*, Report Number 352 (Baltimore: Johns Hopkins University, Center for Social Organization of Schools, 1984); and "Fast Food Jobs" (Washington, D.C.: National Institute for Work and Learning, 1984).

What seems to matter is the quality of the work experience. Jobs high in discretionary decision making, innovative thinking, and challenge, foster greater involvement, self-confidence, and cooperativeness. J. T. Mortimer and J. Lorence. "Work Experience and Occupational Value Socialization: A Longitudinal Study" *American Journal of Sociology*, 1979, 1361–1385; and "Occupational Experience and the Self-Concept: A Longitudinal Study" *Social Psychology Quarterly*, 1979, 307–323.

6. Applied Systems Institute. *Work Patterns of Full-Time College Students in 1974 and 1981*, prepared for National Commission on Student Financial Assistance (Washington, D.C.: Applied Systems Institute, May 5, 1983). These estimates are derived from the Current Population Survey, which is done in the fall. Thus, they tend to underreport the average annual incidence of working, because summer jobs are excluded. Work rates seem to be even higher for part-time students. The Carnegie Foundation for the Advancement of Teaching. *Undergraduate Survey, 1984*.

7. On enrollment effects of grants: W. C. Fuller, C. F. Manski, and D. A. Wise. *The Impact of the Basic Educational Opportunity Grant Program on College Enrollments* (Cambridge, MA: Harvard University, Kennedy School of Government, Number 94D, July 1980); and S. J. Carroll. *Part-time Experience and the Transition from School to Work* (Santa Monica, CA: Rand Corporation, 1970). On the positive effects on persistence: Alexander Astin. *Preventing College Students from Dropping Out* (Washington, D.C.: Jossey-Bass, 1975); Samuel S. Peng and William B. Fetters. "Variables Involved in Withdrawal during the First Two Years of College: Preliminary Findings from the National Longitudinal Study of the High School Class of 1972" *American Educational Research Journal*, Summer 1978, 361–372; and Eric L. Jensen. "Student Financial Aid and Persistence in College" *Journal of Higher Education*, 1981, 280–294. On the neutral effect of grants on grades: M. Betsy Bergen and Donald D. Zielke. "Educational Progress of Basic Educational Opportunity Grant Recipients Compared to Non-recipients" *The Journal of Student Financial Aid*, February 1979, 19–22; and Keith McCreight and Morris LeMay. "A Longitudinal Study of the Achievement and Persistence of Students who Received Basic Educational Opportunity Grants" *The Journal of Student Financial Aid*, February 1982, 11–15.

8. After other forms of student aid (save for Social Security and the GI Bill), loans have been found to have the weakest effect on enhancing students' exercise of choice among colleges. Larry L. Leslie. *Role of Public Student Aid in Financing Private Higher Education* (University of Arizona, Higher Education Program, March 1978), 23–27; Larry L. Leslie, G. P. Johnson, and J. Carlson. "The Impact of Need-Based Student Aid Upon the College Attendance Decision" *Journal of Education Finance*, Winter 1977, 269–285; and Jonathan D. Fife and Larry L. Leslie. "The College Student Grant

186

Study: The Effectiveness of Student Grant and Scholarship Programs in Promoting Equal Educational Opportunity" *Research in Higher Education*, 1976, 317–333.

Several studies report the negative impact loans have on persistence in college. Astin shows this effect to be greater for males than females. Eric L. Jensen. "Financial Aid and Educational Outcomes: A Review" *College and University*, Spring 1983, 287–302; Alexander Astin. *Preventing Students from Dropping Out*; and Peng and Fetters. "Variables Involved in Withdrawal."

A good review of the factors affecting students' decisions to attend and remain in college can be found in Dawn Geronimo Terkla and Gregory A. Jackson. *The State of the Art in Student Choice Research* (Cambridge, MA: Harvard University, MS, January 1984); and Leonard Ramist. "College Student Attrition and Retention," Research Report (Princeton, NJ: Educational Testing Service, 1984).

Recently, it has become more and more difficult to separate out the specific effects of certain kinds of aid from other kinds of aid due to the widespread use of aid packages, which introduces the problem of multi-collinearity into statistical analysis. "We cannot conclude that different types of aid have the same effect because the variables are substantially intercorrelated." Dawn Terkla. *Financial Aid and Undergraduate Persistence*, unpublished Ph.D. dissertation, Harvard University, 1983, 74. Survey data of college freshmen in 1974, 1975 and 1976 found that of those students who received federal financial aid, 64 percent got aid in only one form, i.e., loan, grant, or work/study. Pat Smith and Cathy Henderson. *Federal Student Aid: Who Receives It and How is it Packaged?* (Washington, D.C.: Policy Analysis Service, American Council on Education, 1977). In contrast, in 1981–82, only 28 percent of all students enrolled in college received only one form of student aid. C. Dennis Carroll. "Packaging of Grants, Loans, and Earnings" Bulletin of the National Center for Education Statistics, Washington, D.C., 1983.

9. In addition to the studies cited previously, the bibliography, "Student Aid," will help one to understand the effects of student aid on various educational outcomes.

The studies listed in the bibliography make it clear that cost is not the only factor, not even the most important factor, influencing a student's decision whether to go to college. Aptitude and aspirations (both educational and occupational) are more powerful determinants than cost and the student takes into account the benefits of attending college versus the benefits of doing other things, e.g., working. So the perceived wage differential of college-leavers over non-college-leavers, the condition of the labor market, the terms of military service, and even the convenience of college location, all affect enrollment decisions. All the same, a recent review of 105 empirical studies of the factors influencing college choice places student financial aid fourth out of a list of 12 factors having the greatest impact. Terkla and Jackson. *The State of the Art in Student Choice Research*.

Concentrating upon college drop-outs, what are the factors that account for a student's decision to leave college early and are those factors manipulable by public policy? The simplest model of student persistence pays special attention to the student's aspirations for his college education, his means to achieve those aspirations, and his perception of the college he is attending as helping him toward that end.

187

Aspirations are affected by pre-college experiences, e.g., anticipated future job prospects. Means are affected by parental contribution, financial aid, and student's self-help. Perceptions (or evaluations) of college's relevance is affected by college selectivity, college type (2-year or 4-year), and, most significantly, degree of involvement in the college.

Financial aid is often thought to have a direct effect on *means*. And this is borne out by empirical studies. But it can also have an indirect effect via its influence upon a student's *aspirations* and *perceptions* of the relevance of college. The degree to which financial aid influences aspirations and perceptions depends more upon the *form* of the aid than the amount.

There seems to be great potential for student aid to influence a student's evaluation of the worth of continuing in college. One widely accepted model of student attrition emphasizes the processes of social and academic integration as affecting whether or not a student chooses to remain in college. (See articles by Tinto, Pascarella, and Terenzini.) Assuming that external influences are held constant, the higher the levels of integration into the social and academic systems of an institution, the less likely the student is to withdraw voluntarily. In other words, the more involved a student is in college, the more likely he is to persist. At the same time, the more likely he is to experience the greatest degree of change from a liberal education. Can student aid enhance student involvement or integration within college? If so, how?

Involvement can be divided into three different types: *academic involvement*, as measured by in-class time, studying time, and faculty-student interaction; *athletic involvement*, as measured by participation in on-campus social and extracurricular activities; and *interpersonal involvement*, as measured by participation in on-campus social and extracurricular activities. All these patterns of high involvement result in the greater likelihood of completing college, of implementing career objectives, and of being satisfied with the undergraduate experience, although each mode of involvement has its own set of learning and behavioral outcomes.

Of all forms of student aid why does work/study have the greatest positive effect on persistence? And why do loans have a negative effect? The answer seems to lie in the consequences that each form of self-help has upon increasing student involvement on campus. As Astin has remarked, "any program that involves the student actively in campus life decreases attrition." (Astin, *Financial Aid and Student Persistence*, 23.) Working on-campus is one means of involving students more in college life. But it is important that the work be either on-campus or campus-affiliated. Because off-campus work, unless it has academic affiliations, can have a negative effect on student persistence.

Loans do not involve the student to any degree in college life. Instead, they are apt to sensitize the student to the risks of pursuing a degree and to make him change his mind about the gains to be had relative to full-time working.

A final note on the GI Bill. It has been found to be negatively associated with persistence in college. But this is due to the fact that veterans represent a range of characteristics that themselves correlate with poor college performance, such as age, race, marriage, and educational, income, and occupational disadvantages. David E.

188

Drew and John A. Creager. *The Vietnam-Era Veteran Enters College*, ACE Research Reports, vol. 7, no. 4 (Washington, D.C.: American Council on Education, December 1972). Most studies fail to take this into account. The major exception is Frederiksen and Schrader's study, *Adjustment to College*. They found that the group of veterans that most outperformed themselves in terms of measured potential was also the most disadvantaged group. (See pp. 28–30, passim.) The ROTC program has a strong, positive association with persistence. No studies have looked at Social Security educational payments. Alexander Astin. *Preventing Students from Dropping Out*; and Ramist. "College Student Attrition and Retention."

10. Astin's survey, *The American Freshman: National Norms for Fall 1984* (Los Angeles: University of California, December 1984), found that under 20 percent of college freshmen in 1984 got Pell Grants (down from 31.5 percent in 1980) and 23.4 percent got Guaranteed Student Loans (up from 21.8 percent in 1983).

    A new law introduced by Congressman Montgomery is scheduled to come into effect on July 15, 1985, that will make the existing Veteran's Education Assistance Program (VEAP) more in line with earlier versions of the GI Bill. This law provides that every soldier make an *automatic* (not discretionary, like the original VEAP) contribution of $100 per month with an equal government match, rising to $300 per month after three years of service. The total will be made available to the soldier to finance his education after he leaves the service, *unless* the soldier decides to opt out at any point.

11. The Veteran's Education Assistance Program (see Note 10 above) has attracted rates of participation and levels of funding far below what the three previous GI Bills had managed to achieve. A resurrection of the Social Security program providing funding for college students under the Old Age and Survivors' Dependents Insurance provisions is not recommended. That program may have a rationale as aid to low-income families, but it was inequitable as a means of providing aid to college students. Congressional Budget Office, Congress of the United States. *Social Security Benefits for Students*, Washington, D.C., May 1977; David Paul Rosen. *The Effects of Phasing Out Social Security Student Benefits* (Oakland, CA: Paul David Rosen and Associates, March 1983).

12. On recent borrowing under the Guaranteed Student Loan Program (GSL), see Note 10. In 1983, 883,000 students were estimated to have borrowed under the National Direct Student Loan Program (NDSL). Altogether, 40 percent of all full-time and part-time students borrowed under one or another federal loan program that year. National Commission on Student Financial Assistance. *Guaranteed Student Loans: A Background Paper, Report No. 1* (Washington, D.C.: National Commission on Student Financial Assistance, March 1982).

13. Almost one in 12 medical school graduates have to repay loans of $50,000 and up. The average medical student debt is $26,496, as shown in the Association of American Medical Colleges' (AAMC) survey reported in *Higher Education Daily*, September 14, 1984, 3. While borrowing has risen, scholarships under the National Health Service Corps have been dwindling. In 1983, 16 percent of medical school graduates received such support, compared with only 11.5 percent in 1984. Some medical school

administrators fear that these debt levels will dissuade otherwise capable graduates from pursuing research careers. "[Al]though more than a third of the students reported some research involvement while in medical school, only 13.2 percent indicated that they planned to be extensively or significantly involved in research after graduation." Quoted in "More Than 84 Percent of 1983 Medical Graduates had Debts for Education Costs, Survey Finds" *Chronicle of Higher Education*, September 26, 1984, 16.

14. The Guaranteed Student Loan volume almost doubled from 1971 to 1978, growing from $1.015 billion to $1.958 billion. Over the next three years, the volume almost quadrupled, reaching $7.735 billion by 1981. Sixty percent of the increase over this ten-year period was due to the tripling in the number of students borrowing (1 million in 1971 and 3.5 million in 1981) and 40 percent derived from the doubling in the size of the loans ($998 in 1971 and $2,196 in 1981, on average). National Commission on Student Financial Assistance. *Guaranteed Student Loans: A Background Paper, Report No. 1* (Washington, D.C.: National Commission on Student Financial Assistance, March 1982), 25.

That borrowing is eclipsing scholarships as the major form of financial aid is confirmed by a recent survey of the financial records of 13,200 college students at 324 colleges and universities. Loans comprise the dominant form of student aid for students at lower and lower levels of family income. Using constant 1978 dollars, the cross-over point at which students were more likely to take out Guaranteed Student Loans than to receive Pell Grants was $36,000 in 1979–80, $24,000 in 1981–82, and $15,000 in 1983–84. In 1980, only 23 percent of the aid recipients at private colleges took out loans. In 1984, the figure was 50 percent. For public institutions, it was 35 percent. "Borrowing by Financial-Aid Recipients Is Increasing, 1983–84 Survey Finds" *The Chronicle of Higher Education*, August 1, 1984, 16.

The College Board gives the following breakdown of sources of student aid for the academic year 1983–84:

TABLE N–6

SOURCES OF STUDENT AID

Guaranteed Student Loans	42.9 percent
Other Federal Programs	28.2
Colleges and Universities	15.5
Veterans' Benefits	6.8
State Grants	6.6

Source: Anne MacKay-Smith. "College Financial Aid is Focusing on Loans as a Result of the Pressure of Rising Costs" *The Wall Street Journal*, October 1, 1984, 35.

15. Historically, loans were not intended to serve as the major instrument of financial aid. They were seen as a supplement to other programs. Loans are inherently in-

equitable as they place the heaviest debt burden on the poorest citizens. John F. Morse. "How We Got Here from There—A Personal Reminiscence of the Early Days," in Lois D. Rice (Ed.). *Student Loans: Problems and Policy Alternatives* (New York: College Entrance Examination Board, 1977), 3–15. Dwight Horch has warned of the effects of loans on career choices. Dwight Horch. *Estimating Manageable Educational Loan Limits for Graduate and Professional Students* (Princeton, NJ: Educational Testing Service, 1978). Some observers see the growing reliance on loans as explaining declining graduate school, and business, law, medical, dental, and veterinary school enrollments in the past couple of years. In part, this is due to falling federal support, requiring students to go into debt to attend professional school. It is also due to students' desire not to delay in getting a good-paying job. Gene I. Maeroff. "Enrollment in Professional Schools Declining" *New York Times*, February 10, 1985, 1 and 50. In 1970–71, at Princeton University, total graduate student borrowing was $70,000. Ten years later, in 1980–81, the same number of students borrowed $1.5 million, an increase of 2,000 percent. Raymond B. Anderson and Allen R. Sanderson. *Financial Issues in Graduate Education and an Agenda for Research* (Washington, D.C.: National Commission on Student Financial Assistance, July 1982).

16. In addition to earlier citations see Susan K. Hochstein and Robert R. Butler. "The Effects of the Composition of a Financial Aid Package on Student Retention" *Journal of Student Financial Aid*, February 1983, 21–26.

17. Jacob Stampen reports that minority students receiving federal aid at public schools fell from 34 percent to 28 percent between 1981–82 to 1983–84. American Council on Education. "Who Gets Student Aid: A 1983–84 Snapshot" Summary of a Policy Seminar held July 19, 1984 (Washington, D.C.: American Council on Education, 1984). The reason is the shift in that aid toward loans.

   In 1976, minority students accounted for 35 percent of all financial aid recipients, contrasting with 14 percent of all college students enrolled. Minorities participated most in Pell Grants (43 percent of all recipients), followed by (SEOG) Supplemental Educational Opportunity Grants (40 percent), College Work/Study (29 percent), and (NDSL) National Direct Student Loans (23 percent). The Guaranteed Student Loan Program had the lowest rate of minority participation of all other federal student aid programs, 17 percent. Melanie Reeves Williams and Laura Kent. *Blacks in Higher Education: Access, Choice, and Attainment* (New York: Ford Foundation, June 1982), 35–37. The reason for the different rates of participation by program, of course, is the higher proportion of blacks who fall in low-income categories. Loan programs have been directed at serving the needs of middle-income students. Lower-income parents are demonstrably more reluctant to accept debt-financing of higher education for their children than are higher-income parents. Lorayn Olson and Rachel A. Rosenfeld. "Parents and the Process of Gaining Access to Student Financial Aid" *Journal of Higher Education*, July/August 1984, 455–480.

18. The budget understates the cost of the GSL program each year. A new year of GSLs commits the federal government to 10 years or fewer of interest subsidies, special allowances, default insurance claims, and administrative costs. These costs will show

191

up in the budget only when they must be obligated. D. Bruce Johnstone. "Federally Sponsored Student Loans: An Overview of Issues and Policy Alternatives" in Lois D. Rice and Others. *Student Loans: Problems and Policy Alternatives* (New York: College Entrance Examination Board, 1977), 16–42. Johnstone estimated that for each $100 lent out under GSL, the federal government would have to pay $41, with $31 of this being accounted for by interest subsidies and special allowances (pp. 37–39). In FY 1982, the federal government committed itself to future payments of $2.9 to 3.6 billion (not at present value) on the $6.2 billion disbursed in loans. This comes to 47 cents to 59 cents on each dollar lent. The special allowance and in-school interest subsidy together account for 72–77 percent of the program outlays, or 34 cents to 45 cents per dollar. Reinsurance costs 16–19 percent, or 7 cents to 11 cents per dollar. Touche Ross and Company. *Study of the Cost and Flows of Capital in the Guaranteed Student Loan Program*, Final Report, prepared for the National Commission on Student Financial Assistance (Washington, D.C.: Touche Ross and Company, March 1983).

19. Because the loan program operates on leverage, it delivers more capital to students than would a grant program by a multiplier of 2:1. From the government's point of view, the loan program is cheaper. From the student's point of view, a grant is cheaper. Taking out a loan under the federal and state program is cheaper for the student than taking out a loan in the private market without the program. In fact, one estimate puts the effective interest rate at close to or below zero, due to the delay in repayment until after school and the below-market interest rates charged. Touche Ross and Company. *Study of the Cost to Borrowers of Participating in the Guaranteed Student Loan Program*, Final Report (Washington, D.C.: National Commission on Student Financial Assistance, March 1983). Nevertheless, the loan does represent a claim on a student's future income and many have begun to question the cost to the student in foregone alternatives for allocating his income after leaving school. To what extent do the educational loan repayments "distort" the spending and saving patterns of students following graduation?

Using consumption budget data from the Bureau of Labor Statistics, it has been estimated that a manageable educational loan limit would be one where monthly repayments ranged from 5.4 percent to 6.5 percent of after-tax income. Dwight H. Horch. *Estimating Manageable Educational Loan Limits for Graduate and Professional Students* (Princeton, NJ: Educational Testing Service, March 1978). This recommended limit is often exceeded. "The average doctoral recipient has a debt burden of, at most, 8 percent of discretionary earning, during the repayment period." Terry W. Hartle and Richard Wabnick. *The Educational Indebtedness of Graduate and Professional Students* (Washington, D.C.: Educational Testing Service, July 1983).

The burdensomeness of loans varies with occupation (and income level) and manner of repayment. Physicians and lawyers are able to handle the largest loan limits, followed by doctoral scientists and engineers, with teachers and nurses coming in last. But even physicians and lawyers have begun to feel the pinch. One recent study concluded that "Assuming the conventional 10-year repayment period with equal monthly installments, about 46 percent of the arts and sciences borrowers had unmanageable, or burdensome, loans compared to 86 percent of the law students and 83 percent of the medical students." H. J. Flamer, D. H. Horch and S. Davis. *Talented and Needy Graduate and Professional Students: A National Survey of People Who Applied for Need-Based Financial Aid to Attend Graduate and Professional Schools in 1980–81* (Princeton, NJ: Educational Testing Service, April 1982), 7–11.

The limits educational debt places on further borrowing after graduation began to constrain consumer purchasing in the 1980s. Under current projections, by 1989 educational debt will absorb *total debt capacity* of most college graduates. Credit Research Center. *The Role of Educational Debt in Consumer's Total Debt Structure* (Lafayette, IN: Credit Research Center, Purdue University, January 31, 1983).

20. Mandatory service requirements, even for military service, have always had loopholes and would continue to be full of exceptions in the future. James L. Lacy. "Military Manpower: The American Experience and the Enduring Debate" in Andrew J. Goodpaster and Others (Eds.). *Towards A Consensus on Military Service* (New York: Pergamon Press, 1982). Voluntary service certainly seems more attractive to the young. A Gallup poll in February 1984 registered that 65 percent of respondents support mandatory national service as a good idea and 30 percent oppose it as a bad idea. In a 1977 poll, 18- to 24-year-olds supported voluntary national service by 77 percent to 14 percent. Don Eberly. " A National Service Model Based on Experience and Research," prepared for the American Political Science Association Annual Meeting, Washington, D.C., August 31, 1984.

21. A similar proposal, including the adoption of a service unit as a measure of students' service performance, has been put forth in Ernest L. Boyer. *High School*, Report of The Carnegie Foundation for the Advancement of Teaching (New York: Harper & Row, 1983).

22. One problem is that advisors often counsel against public service, particularly when it interferes with professional preparation.

23. Brown University's National Service Scholarship Program began in 1982 with a million dollar grant from the C. V. Starr Foundation. That year, 13 students received awards of $1,000 to $3,000 for having contributed time to voluntary public service. Cornell University's CIVITAS program allows the use of federal college work/study money to finance students working off-campus in public service organizations. Georgetown University operates a liaison center that puts university students in touch with community service groups in the Washington area. The University of Minnesota, Duluth, has an off-campus service program, called Human Resources Bank (HRB) run by students that places them in local community service agencies. A university committee review of HRB determined that "the program provided for the development of life skills, career awareness opportunities, and interpersonal and helping skills." Robert J. Falls and Marion G. Agre. "The Human Resource Bank" *Synergist*, Winter 1981, 22.

Stanford University began granting competitive awards to students in 1984 for summer projects involving service-oriented work anywhere in the world.

Vanderbilt University has been running the Center for Health Services since 1969. The Center accepts students from around the country to help in delivering health

193

care to underserved rural communities and in mobilizing these communities to provide for their own needs.

Yale University's Dwight Hall, in operation for almost one hundred years, involves student volunteers in both community service and social action. Most projects are initiated by students, who then work with existing non-profit organizations in New Haven. Similar programs function at Columbia University, through its Earl Hall, and at Dartmouth College, through support from the Tucker Foundation.

24. New York City runs the National Service Corporation's City Volunteer Corps. Fall 1984 was the start of their first term of operation. They selected 56 volunteers from over 300 applicants. Initial work has been on city park restoration, delivering food to the poor, helping senior citizens relocate, working with terminally ill children, and cleaning up public places. This program offers remedial education through City University of New York (CUNY) during the term of service and a "golden handshake" in the form of a scholarship at the end.

Maryland's state superintendent of schools has proposed 100 hours of community service as a high school graduation requirement. There already has been a pilot program at two high schools resulting in improvement in school attendance, a fall in truancy, and a rise in measures of student self-esteem. "Community Service Eyed as Maryland High School Graduation Requirement" *The Washington Post*, January 23, 1984, D8.

25. An effective national service model must meet the diverse needs of its constituents. "Generally, it seems that college-oriented youth view national service as an opportunity to learn about themselves; working class/non-college-bound youths are interested in the possibility of a job or in learning skills which could help them in future employment." James L. Lacy. "NYC National Service Demonstration Project— Compensation of Participants," report to Carl Weisbrod (Chevy Chase, MD: MS, May 14, 1984), 11.

26. California has been notably active in this area. Not only is there the California Conservation Corps, there is also the San Francisco Conservation Corps, and other community service programs operating in Marin County and the East Bay.

27. The surfeit of teachers in the late 1970s has been replaced by a shortage of teachers in the 1980s, particularly of teachers in specific academic specialties and certain geographic areas. In New York City, for example, there were 300 vacancies for teachers in 1983 and 600 in 1984. The greatest problem remains getting white teachers to teach in black school districts. Joyce Parnick. "Gains Seen in City's Hiring of New Teachers" *New York Times*, September 23, 1984, 42.

Georgia has been importing teachers from West Germany to fill vacancies in math and science. Louisiana has had a longstanding program of seeking French teachers in Belgium, France, and Canada.

The National Center for Education Statistics estimates that as early as this year, the supply of new teachers will fall short of the demand. If current trends continue, by the 1990s there will be three jobs for every two education graduates. The shortage is due to rising elementary and secondary school enrollments compounded with declining college graduates in education. Nationwide, there were 317,000 such grad-

194

uates in 1972, compared to only 140,000 in 1984. Edward B. Fiske. "Teacher Glut is Coming to an End; Take Notes" *New York Times,* June 24, 1984, 24E.

Education Secretary Terrel Bell announced before an August 1984 meeting of the National Education Association that the poor quality of teachers is the number one source of problems in the nation's schools. "We're drawing most [teachers] from the bottom 25 percent of the barrel," he said. *Education Daily,* September 4, 1984. Bell estimated that 15,000 more high school math and science teachers are needed. Higher salaries in business and engineering are drawing qualified people out of the teaching field. A task force of the American Chemical Society concluded last year that chemistry courses are often taught by ill-trained teachers. Thomas Toch. "Problems in Math, Science Education Spur Varied Policy Initiatives" *Education Week,* August 22, 1984, 15. A report from the National Center for Education Information based on a nationwide survey, placed the blame on teacher education programs. It recommended that up to half of them be shut down due to poor standards. Emily Feistritzer. *The Making of a Teacher: A Report on Teacher Education and Certification* (Washington, D.C.: National Center for Education Information, 1984). This point of view has been seconded in Linda Darling-Hammond. *Beyond the Commission Reports: The Coming Crisis in Teaching* (Santa Monica, CA: The Rand Corporation, 1984). That report documents shortages in physics, computer programming, chemistry, bilingual education, earth science, geology and English. They estimate that 30 percent of math and science teachers are not qualified to teach those subjects.

28. The body that selects program participants should be a statewide panel appointed by the Secretary of Education from among faculty at the universities and colleges, school superintendents, school board members, principals and master teachers. It is essential that it be external to the universities, lest the departments of education simply select the same students that they already enroll rather than seeking the most able students from any discipline.

29. The Talented Teachers Act, which was signed into law in late 1984, establishes a program of Perkins Scholarships to go to 10,000 high school students per year interested in becoming teachers. Students would receive a maximum of $5,000 a year for up to four years in return for two years of teaching for each year of assistance, to be reduced to one year for those working in economically depressed areas.

In many respects, the Talented Teachers Act is the offspring of the National Defense Education Acts' National Defense Student Loans, which originally had cancellation clauses for graduates entering the teaching profession.

Texas currently uses a policy of loan forgiveness to attract graduates into teaching. Students going to teach in designated areas will not have to pay back educational loans. Previous loan-forgiveness programs have not worked well. James Stedman. *The Experience with Loan Forgiveness and Service Pay Back on Federal and State Student Aid Programs* (Washington, D.C.: Congressional Research Service, January 1983).

30. Contrary to misconceptions, ROTC does not attract students disproportionately from the middle class, from white families, or from families with a history of military service. At the same time, because ROTC demands only a *limited* term of service in

the military, it brings in high quality individuals who would otherwise never have joined the military. This is seen as its greatest attraction to the military services. Ronald Lloyd Cummings. *Army ROTC: A Study of the Army's Primary Officer Procurement Program, 1962–1977*, unpublished Ph.D. dissertation, University of California, Santa Barbara, 1982. A similar program for teachers would attract individuals who otherwise would not have gone into teaching due to doubts about the teaching profession.

31. Cummings. *Ibid.*, found that ROTC graduates were more likely than career military officers to accept dangerous or uninviting assignments. They knew that by doing so they would not put their future careers into jeopardy.

32. Even by the standards of the Reagan administration, this is not a large sum. A two-year program costing $965 million was accepted beginning in 1984 to address the problem of math and science education in schools. Also, the National Science Foundation began a $70 million program in 1984 and a $140 million program in 1985 to improve math and science teaching. Thomas Toch. Op. cit.

33. But not even the military guarantees every graduate of its ROTC program a military commission. If they are not needed, they are simply left to pursue other options.

34. How responsive would today's student be to the ROTC as a model? It is worth noting that the ROTC after years of abuse is back in favor on college campuses. Today there are 529 units across country, contrasted with 485 in 1981, enrolling 110,145 in 1984, which was 17,000 more than in 1980. Elizabeth Greene. "CIA Recruiters Find Students Welcome Them" *Chronicle Of Higher Education*, August 29, 1984, 1 and 24; and three articles in the *Educational Record*, Winter 1985: Dewitt C. Smith, Jr. "To Protect a Free Society: Maintaining Excellence in the Military," 10–13; Leslie F. Malpars. "The Benefits of ROTC on Campus: A President's Perspective," 14–21; and James E. Shelton. "The ROTC Wants You: Why Military Training Programs Need Campus Support in the '80s," 22–25.

35. It is important to bear in mind that the Public Service Teaching Fellows program is not a reincarnation of the Teacher Corps, which was abolished in 1981. The Teacher Corps changed greatly over the years in its programmatic goals, its recruits, its operations, its success. It was more successful as a strategy for attracting a different kind of individual into teaching than as a strategy for institutional change. David D. Marsh. "Teacher Corps" *Encyclopedia of Educational Research*, 5th ed. (Glencoe, IL: The Free Press, 1982), 1876–1880.

Also, these Public Service Fellowships should not be confused with the Higher Education Acts' Title IX Public Service Fellowships. The latter provide financial support to graduates in public administration.

36. The National Health Service Corps has provided scholarships paying full tuition plus living and book allowance to physicians and dentists in return for equivalent-time service in areas suffering from physician shortages. According to Gary Wald, director of the program, some parts of the country would have no doctors were it not for this program. The National Health Service Corps has had about 13,000 members since its inception in 1974. The program is currently being reduced, due to the physician

glut and to past successes at building up areas that earlier had shortages, as well as to general federal budget contraints.

New York State has proposed a Police Corps. The goal of that proposal is to attract more minorities into police work. Corps members would be bound to do three years of police work in return for educational assistance. They would not be professionals, as they would be ineligible for tenure or for pension benefits.

37. The VEAP was changed in 1984 in a manner causing some to herald the return of the GI Bill. In our estimation, the changes represent an improvement over the old VEAP but they do not go far enough. See Note 10.

38. Charles C. Moskos. "Making the All-Volunteer Force Work: A National Service Approach" *Foreign Affairs*, Fall 1981, 17–34; and Michael W. Sherraden and Donald J. Eberly (Eds.). *National Service: Social, Economic and Military Impacts* (New York: Pergamon Press, 1982).

Americans are increasingly coming to consider public service as a very important purpose of colleges and universities: 62.1 percent said so in 1983, up from 39.2 percent the year before. Group Attitudes Corporation. "American Attitudes Toward Higher Education—1983" paper prepared for the New England Board of Higher Education (New York: Group Attitudes Corporation, October 3, 1983).

39. Harvard has Phillips Brooks House, whose public service program is growing. The class of 1983 had 34.9 percent give some time to volunteer work. The class of 1984 had 48 percent do so. Of 1,600 students at Connecticut College, 230 were in volunteer work in 1983, compared with only 142 students in 1980. Madison House at the University of Virginia had 1,200 out of 11,000 students participating in community service. Rhoda M. Gilinsky. "When Helping Others is Part of Learning" *New York Times*, Higher Education Winter Survey, January 6, 1985, 23–24.

Although the Peace Corps has changed from recruiting young students to recruiting older people equipped with skills and experiences useful in Third World countries, it still remains popular on college campuses. More members of Yale's graduating class sign up with the Peace Corps than with any other employer. Even so, the younger recruit is more career-oriented than in the past, viewing his term of service as a step up in the job market. The Peace Corps operates at only one-third the level of its peak in 1966 when it had 15,556 recruits and spent $114 million. In 1984 there were 5,200 recruits with a budget of $117 million. William R. Greer. "Face of Peace Corps Today" *New York Times*, January 23, 1985, C1 and C8.

Project HELP (Helping Experiential Learning Program) at Stephen F. Austin State University is an example of the successful use of volunteer student paraprofessionals in rural human service agencies. Begun in 1970, HELP now involves 20 different agencies and by 1983 had enlisted the services of over 2,000 students for over 200,000 hours of service. Bruce E. Bailey and Patricia E. Ray. *Student Human Services Volunteer Programs for Rural Communities—A Practical Guide* (Nacagdoches, TX: Stephen F. Austin State University, 1983).

Since its funding in 1971, ACTION's University Year for Action (UYA) has stimulated colleges and universities to move in this direction. Over 100 post–secondary

197

institutions involving 10,000 students have taken part in UYA. These students have tended to be majors in sociology, psychology, and education. "University Year for Action" *Synergist*, Winter l981, 25.

40. Congressman Panetta reintroduced his bill into the 99th Congress as H.R. 888, Voluntary Youth Service Act.

The American Council on Education supports legislation to establish a national commission to study the desirability, feasibility, costs, and broader social effects of national service.

41. Some would argue that the modern military needs long-term, career-oriented, and highly skilled recruits to handle increasingly sophisticated military technology. Martin Binkin and Irene Kyriakopoulos. *Youth or Experience? Manning the Modern Military* (Washington, D.C.: The Brookings Institution, 1979). These arguments seem persuasive. More research should be done before a large-scale program is adopted. But a small-scale program of 10,000 or so volunteers could be implemented experimentally at relatively little cost.

42. "The Civilian Conservation Corps, the Job Corps, and the Program for Local Service have had impacts on the lives of participants in a variety of ways. Specific results vary from program to program, but the general picture is that participants have gained self-confidence, social maturity, employability, and avoidance of criminal behavior." Donald J. Eberly and Michael W. Sherraden (Eds.). *National Service: Social, Economic and Military Impacts* (New York: Pergamon Press, 1982), 186.

A study of VISTA and Peace Corps volunteers found that most of them felt they gained more from the experience, in terms of improved skills, enhanced job choice afterwards, and greater interest in political activities and social service, than did the communities in which they served. Peace Corps service created more mature and tolerant individuals having broader knowledge of and interest in national and international affairs. Ester Gottlieb Smith and Others. *The Impact of Peace Corps and Vista Service on Former Volunteers and American Society*, draft Final Report prepared for ACTION (Belmont, MA: CRC Education and Human Development, 1978).

One study of how participating in a University Year for Action program affected participants' attitudes and career choices seven to ten years afterwards, found that students considered UYA to be the most important part of their education and, although participants were no more likely to be politically or socially active than the normal student, they were significantly more likely to enter a career in human service and to be active in voluntary community activities. Nancy J. Gansneder and Paul W. Kingston. "University Year for Action Internships and Post–Graduate Career Choice: A Retrospective Study," Undergraduate Internship Program, University of Virginia, MS, n.d.

Participants in the Syracuse Youth Community Service Project, mostly inner-city youth, showed greater community awareness and greater community commitment. Marilyn Gittell, Marguerite Beardsley, and Marsha Weissman. *Final Evaluation Report on Syracuse Youth Community Service Ethnographic Research* (New York: Graduate School and University Center of the City University of New York, May 1981).

198

For these experiences to have an impact on a student's ability to conceptualize or judge morally, a discussion group that enables students to express opinions about the learning experience before their peers is needed as an adjunct. Darwin D. Hendel and Robert Enright. "An Evaluation of a Full-Time Work Study Program for Undergraduates" *Alternative Higher Education*, Fall 1978, 21–30.

43. Eleanor Law, who designed a successful professional volunteer program at the University of Southern Maine (USM), argues that colleges and universities can use volunteers from the community to solve staffing shortages. This also improves relations with the community and gives students working models of volunteer servers. In USM's program, many of the volunteers are also recent college graduates looking for needed job experience. Greg McCaffery. "Volunteers Valuable Supplement to Staff, CUPA Told" *Higher Education Daily*, August 13, 1984, 3.

44. The original intent of the College Work/Study program when it fell under the Office of Economic Opportunity, 1964 to 1968, was to enable students to perform services in their local community while helping to pay the cost of their higher education. In some cases, for example the New York City Urban Corps, work/study money helped fund the participation of thousands of college students in community development projects. The shifting of the program to the Office, and later the Department, of Education debased it from its original conception. Nevertheless, statutorily there are no restrictions on the use of federal work/study money for off-campus public service jobs. Don Eberly. "The Educational Integrity of Community Service and the Need for Federal Support" *New Directions for Higher Education*, Summer 1977, 53–63. A number of colleges already allocate a share to off-campus service. Amherst College, as an example, allocates 20 percent.

45. On the positive effects of cooperative education on persistence, see internal reviews of cooperative education programs at Pace University and Northeastern University cited in Note 5. The nature of work in college appears to have no effect on a student's grades in college. Surjit K. Bella and Mary E. Huba. "Student Part-time Jobs: The Relationship Between Type of Job and Academic Performance" *Journal of Student Financial Aid*, November 1982, 22–27. For evidence that type of job affects students in other ways, particularly in their assessments of their abilities and in their career aspirations, see Jeylan T. Mortimer and Michael P. Finch. "The Effects of Part-Time Work on Adolescent Self-Concept and Achievement" in Kathryn Borman and Jane Reisman (Eds.). *Becoming A Worker*.

46. For ideas on the many areas in which students can work in colleges, see Steven C. Ender and Roger B. Winston, Jr. (Eds.). *Students as Paraprofessional Staff, New Directions for Student Services #27* (San Francisco: Jossey-Bass, 1984).

47. The Student Work Conference held at Berry College in the fall of 1982 reaffirmed the value of in-college work programs. Ten colleges, Alice Lloyd, Berea, Berry, Bethune-Cookman, Blackburn, Bluffton, LeMoyne-Owen, Oakwood, Tuskegee, and Warren Wilson, participated. All are small. All have extensive work/study programs. All agreed that such programs teach their students more about life and leave them better equipped for dealing with the world after graduation. Although the programs do not net a profit, due to the support services that students require, they nonetheless

do pay for themselves by permitting the replacement of full-time professional staff. Berry College. *Report on Student Work Programs Leadership Conference*, funded by the Charles Stewart Mott Foundation (Mount Berry, GA: Berry College, 1982).

48. Cornell has four scholarship programs, known as the Cornell Tradition, designed to reward both academic achievement and hard work. Two of the programs offer students up to $2,000 in grant aid each year to replace student loans. To qualify, a student must have a good academic record and must have worked during the academic year to help pay for college costs. They also offer summer fellowships to defray the added cost of accepting a summer job away from home that may be more challenging though less remunerative. Also, they operate a summer job network that helps undergraduates find career-related summer jobs and that will subsidize an off-campus employer who accepts a Cornell student. The Dana Foundation has begun a program to encourage liberal arts colleges in the northeast in the same direction.

Currently there are 16 states that have programs to support work/study. But only five of them, Colorado, Minnesota, Florida, Washington, and Pennsylvania could be considered major initiatives. The federal government could encourage more such programs in the states through a formula-grant program similar to State Student Incentive Grants (SSIG) but specifically for college work/study. Jerry S. Davis. "Brief Descriptions of State-Supported College Work-Study Aid Programs" (Harrisburg, PA: Pennsylvania Higher Education Assistance Agency, November 1984).

49. For an overview of possible changes in future federal student aid policies, including a discussion of national service for student aid, see Lawrence E. Gladieux. "The Future of Student Financial Aid" *The College Board Review*, Winter 1982–83, 2–12.

CHAPTER VII.

1. Carol Frances. *Basic Facts on College-Going Rates by Income, Race, Sex, and Age, 1970 to 1980* (Washington, D.C.: National Commission on Student Financial Assistance, October 22, 1982).

2. H. A. Hodgkinson in Henry A. Giroux. "Public Philosophy and the Crisis in Education" *Harvard Education Review*, May 1984, 191; and Kenneth S. Tollett. "The Propriety of the Federal Role in Expanding Equal Educational Opportunity" *Harvard Educational Review*, "Special Issue: Rethinking the Federal Role in Education," 1982, 431–443.

3. Black enrollment in graduate schools leveled off in 1976 and has declined since 1981–82. The drop from 1980 to 1982 was 15 percent for blacks in graduate school, contrasted with 8.4 percent for whites. For undergraduates, 1978 was the peak year when blacks were 10.4 percent of enrollment. In 1982, black enrollment fell to 9.8 percent. Gene I. Maeroff. "The Class of '84 is Another Disappointment for Blacks" *New York Times*, June 10, 1984.

The percentage of black high school graduates going on to college dropped from 32.0 to 27.8 and the percentage of Hispanics decreased from 35.4 to 29.9 between 1975 and 1980. Greg Anrig. "A Challenge for State Boards of Higher Education: Protecting Minority Access Within Systemwide Admission Standards" (Princeton, NJ: Educational Testing Service, 1985).

4.

TABLE N-7

ENROLLMENT IN TWO-YEAR INSTITUTIONS BY RACE/ETHNICITY

	NUMBER IN THOUSANDS				PERCENTAGE			
	1976	1978	1980	1982	1976	1978	1980	1982
White	3,077	3,167	3,532	3,657	79.3	78.6	78.7	77.8
Total Minority	761	810	894	981	19.6	20.1	19.9	20.9
Black	429	443	468	483	11.1	11.0	10.4	10.3
Hispanic	210	227	255	291	5.4	5.6	5.7	6.2
Asian/Pacific Islander	79	97	124	158	2.0	2.4	2.8	3.4
Am. Indian/ Alaskan Native	41	43	47	49	1.1	1.1	1.1	1.0

Source: National Center for Education Statistics. *The Condition of Education, 1984 Edition*, Washington, D.C., 1984, Table 2.5.

TABLE N-8

TRENDS IN FIRST-TIME, FULL-TIME FRESHMAN ENROLLMENTS, 1966–1980 (THREE-YEAR MOVING AVERAGES)

	PERCENTAGE OF FRESHMAN CLASS			
Year	*Blacks*	*Chicanos*	*Puerto Ricans*	*American Indians*
1966	5.0	N/A	N/A	0.6
1967	5.0	N/A	N/A	0.7
1968	5.4	N/A	N/A	0.6
1969	5.9	N/A	N/A	0.5
1970	6.2	N/A	N/A	0.6
1971	7.5	1.1	0.2	1.0
1972	7.6	1.3	0.4	1.0
1973	8.0	1.4	0.5	1.0
1974	8.1	1.5	0.6	0.9
1975	8.3	1.6	0.6	0.9
1976	8.7	1.6	0.7	0.9
1977	8.4	1.4	0.8	0.8
1978	8.7	1.2	0.9	0.9
1979	8.8	1.4	0.9	0.9
1980	9.2	1.7	0.9	0.9

Source: Figures on full-time freshman enrollment are from Alexander Astin. *Minorities in American Higher Education* (San Francisco: Jossey-Bass, 1982), 80. Originally from the Cooperative Institutional Research Program (1966–1980).

5. Gary Orfield and Others. *The Chicago Study of Access and Choice in Higher Education: A Report to the Illinois Senate Committee on Higher Education* (Chicago: University of Chicago, Committee on Public Policy Studies Research Project, September 1984), 22.

6. Bureau of the Census. *Current Population Surveys.* Washington, D.C., Department of Commerce, December 1983, Tables 33 and 44.

7. James Blackwell notes that despite the growth in the 1970s in the absolute numbers of minority group professionals in law, medicine, dentistry, and engineering, their percentages remain small (under 3 percent) and "at the rate of production of Black professionals witnessed in the seventies, it will probably take another forty years before parity is reached in most professions." James E. Blackwell. *Mainstreaming Outsiders: The Production of Black Professionals* (Bayside, NY: General Hall, 1981).

8. In Chicago, underrepresentation of blacks and Hispanics was widely pronounced. Gary Orfield and Others. Op. cit., Chapter 3. At the faculty level, the problem will remain for a long time. The number of black faculty is small and has remained so throughout the past decade despite the gradual increase in black enrollment in professional schools. Moreover, blacks are no greater a proportion of the younger faculty than of the older faculty and remain concentrated in less notable institutions. Charles J. Elmore and Robert T. Blackburn. "Black and White Faculty in White Research Universities" *Journal of Higher Education*, 1983, 1.

It should be noted that the increase in the percentage of minority students, particularly black and Hispanic, at the *doctorate* level in science and engineering is due largely to the decrease in the absolute number of white students, not to an increase in the absolute number of blacks and Hispanics. But the absolute number and the percentage of the blacks and Hispanics at the *bachelor* degree level has increased dramatically in the last five years. This is a particularly encouraging sign since it is from recent bachelor recipients that the new generation of advanced degree recipients will come.

TABLE N-9

ENGINEERING BACHELOR DEGREE RECIPIENTS BY RACE, 1968–1983

YEAR	TOTAL	BLACK		HISPANIC		ASIAN	
		N	Percent	N	Percent	N	Percent
1968–69	39,972	314	.79	N/A		N/A	
1969–70	42,966	378	.88	N/A		N/A	
1970–71	43,167	407	.94	N/A		N/A	
1972–73	43,429	657	1.51	866	1.99	684	1.58
1973–74	41,407	756	1.83	1,037	2.50	957	2.31
1974–75	38,210	734	1.92	1,060	2.77	883	2.31
1975–76	37,970	777	2.05	1,019	2.68	1,074	2.83
1976–77	40,095	844	2.11	1,035	2.58	1,146	2.86
1977–78	46,091	894	1.94	1,072	2.33	1,195	2.59
1978–79	52,598	1,076	2.05	1,212	2.30	1,532	2.91

YEAR	TOTAL	BLACK		HISPANIC		ASIAN	
		N	Percent	N	Percent	N	Percent
1979–80	58,742	1,320	2.25	1,332	2.27	1,922	3.27
1980–81	62,935	1,445	2.30	1,513	2.40	2,267	3.60
1981–82	66,990	1,644	2.45	1,608	2.40	2,577	3.85
1982–83	72,471	1,842	2.54	1,883	2.60	3,098	4.27

Source: Scientific Manpower Commission. *Professional Women and Minorities*, Washington, D.C., August 1984, Table 7.12.

9. Harold L. Hodgkinson. *Guess Who's Coming to College: Your Students in 1990* (Washington, D.C.: National Institute of Independent Colleges and Universities, January 1983).

10. The American Council on Education has drawn attention to this issue. They also point out that blacks and Hispanics are unevenly distributed across the nation. Blacks tend to be concentrated in most states east of the Mississippi, with heaviest concentration in the southeast. Hispanics are concentrated west of the Mississippi, largely in the southwest, but including New York, New Jersey, and Florida. American Council on Education and Others. *Demographic Imperatives: Implications for Education Policy*, Report of the Forum on "The Demographics of Changing Ethnic Populations and their Implications for Elementary-Secondary and Postsecondary Educational Policy," June 8, 1983, 8 and 9. Connecticut, Pennsylvania, New Jersey, and New York have all registered declines in the rate of college-going by blacks that have exceeded declines in the college-going rate of the general population. New Jersey is studying the causes of this phenomenon. The tentative hypothesis is that it is the result of increased college costs combined with reduced grant aid. New Jersey Department of Higher Education. *Declining Black Enrollments Among Full-Time Undergraduates in New Jersey Colleges and Universities*, Special Report Series, vol. 5: Report No. 1, December 1984, 4, passim.

    States in the southwest have come to recognize that minorities, largely Hispanics, will make up a larger and larger proportion of college-age youth in those states. Western Interstate Commission for Higher Education. *The Changing Demographics of the Southwest: Data and Issues Relating to Minority Representation in Postsecondary Education in Seven Southwest States* (Boulder, CO: Western Interstate Commission for Higher Education, 1983).

11. This is an immediate problem that will take many years to overcome. Franklin Thomas was right in spirit when he said, "after 10 to 15 years of residence legal immigrants have incomes and (rates of) civic participation at least equal to that of the native born." But his time frame seems too optimistic, at least for levels of civic participation. Franklin Thomas. *The New Migration*, Commencement address at Cooper Union, May 23, 1984, 7.

12. There are many private initiatives that have impressive records of achievement in successfully placing minority students into prestigious programs. One example is the

Wadleigh program, affiliated with the Boston-based "A Better Chance" (A.B.C.) and operating for the last 20 years. "Over the years, the Wadleigh Scholarship Program, which identifies and prepares, with intense after-school instruction, seventh and eighth graders for admission to preparatory schools, has sent 210 children to 70 top schools from Maine to Arizona, schools such as Phillips, Phillips Exeter, Deerfield, Hotchkiss, Lenox, Fieldston and Lawrenceville. Of those, 108 have graduated from Harvard, Yale, Columbia, Princeton, the University of Pennsylvania, Sarah Lawrence, Vassar, the Massachusetts Institute of Technology and other institutions." Dorothy J. Gaiter. "Harlem Marks 20th Year of Prep-School Program" *New York Times*, Sunday, July 8, 1984.

The National Research Council and the Ford Foundation jointly run the Postdoctoral Fellowship for Minorities program. All recipients are current or prospective university teachers. Thirty-five scholars received the one-year award in 1984, for a total of 175 recipients since the program began in 1979.

13. For a list (with comments) of some of the more noteworthy examples of linkage programs, see Clifford Adelman. "Starting With Students: Notable Programs, Promising Approaches, and Other Improvement Efforts in American Postsecondary Education," vol. I (Washington, D.C.: National Institute of Education, December 1983). From a list of about 230 programs linking high schools and colleges, the Council of Chief State School Officers identifies fewer than 10 as being directly concerned with improving minority access. Also, see Appendix.

14. The Fund for the Improvement of Post-Secondary Education (FIPSE) was established by Congress in the Education Amendment Act of 1972. It was designed to be non-bureaucratic, i.e., responsive, flexible and sensitive. Unlike most granting agencies, FIPSE yields the initiative to applicants as to what problems they consider to be important and what approaches they may wish to try. It thereby nurtures and rewards enterprise.

Funding is awarded either in the form of grants or cooperative agreements. Competition is keen, with an average of 2,000 proposals each year for only 100 grants. In its first 10 years, FIPSE awarded $111.47 million in 1,040 grants chosen from a collection of 22,000 applications. Grants are small, ranging from a low of $5,000 to a high of $200,000 with an average of $70,000. Funding is open to virtually any type of organization. It is directed not at "pure" research but at action-based programs for reform. FIPSE has proved itself willing to support unproven ideas. One-third of its grantees had never before applied for federal support.

Besides stimulating innovative programs, FIPSE has an excellent track record at stimulating long-lasting programs. Over 70 percent of FIPSE-funded projects persist after the period of funding has ended, which can vary from one to three years. This contrasts with a 5–15 percent rate of continuation for most other seed-grant programs.

One of the major categorical areas that FIPSE has funded has been minority access. For example, it provided initial funding behind the University of California at Berkeley's Professional Development Program (PDP). This program takes low-achievers, puts them in math and science workshops, and engages them in a community of peers with whom they can socialize, work and learn. It has substantially improved math performance and retention rates.

204

FIPSE also provided seed-money to *Solidaridad Humana* in New York City. This program offers literacy training, basic education, college credit courses, and vocational training to youth from the Latin community. It draws on the services of five public colleges and has an impressive record of improving college enrollment and retention rates.

Friends of FIPSE. *Salute to FIPSE*, Washington, D.C., n.p., n.d.; Richard Hendrix (Ed.). *Priorities for Improvement* (Washington, D.C.: American Association for Higher Education, 1984); and Norman Smith. "Innovation in Education: The FIPSE Model," qualifying paper submitted to Harvard University School of Education, September 1983.

15. Another possibility is for the federal government, perhaps through FIPSE, to set up seed-grants in states to encourage them to set up their own FIPSE-like organizations.

16. There is a fifth program to train counselors, tutors, and others for working in the four client-directed programs.

17. Kenneth C. Green. *Government Support for Minority Participation in Higher Education*, AAHE/ERIC Research Report (Washington, D.C.: American Association for Higher Education, 1984); Graham J. Burkheimer with Thomas P. Novak. *A Capsule Description of Young Adults Seven and One-Half Years After High School*, National Longitudinal Study Sponsored Reports Series NCES81–255 (Research Triangle Park, NC: Center for Educational Research and Evaluation, Research Triangle Institute, August 1981); Graham J. Burkheimer, Jr. and Others. "Evaluation Study of the Upward Bound Program: A Second Follow-up," Final Report (Durham, NC: Center for Educational Research and Evaluation, Research Triangle Institute, November 1979); J. N. Pyecha and Others. "A Study of the National Upward Bound and Talent Search Programs," Final Report, vol. III, *Descriptive Study of the Talent Search Program* (Durham, NC: Center for Educational Research and Evaluation, Research Triangle Institute, December 1975); J. Davis and Others. *The Impact of Special Services Programs in Higher Education for 'Disadvantaged' Students* (Princeton, NJ: Educational Testing Service, 1975); V. Tinto and R. H. Sherman. *The Effectiveness of Secondary and Higher Education Intervention Programs: A Critical Review of the Literature* (New York: Teachers College, Columbia University, 1974); and Paul L. Franklin. *Helping Disadvantaged Youth and Adults Enter College* (Washington, D.C.: The College Board, 1985).

These federal programs have also stimulated the proliferation of state and institutional campus-based assistance and outreach programs for disadvantaged students. A survey in 1977 found that 86 percent of the nation's *public* higher education institutions offered some sort of special services or programs to their disadvantaged students. Up to 95 percent of community colleges and 77 percent of 4-year colleges had such programs. The number of similar programs in private institutions is large but undetermined. John E. Rouche and J. R. Snow. *Overcoming Learning Problems* (San Francisco: Jossey-Bass, 1977).

18. There are other federal efforts:

In 1983 and 1984, NSF awarded 10–15 science and engineering grants to minority institutions to support faculty research, instrumentation purchases, and cooperative research activities.

The Health Careers Opportunities Program (HCOP) has been operating since 1972, funding health profession schools to help them recruit disadvantaged students into the health professions. About one-quarter of FY 85's $24 million budget is awarded for competitive grants. And there is the Cooperative Legal Education Opportunities (CLEO) Program to provide pre-law preparation and law school fellowships to minority students wanting to enter law.

CHAPTER VIII.

1. Michel Oksenberg. "U.S. Markets in China: The Importance of Understanding the Chinese" in "Education and Economic Competitiveness Abroad" papers presented at a congressional seminar on July 19, 1983 (Washington, D.C.: Consortium of Social Science Associations, 1983).

2. The Commission on International Education. *What We Don't Know Can Hurt Us* (Washington, D.C.: American Council on Education, January 1984), 6; Stephen K. Bailey. "International Education: An Agenda for Global Interdependence" *The College Board Review*, Fall 1975, 2–21; and "Special Issue: Educating for the World View" *Change*, May-June 1980.

3. This concern has been expressed by the Carlucci Commission on Security and Economic Assistance, the United States Advisory Commission on Public Diplomacy, and the National Bipartisan Commission on Central America. *Congressional Record*, 98th Congress, Senate, Second Session, vol. 130, no. 81, Thursday, June 14, 1984.

4. The United States spends 2,000 times more on the military than on the Fulbright and other exchange programs. "Can you cite a single country in which the U.S. has 'lost' because of insufficient military strength? There are numerous examples where America has lost because of a failure to understand the cultural dynamics of a region or country." Cassandra Pyle. "Our Shortfall in International Competence" *AGB Reports*, March/April 1984, 34.

5. Fritz Stern comments about European leaders: "It is a commonplace to talk today with some concern, justified concern, of the successor generations in Europe and the U.S. The younger generations bring with them no automatic memories of America's beneficent role in the immediate postwar era. Nor are the personal and academic ties as strong as they once were." "The Role of Cultural Understanding in U.S.-European Relations," in "Education and Economic Competitiveness Abroad," 7. Michel Oksenberg makes the same point with respect to China: "There is a lack of familiarity with the U.S. among the generation now coming to power in China, while those who are most familiar with us are passing from the scene." "U.S. Markets in China: The Importance of Understanding the Chinese," 15.

6. International studies were peripheral to academia until World War II and the Cold War, then international studies became a promotable national asset. Robert A. McCaughey. *International Studies and Academic Enterprise* (NY: Columbia University Press, 1984). The Council on Learning's Education and the World View project has shown that, despite a few model programs, most college students come away with little knowledge about the world. Council on Learning. *Education and the World*

View, vol. IV (New Rochelle, NY: Change Magazine Press, 1980); Council on Learning. *Handbook of Exemplary International Programs*, vol. III (New Rochelle, NY: Change Magazine Press, 1981); and Thomas S. Barrows and Others. *College Students' Knowledge and Beliefs: A Survey of Global Understanding*, prepared for the Council on Learning (Princeton, NJ: Educational Testing Service, 1981).

7. The growth rate has now leveled off to about 1 percent per year. Edward B. Fiske. "Recruiting Abroad" *New York Times*, July 17, l984, C1 and C5.

8. There are other federal programs that promote international exchanges outside higher education in the professions and business: the business and international education programs under Title IV in the Department of Education, some of the private sector programs run by the United States Information Agency, and the Hubert Humphrey Fellowships for mid-career professionals from abroad. Private sector programs include the American Field Service, Youth for Understanding, and the Experiment in International Living in Brattleboro, Vermont.

   International exchange is only one leg of the triad of federal programs fostering international ties in higher education. The other two legs, technical and developmental assistance programs and foreign language and area study programs, are important. They are not emphasized in this chapter because they seem to be working satisfactorily. The Peace Corps is largely uninvolved with universities, serving as a way-station between graduation and enrollment in graduate school for some. We are also neglecting two massive learning programs in the military: the International Military Education and Training Program (which has trained over half a million foreign military personnel since 1950) and the non-ROTC tuition assistance programs for 650,000 servicemen in hundreds of colleges and universities here and abroad. Sven Groennings. "The American Democracy in the Global Community: The Second Triad," delivered at American University, March 2, 1984, 19–25.

9. These reports represent a variety of constituencies: business, in the American Council on Educations' Task Force on Business and International Education's 1979 report and the Conference Board's 1982 report; government, in the President's Commission on Foreign Language and International Studies' 1979 report; higher education, in the Commission on International Education's 1984 report; and the military, in Robert D. Lambert and Others. *Beyond Growth: The Next Stage in Language and Area Studies* (Washington, D.C.: Association of American Universities, April 1984), commissioned by the Pentagon. For citations of other reports see *What We Don't Know Can Hurt Us* (Washington, D.C.: American Council on Education, 1984).

10. The Ford Foundation provided $27 million annually for advanced training and research in international affairs between 1960 and 1967. This has been cut back to $3–4 million a year. *What We Don't Know Can Hurt Us*, 10 and passim.

    In 1981, the Reagan administration proposed cutting funding for the Fulbright program by one-half and eliminating 60 of the 120 countries from the program. This was defeated by a coalition of congressmen and interest groups. This position, partly reversed, has been in later budgets. Malcolm G. Scully. "Fortunes Improve Dramatically for Academic Exchanges" *Chronicle of Higher Education*, March 28, 1984, 1–17. The administration proposals for FY 1986 also indicate a new interest in exchange.

11. Based on remarks by Richard Brod of the Modern Language Association reported in *Higher Education Daily*, Thursday, August 30, 1984, 1; Cassandra Pyle. "Our Shortfall in International Competence" *AGB Reports*, March/April 1984, 33; and National Advisory Board on International Education Programs. *Critical Needs in International Education*, a Report to the Secretary of Education, December 1983. In 1982, only 47 percent of the nation's colleges and universities required foreign language study for the baccalaureate degree. There was a 4.5 percent increase in language course enrollments from 1980–81 to 1983–84, with Japanese (+40 percent) and Russian (+27 percent) sharing the greatest growth, according to Brod. Also, fully 77 percent of college preparatory high school seniors had taken at least one foreign language course and one-third had taken two courses in 1982. *Higher Education and National Affairs*, July 2, 1984, 3.

12. *UNESCO Statistical Yearbook* (Paris: United Nations Educational, Social, and Cultural Organization, 1982 and 1983 editions) estimates 20,838 Americans studied abroad in 1979 and 19,843 in 1980.

   The *Digest of Education Statistics*, 1983–84 edition, Table 160, p. 1974, estimates in 1980–81 there were 19,815 Americans studying abroad in the 23 most frequently chosen countries. A more generous estimate of 120,000 American students abroad in 1978 comes from Barbara Burn. *Expanding the International Dimensions of Higher Education*, prepared for the Carnegie Council on Policy Studies in Higher Education (San Francisco: Jossey-Bass, 1980), 70. The number of students going abroad seems to have risen recently due to favorable exchange rates. Thomas J. Meyer. "Strength of Dollar Adds to Popularity Abroad" *Chronicle of Higher Education*, October 10, 1984, 1 and 20.

13. Council for International Exchange of Scholars. *Fulbright Scholar Program, Annual Report 1983* (Washington, D.C.: C.I.E.S., 1984).

14. Many Canadian students come to the United States for their higher education. But the reverse flow of Americans to Canadian colleges and universities is a trickle.

15. *Fulbright Scholar Program, Annual Report 1983*. A conservative estimate by Ronald A. Ungaro of the United States Information Agency is that 25,000 American academics, mostly faculty but including graduate students, teach at a college or university in another country. That represents .03 percent of all faculty in the United States. Barbara S. Kraft. "Scholars Hail Rewards of Teaching Overseas but Warn that Planning Ahead is Essential" *Chronicle of Higher Education*, April 4, 1984, 21.

16. 37,000 students went to Russia from Africa in 1982. Senator Mathias in *Congressional Record*, 98th Congress Senate, vol. 130, no. 81, Thursday, June 14, 1984. The Soviet Union funds nearly as many exchanges with Latin America as the United States does with the entire world. Sven Groennings. "The American Democracy in the Global Community," 17. In 1984–85, close to 7,000 students fom Latin America studied in the U.S.S.R., about 3,000 in Eastern Europe, and 6,400 in Cuba. Paul Desruisseaux. "Plan to Bring Central American Students to United States Colleges Will Get 2-year Trial" *The Chronicle of Higher Education*, April 3, 1985, 33–34.

17. Japan has nine Fulbright Alumni Associations. Their members include presidents of corporations, newspaper editors, university professors, and a retired chief justice of

the Japanese Supreme Court. "Going to Take a Sentimental Journey—And They Did" *Higher Education and National Affairs*, May 21, 1984, 6.

18. This may be difficult to achieve, primarily because a foreign country's own education system may be biased against those from a poor socio-economic background early in their educational career. The Central American Plan (see Note 29) is attempting to address this issue. It is a longstanding problem that needs to be discussed more openly and thought about more seriously.

This has been recognized as a problem for over 20 years. In the State Department's 1973 report on international cultural and educational exchange programs, the United States Advisory Commission recommended that "the exchange program make a concerted effort to seek out and select more 'have nots' with particular promise and talent so, that, in keeping with this country's traditions, an American exchange experience never becomes a privilege restricted to the elite." United States Advisory Commission on International Educational and Cultural Affairs. *A Beacon of Hope*, Washington, D.C., April 1963, 3–4.

19. These difficulties are discussed in a June 1984 study done by the Council for International Exchange of Scholars but not released for attribution, and in their follow-up study, "The Fulbright American Scholar Program: How It Compares with Other Grant Programs," n.d.

20. The effects of studying abroad upon a student's attitudes and personality are uncertain. Dennison Nash. "The Personal Consequences of a Year of Study Abroad" *Journal of Higher Education*, March/April 1976, 191–203. It is known with certainty that there is an increased proficiency in the language of the country of residence. Some studies suggest there are positive effects upon a student's sense of autonomy and self-actualization; others argue there are no effects. It is the nature of the experience abroad and the characteristics of the individual involved that matter. Jerold Martin Starr. *Cross-Cultural Encounter and Personality Change: Peace Corps Volunteers in the Philippines*, Ph.D. dissertation, Brandeis University, 1970.

21. Richard D. Lambert and Others. *Beyond Growth: The Next Stage in Language and Area Studies* (Washington, D.C.: Association of American Universities, April 1980) and National Advisory Board on International Education Programs. *Critical Needs in International Education*, Washington, D.C., December 1983.

22. "The actual experience of living in another country . . . provides a perspective and perceptual lens of inestimable value in understanding what it means to be a global citizen. You begin to realize that, had you been born in another country, with different cultural and historical roots, different interests and outlooks, you would be a different person; in fact probably rather like individuals you have come to know in that country. . . . How obvious once learned, yet how many have not learned it yet today." Barbara M. White. "Global Citizens: Are They Born or Made?" Kenneth M. Gould Address to the 57th Annual Meeting of the National Council for the Social Studies, Cincinnati, Ohio, November 26, 1977.

23. More than 200 American colleges and universities send students abroad in special international education programs. Kalamazoo College in Michigan and Goshen College in Indiana operate on-going, extensive study abroad programs. Kalamazoo has

sent 85 percent of each graduating class since 1961 overseas. The course of study lasts from one to three quarters. Goshen has had an international studies requirement since 1968 that 85 percent of its students fulfill by spending one trimester abroad for study and service. Association of American Colleges. "Internationalizing the Curriculum" *The Forum for Liberal Education*, March 1984, 3–6.

24. Cornell University has such links with the University of the Philippines, as does the University of Rhode Island with the University of the Azores.

25. One advantage of the direct institution-to-institution approach is that it enables the American college to have more control over its students abroad and to know what they are studying. Fear of losing control inhibits many schools from undertaking overseas programs. Margaret B. Matson and Robert Kirkwood. "Study the Issues Before Offering Study Abroad" *Educational Record*, Spring 1983, 48–51.

26. Many students presently choose to "stop-out" for a year or more to pursue extra-collegiate interests before finishing college.

27. Italy has a privately funded program where American faculty members and American graduate students teach writing.

28. Yale's Dwight Hall has begun a pilot exchange program with Japan that provides public service opportunities for Americans in Japan and for Japanese in America. Operation Crossroads Africa, a non-profit organization based in New York, sends American students to work on African development projects at a cost of about $3,000 to the student. "Organization Helps U.S. Students Aid Africa" *New York Times*, July 8, 1984.

29. The Reagan administration, following recommendations of the Kissinger Commission, proposed more dollars for Central America—$25 million to the United States Information Agency and $25 million to the Agency for International Development in 1985, for a five-year cost of $290 million. Congress allocated some $3.8 million to the United States Information Agency to bring as many as 143 undergraduates from Central America for a two-year trial. The same program will spend $5.1 million to finance the visits of 200–250 Fulbright scholars from Central America. The focus will be on non-elites. Paul Desruisseaux. "Plan to Bring Central American Students to United States Colleges" *Chronicle of Higher Education*, April 3, 1985, 33–34. Senator Mathias and Representative Michael Barnes have proposed separate bills to direct new monies to economically disadvantaged students and generally to students in Latin America. Africa and Southeast Asia are considered to be of equal importance.

30. The Agency for International Development signed a $30 million contract with Florida State University to manage a consortium of American Universities. This five-year program is to assist selected developing nations to improve their education systems.

31. There has been a small set-aside in the Fulbright Scholars program for sending high school faculty and administrators abroad. This should be revised and enlarged.

32. The legislative goal of the Fulbright program is "to enable the government of the United States to increase mutual understanding between the people of the United States and the people of other countries." Text of the Mutual Educational and Cultural Exchange Act of 1961. Quoted in *Fulbright Scholar Program, Annual Report 1983* (Washington, D.C.: Council for International Exchange of Scholars, 1984), 2.

210

CHAPTER IX.

1. The form of the American research system is unusual. In most industrialized countries basic research is carried on at specialized institutes, e.g., the Max Planck Institutes in Germany. In the United States approximately 60 percent of all basic research is done within the university system, approximately 50 percent if Federally Funded Research and Development funding is removed. National Research Council. *Outlook for Science and Technology, The Next Five Years* (San Francisco: W. H. Freeman and Company, 1982).

2. In the nineteenth century Americans created their own version of the research university even as they attempted to copy the German system. The differences provided important advantages. Graduate programs were superimposed on the traditional undergraduate degrees. This allowed the universities to select only a small number of advanced degree candidates who were interested in and able to do research while not inhibiting the opportunity of the growing numbers interested in a general college education. The American academic department, as opposed to the European system dominated by a single professor in each discipline, provided more room for new people, new ideas, and new disciplines to come forward.

   The debates surrounding the emergence of Johns Hopkins, Cornell, and Clark showed the concern for the importance of research and the assumption that the logical location for it was the university.

3. Vanevar Bush. *Science: The Endless Frontier* (Washington, D.C.: Government Printing Office, 1945).

4. This is what the scientists themselves had proposed in their original conception of the National Science Foundation. *Ibid.*

5. For level of federal support in early 1950s, see National Science Foundation. *National Patterns of R & D Resources, 1953–70*, Report 69–30, Chart 1.

   Despite the increase in the number of federal agencies supporting academic research, 95 percent of the support continues to come from half a dozen agencies. National Science Foundation. *Federal Support to Universities, Colleges, and Selected Nonprofit Institutions*, Report 82–308, Washington, D.C., 1982, Chart 8.

6. Personal communications from Stanford University.

7. National Science Foundation. *Federal Support to Universities, Colleges, and Selected Nonprofit Institutions*, Washington, D.C., 1982.

8. The National Science Foundation statistics report an impressive performance for the U.S.:

   Ninety-one of the 183 Nobel Prizes awarded after World War II up to 1973 were won by United States scientists. (Prior to World War II only 15 of 128 were won by Americans.)

   The United States produced 65 percent of 492 major technological innovations in the period 1953–1973. Great Britain was second with 17 percent; Japan was third. National Science Foundation. *Science Indicators 1974* (Washington, D.C.: National Science Foundation, 1976).

9. *Science*, May 6, 1983.

10. Jacob Rabinow (himself an inventor) reports that the propensity to patent may be industry-specific—chemical companies choose to patent but electrical and computer companies do not. Jacob Rabinow. "We Have to Keep Inventors Inventing" *Research Management*, November 1982, 7–9. Patents are a flawed measure of innovation. They only measure successful, revealed processes. The legal procedures vary from country to country so international comparison is difficult. And if the industry (or technology) changes rapidly, no patents may be sought. Committee for Economic Development. *Stimulating Technological Progress* (New York: Committee for Economic Development, 1980), 66–67.

11. Diane Couto. "Brain Drain: European Nations Fret Over Mounting Losses of Scientists to the U.S." *The Wall Street Journal*, October 21, 1983, 1. When the Max Planck Society needed a divisional director recently they mounted a worldwide talent hunt. Eventually they focused on a West German scientist temporarily working in the United States. "We made him an offer he couldn't turn down," said Robert Gerwin, the Society's spokesman. "He turned us down. He told us that only America provides the right 'atmosphere' for doing good scientific research."

12. Now the Japanese have made inroads into our university research network. Georgia Tech, for example, is currently receiving funds from Japan to do basic electronics research and translate technical works into Japanese.

13. Americans play a key role at CERN (The European Consortium for Nuclear Research).

14. Even to ask these questions reminds us that they are not easily answered. What are the criteria for effectiveness? Should we attempt to assess the number of breakthroughs? One problem is that most scientific and technical progress comes through steady, undramatic progress. There are few DNAs and transistors.

    Ralph Gomary, Vice President and Director of Research at IBM stated: "Real breakthroughs do occur; they are rare and stunning events. The common course of technological evolution is steady year-to-year improvement, and when that is rapid and persistent, the results are just as revolutionary."

15. Bruce L. Smith and Joseph L. Karlesky. *The State of Academic Science: The Universities in the Nation's Research Effort* (New York: Change Magazine Press, 1977), 190.

16. See Chapter IV for documentation.

17. Research and Development spending in the FY 1984 budget was designed to have the greatest long-term impact on new technologies. Basic research in physical sciences and engineering received large increases directed at math, physics, plant biology, material science, astronomy, and space sciences. Much of the increase went to universities. Basic research rose 10 percent overall but it rose by 15 percent in agencies that primarily support physical sciences and engineering and by up to 25 percent for mathematics and electrical engineering. George A. Keyworth. "Federal R & D: Not an Entitlement" *Science*, February 18, 1983, 1.

18. David Crockett, President of Dataquest, as reported in Robert Batt. "U.S. High Tech Must Return to Basics" *Computerworld*, January 9, 1984, 73.

    In fact, the major Japanese producers of the 256K-byte RAM (Hitachi, Ltd.; Fugitsu, Ltd.; Nippon Electric Co.; and Toshiba) planned to increase shipments from 800,000 in 1983 to 14 million in 1984. The RAM market is still immature, but the Japanese control 76 percent of the world market.

19. The National Academy of Engineering Panel chaired by E. Ray McClure, head of the precision engineering program of Lawrence Livermore Laboratory, held that the United States machine tool industry is in serious trouble because it has lost its technological lead to the Japanese and West German industries and has difficulty competing in world markets. Steve Lober. "The Japanese Challenge" *The New York Times Magazine*, July 8, 1984, 23.

This trend is tempered by the Japanese tendency to mistrust their domestically developed technology. Stephen K. Yoder. "Magnetic-Train Saga Indicates Japan's Distrust of Its Home-Grown Technology" *The Wall Street Journal*, September 20, 1984, 34.

20. The European Economic Community (EEC) is moving to catch up with the growing technological lead of America and Japan in information technology by launching "ESPRIT"—the European Strategic Program for Research and Development in Information Technology. The EEC plans to spend $585 million over the next five years to back key projects in microelectronics, software technology and information processing.

An assessment by the Chief Executives of 200 European Firms (sponsored by the Wall Street Journal and Booz-Allen and Hamilton) ranked the United States and Japan as clearly dominant in *all* high technology fields surveyed.

John Markum. "High Technology and the Economy" *OECD Observer*, November 1984, 5.

CHAPTER X.

1. National Science Foundation. *Federal Funds for Research and Development, Detailed Historical Tables: Fiscal Years 1955–1984*, Tables 4A–5B, 16A–16B, 26A–26B, 36A–36B, 46A–46B. Figures for 1983 and 1984 are estimates.

2. "Science and the Citizen" *Scientific American*, June 1984, 74.

Reagan's first budget included cuts in research. The second budget provided healthy increases. George A. Keyworth II, Reagan's science advisor and head of the White House Office of Science and Technology, is credited with the turn-around. Concern has arisen that the legacy of Reagan's large budget deficits threaten the future growth in research and development funding. American Association for the Advancement of Science. *AAAS Report IX: Research and Development, FY 1985* (Washington, D.C.: AAAS, 1984).

3. National Science Foundation. *Federal R & D Funding, the 1975–85 Decade*, Washington, D.C., March 1984, 16–17.

4. If university-operated Federally Funded Research and Development Centers (FFRDCs) are included, the university share is approximately 60 percent of the funds for basic research.

5. FY 1981 to FY 1985, federal research and development support at universities rose 26 percent in real terms. George A. Keyworth. "Four Years of Reagan Science Policy"

213

Science, April 6, 1984, Figure 3. National Science Foundation. *Historical Tables,* Tables 8C–D, 17A–B, 27A–B, 37A–B, and 47A–B. The figures for 1983 and 1984 are estimates.

6. In 1983 the House Science and Technology Committee debated whether the United States research system needed to be more centralized and directed, in imitation of our major international competitors. They also debated the need to create a separate National Science Foundation for Engineering, a National Technology Foundation. *Science and Government Report.* "A Federal Research & Development Reorganization? Interest Rising," July 15, 1983, 1–2.

7. In 1976 the Committee on Science and Technology of the United States House of Representatives, 94th Congress, Second Session, held six days of hearings into the National Science Foundation peer review procedures. A principal finding of that report was that "no method superior to peer review has been found for judging the scientific competence of proposers." Committee on Science and Technology. *National Science Foundation Peer Review,* vol. 1, Washington, D.C., 1976.

8. France has one of the most targeted research systems in the world. It is quietly acknowledged to have mounting problems. Critics suggest that President Mitterand's effort to make French science flourish is suffering from some bad mistakes: too much bureaucratic control from the top and too much inefficient spending.

9. It is interesting to consider that the ranking of the universities, in terms of dollars earned, has changed significantly over time. This dynamism is a strong argument against targeting.

TABLE N–10

UNIVERSITIES RANKED AS RECIPIENTS OF FEDERAL RESEARCH FUNDS, 1964, 1974 AND 1982

		RANKING	
INSTITUTION	1964	1974	1982
University of California, San Diego	37	5	5
Washington University	28	18	19
University of California, San Francisco	36	19	15
University of Alabama, Birmingham	80	40	49
University of Hawaii	71	41	66
City University of New York–			
Mt. Sinai School of Medicine	*	44	67
Colorado State University	68	45	58
Boston University	83	50	46

* Not in top 100 in 1964.
Source: General Accounting Office. *Geographical Distribution of Federal Science Funds to Colleges and Universities,* GAO Report B–117219, Washington, D.C., 1976, p. 11.; National Science Foundation. *Federal Support to Universities, Colleges, and Selected, Non-Profit Institutions, FY 1982,* Washington, D.C., Table B22.

10. Bruce L. Smith and Joseph J. Karlesky. *The State of Academic Science* (New York: Change Magazine Press, 1977), 6.

11. In 1983, Catholic University in Washington, D.C. and Columbia University in New York City got two amendments to legislation passed in the House directing the Department of Energy to provide them with new laboratories. These new programs put a claim on research funds that would otherwise have gone through peer review. "Take from the Pork Barrel Route to Research & Development Money" *Science and Government Report*, June 1, 1983, 1–5. A special five-member panel of the National Science Board has begun to study this issue. Erich Bloch, director of the National Science Foundation, has said, "If political criteria are used in place of merit-based peer review, scarce research and educational dollars will be allocated to projects of questionable technical merit." Kim McDonald. "NSF Seeks Ways to Prevent Universities from Bypassing 'Peer Review' System" *Chronicle of Higher Education*, January 1985, 25–26.

12. Evidence cited in conversation with historian of science, A. Hunter Dupree.

13. Looking at the priority areas for government research and development funding between 1975 and 1982, for all Organization for Economic Cooperation and Development (OECD) countries, Health and Welfare was at the bottom of the list, except in the United States where it ranked second only to Defense and Space. Organization for Economic Cooperation and Development. "Science and Technology Indicators" *Science Resources Newsletter*, 1983, nos. 7, 3.

14. The President's Commission on Industrial Competitiveness had three recommendations on how education could better put America back on the path to industrial competitiveness. They called for increased business-school partnerships, better computer training, and expansion in fellowship support for graduate students in engineering. The Commission also supported the National Science Foundation's proposed program of on-campus, cross-disciplinary engineering research centers. Support for health and defense was conspicuously absent. *Higher Education Daily*, May 7, 1984, 4.

15. Office of Technology Assessment. United States Congress. *Commercial Biotechnology: An International Analysis*, Washington, D.C., January 1984.

16. It is well known that the academic fallout is limited. Only nine universities fell within the top 100 Defense Department contractors in 1982. Twenty-six were within the top 200, and 86 made the top 500 institutions getting funding from the Department of Defense. "Fact-File" *Chronicle of Higher Education*, April 6, 1983, 16.

17. Federal funding for basic research in industrial laboratories grew by 6.2 percent, in non-profit organizations by 8.4 percent, and in Federally Funded Research and Development Centers (FFRDCs) by 10.2 percent.

    The 1979 budget of two federal labs, Sandia and Livermore, was more than the combined research funding of the top six research universities. The 1983 budgets of these two labs exceeded the combined budgets of those same six universities plus the next six as well. Neils Reimers. "Improving Innovation—Government, Industry, Universities" in James S. Coles (Ed.). *Technological Innovation in the '80s* (Englewood Cliffs, NJ: Prentice-Hall, 1984), 129.

18. Research and Development Task Force (The Grace Commission). *Report of The Pres-*

ident's Private Sector Survey on Cost Control, Washington, D.C., December 8, 1983; and Stanley Wellborn. "Why National Laboratories are Under Fire" *U.S. News and World Report*, November 8, 1982, 54. Federal labs account for one-third of the $45 billion budgeted in FY 1984 for federal research and development.

19. As early as 1968, a report on improving the effectiveness of federal laboratories suggested 1) encouraging interagency transfers of labs and programs; 2) encouraging interagency transfer of technology; and 3) eliminating manpower ceilings for cross-agency work. The general thrust was toward broadening interchange of personnel, equipment, ideas, and projects between government agencies. Donald MacArthur. *Effective Use of Federal Laboratories* (Washington, D.C.: Office for Laboratory Management, April 2, 1968). This should be taken further by promoting exchanges with academe and industry, too.

20. James S. Coles (Ed.). *Technological Innovation in the '80s* (Englewood Cliffs, NJ: Prentice-Hall, 1984), 54.

    Other studies include those by the General Accounting Office, the Department of Energy (DOE), the President's Private Sector Survey on Cost Control (The Grace Commission), the House of Representatives' Committee on Science and Technology, the Congressional Office of Technology Assessment, and Georgetown University's Center for Strategic and International Studies. "Will House Advisors Urge Significant Changes?" *Physics Today*, September 1983, 39.

21. Office of Science and Technology Policy. *Report of the White House Council*, May 1983, 5. The White House Panel was especially critical of micromanagement and of a tendency for federal labs to isolate themselves from university and industry labs.

22. About 70 percent of the federal labs are very small, with fewer than 50 people. But almost 90 percent of the operating costs of all federal labs is concentrated in the 146 labs (20 percent of the total) with over 100 employees. Moreover, 70 percent of the total operating costs for federal labs comes from just two agencies, the Defense Department and the Department of Energy. Research and Development Task Force (Grace Commission), op. cit., Exhibit II–9.

23. The White House Panel felt that competition between Lawrence Livermore and Los Alamos was important in the high quality of their weapons development work.

24. The private sector has a relatively lean hierarchy. Federal labs tend to be top-heavy with higher ratios of managers to workers, between 16 percent and 21 percent, and a greater percentage of technical staff working on evaluation rather than research. The major corporations have management ratios in the range of 12.5 percent to 17 percent. Research and Development Task Force (Grace Commission), op. cit., Table 2. However, in the last 12 years, the cost of performing research has risen faster in academia (up 136.3 percent) than overall (up 123 percent). Battelle Memorial Institute. *Probable Levels of R & D Expenditures in 1984* (Columbus, OH: Battelle Memorial Institute, 1984).

25. *Report of the White House Science Council*, May 1983, 5.

26. George Keyworth pledged to change federal labs, to make them more open to universities and industry. He saw them as the linchpin in a three-way alliance between government, industry and academe. "If you take a hard look at the national labo-

216

ratories today, you'll see that a very substantial amount of work . . . has very little impact on industrial competitiveness, very little impact on training of people, and very little impact on defense. So, naturally, you ask yourself, 'What does it have impact on?' The answer is not absolutely clear to me." The Stanford accelerator, the Fermilab, and the new Materials Center at Lawrence Laboratory at Berkeley are to be models of the new national labs. Interview in "Q & A with Keyworth on FY 1984 Budget" *Science and Government Report*, February 15, 1983, 6–7.

27. Congress in 1983 and 1984 introduced legislation to promote technological development. H.R. 481, The National Technology Foundation Act, would establish a foundation along the lines of the National Science Foundation but exclusively devoted to funding engineering research. The High Technology Morrill Act (H.R. 3334 and S. 631) would establish a national education grants program to provide matching federal assistance to industry, states, and academe to strengthen science, engineering, and technical education. House Bill H.R. 4974 proposed to amend the National Science Foundation charter to include engineering, along with research and education, as the primary mission objectives of the National Science Foundation.

28. In the 1980s industry's support for academic research has grown faster (+ 7 percent per year) than the federal government's support (+ 4 percent per year) although industry still provides far less support, $700 million contrasted with the federal government's $7.9 billion in 1984. Battelle Memorial Institute. *Probable Levels of R & D Expenditures in 1984* (Columbus, OH: Battelle Memorial Institute, 1984).

29. The National Governors' Association. *Final Report: Technology and Growth: State Initiatives in Technological Innovation* (Washington, D.C.: National Governors' Association, October 1983); and Herb Brody. "States Vie for a Slice of the Pie" *High Technology*, January, 1985, 16–28.

30. The National Science Foundation launched a new program in 1985 to create university centers for cross-disciplinary research in engineering. These centers will serve three functions: 1) to change how universities educate engineers; 2) to develop a body of knowledge for integrating different disciplines; and 3) to improve industry/university linkages. It will spend up to $94.5 million over the next five years to establish and operate six such centers with grants to eight major universities: the University of California at Santa Barbara; Columbia University; the University of Delaware in collaboration with Rutgers University; the Massachusetts Institute of Technology; Purdue University; and the University of Maryland in collaboration with Harvard University. "National Science Foundation Establishes Engineering-Research Centers at 6 Universities" *Chronicle of Higher Education*, April 10, 1985, 9; and "8 Universities Get Industrial Grants" *New York Times*, April 4, 1985, A21.

31. National Academy of Science. Ad Hoc Committee on Government University Relationships in Support of Science. Committee on Science, Engineering, and Public Policy. *Strengthening the Government-University Partnership in Science* (Washington, D.C.: National Academy Press, 1983); Thomas Langfitt and Sheldon Hackney and Others (Eds.). *Partners in the Research Enterprise: University-Corporate Relations in Science and Technology* (Philadelphia: University of Pennsylvania Press, 1983); and United States General Accounting Office. *The Federal Role in Fostering*

217

University-Industry Cooperation, Washington, D.C., 1983. The National Science Foundation is funding a study. The Carnegie Corporation of New York is also funding a study by James Botkin and Dan Dimencescu.

32. This process began many years ago. The Daddario-Kennedy Amendment of 1968 to the National Science Foundation Act marked a turning point for the National Science Foundation. It became more concerned with *applied* research, particularly research related to the problems of society. The first applied research initiative at the National Science Foundation was the program, Research Applied to National Needs, replacing the smaller program, Interdisciplinary Research Relevant to Problems of our Society (IRRPOS), begun in 1970. John Wilson. *Academic Science, Higher Education, and the Federal Government, 1950–1983* (Chicago: The University of Chicago Press, 1983), 34–42.

CHAPTER XI.

1. A symposium of chemists at the American Association for the Advancement of Science meeting in New York in 1984 noted the importance of new instrumentation—lasers, computers, molecular beams, ion cyclotron resonance, and others—in studying the why and how of chemical changes. Increasingly, research at the frontiers of knowledge is predicated upon state-of-the-art instrumentation. Philip H. Abelson. "Chemistry Without Test Tubes" *Science*, June 22, 1984. The President's Commission on Industrial Competitiveness, chaired by John A. Young, president of Hewlett-Packard, saw as part of its agenda replacing obsolete research equipment at universities. The American Council on Education has made federal funding for research instrumentation part of its higher education agenda.

2. Edward Knapp, Director of the National Science Foundation, has voiced his preference for funding instrumentation through project grants rather than through separate instrumentation grants. Interview in "New NSF Director Sets Out Policy Views" *Science and Government Report*, December 15, 1982, 4.

3. Charles E. Young, Chancellor of the University of California at Los Angeles, estimates that the University of California will need to spend $4 billion over the next decade to construct, renovate, and maintain research buildings, libraries, hospitals, and instructional facilities. This extrapolates into a nationwide need of $40 billion. "Fourth of Equipment for Research Found Obsolete, Unused" *Chronicle of Higher Education*, May 16, 1984, 1 and 18. In their 1982 research equipment inventories, university researchers classified one-fourth of their equipment as obsolete. Only 16 percent was considered "state-of-the-art." Over 90 percent of the respondents felt that this situation inhibits the conduct of critical research. About two-thirds of equipment acquired in 1982 was done so wholly or in part with federal funds. National Science Foundation. "One-fourth of Academic Research Equipment Classified Obsolete" *Science Resources Studies Highlights*, April 18, 1984.

4. Quoted in Frank Rhodes' Testimony before the House Committee on Science and Technology. "Nation Faces 'Serious' R & D Problems" *Higher Education and Na-*

218

tional Affairs, June 4, 1984, 3. Also, Robert M. Rosenzweig. *The Research Universities and Their Patrons* (Berkeley, CA: University of California Press, 1982), Chapter 5; Association of American Universities. *The Scientific Instrumentation Needs of Research Universities*, Report to National Science Foundation (Washington, D.C.: Association of American Universities, June 1980); and Association of American Universities. *The Nation's Deteriorating University Research Facilities* (Washington, D.C.: Association of American Universities, July 1981).

5. Robert Rosenzweig. Op. cit., 87. In 1979, over three-quarters of all federal support for research and development plants went to federal and industrial labs, not to university labs.

6. About 30 percent of a Biomedical Research and Support Grant (BRSG) goes to equipment purchases and maintenance. The remainder covers salaries and related support costs. From 1976 to 1982, the amount of money under the BRSG program fell 6.2 percent in nominal terms and 25.8 percent in real terms. Robert Rosenzweig. Op. cit., 1982, 88.

7. A similar program operated during the 1950s and 1960s when United States researchers took the lead in scientific computation. The initial outlay is dwarfed by the estimated $400 million needed over the next three years to deal with this problem. John Walsh. "NSF Plans Help with Big Computer Problems" *Science*, February 24, 1984, 797–798.

8. Out of these applications, 204 awards were made, averaging $148,000. "That represents an award rate of eight percent and a funding level four percent of the amount requested." Testimony of Dean Charles Hess of the University of California at Davis, quoted in Committee on Science and Technology. United States House of Representatives. *Summary and Analysis of Hearing on "Improving the Research Infrastructure at U.S. Universities and Colleges,"* Washington, D.C., July 1984, 4.

9. Dr. George A. Keyworth, quoted in *ibid.*, 5.

10. At present, the National Science Foundation is the leading federal funder of research equipment in the physical and computer sciences; the National Institutes of Health is the leading federal funder in the biological and medical sciences; and the Department of Defense is the leading federal funder in engineering. Frank Rhodes' testimony in *ibid.*, 4.

11. The National Center for Education Statistics has reported recent increases at academic libraries in book volume and periodical subscriptions, and expects reference transactions and inter-library loans to continue to increase into the 1980s. *Higher Education and National Affairs*, July 2, 1984, 5.

12. In 1979–1980, American research universities spent over $500 million to operate their libraries. Robert Rosenzweig. *The Research Universities and Their Patrons*, 64.

Serials constitute a growing and books a declining portion of expenditures at libraries. The National Enquiry into Scholarly Communication. *Scholarly Communication* (Baltimore, MD: Johns Hopkins University Press, 1979), Table 4.1.

13. Print publishers are beginning to distribute their products in a wide variety of electronic forms, over phone lines, through computer programs, and on videotapes. This is substituting for printed copies to some extent. For example, when Chemical Ab-

stracts Services offered electronic versions of its abstracts, the number of subscription non-renewals doubled. "Publishers Go Electronic" *Business Week*, June 11, 1984, 84–97.

14. Robert Rosenzweig. Op. cit., 61.

15. *Ibid.*, 62.

16. The use of computers to give bibliographic information to researchers has raised the cost of using libraries. This threatens to create an "information elite" of those with access to research grants. One estimate puts the number of data bases at 1,596 from 244 different sources. Judith Axler Turner. "Computerized Data-Base Services for Research Bringing Era of 'Free' Library Service to End" *Chronicle of Higher Education*, September 19, 1984, 23–27.

17. The National Enquiry into Scholarly Communication. Op. cit., 18–20, recommended the establishment of a national periodicals center. So did Robert Rosenzweig. Op. cit., 72–74.

18. The National Technical Information Service (NTIS) can deliver via "electronic mail" abstracts of technical reports to anyone with a computer terminal and a telephone line.

   The National Institutes of Health has begun a five-year program to establish a commercial national computer resource for molecular biology. Called BIONET, this system will give researchers access to national databases and will provide software for sequence searching, matching and manipulation. This program is an outgrowth of collaboration between molecular biologists and artificial intelligence experts at Stanford University. Access will be reviewed by an advisory committee. A user fee will be charged. Roger Lewin. "National Networks for Molecular Biologists" *Science*, March 30, 1984, 1379–1380.

   EDUCOM's BITNET has developed into a self-sustaining, user-oriented, international computer network. It has direct links to over 200 computers at 60 campuses. Originally begun as a communications channel for systems programmers, BITNET has come to be used by scholars in many different disciplines for innovative collaborative efforts. John W. McCredie. "BITNET's Changing Role in Higher Education" *EDUCOM Bulletin*, Summer 1984, 2.

19. Computer manufacturers have been perfecting the technique for linking computers into a network, allowing an entire office, for example, to replace paper communications with electronic communications. Dennis Kneale. "Networks Connecting Diverse Computers Are Expected to Undergo Rapid Growth" *Wall Street Journal*, August 31, 1984, 15.

20. The Library of Congress has formed an Optical Disk Pilot Program Advisory Committee to deal with issues such as a fair return to publishers of journals accessed on optical disk, the degree of subsidy for browsing on optical disk, and relations with other libraries desiring access to this technology. *Library of Congress Information Bulletin*, May 21, 1984, 167.

21. "[B]ecause of a decade of intensive automation activity in libraries, librarians probably know far more about computing than computer specialists know about libraries." Patricia Battin. "The Electronic Library—A Vision for the Future" *EDUCOM Bulletin*, Summer 1984, 12.

22. "Basically, it's a matter of whether the academic research library is to function as a source of information or as the agency for assuring that the record is preserved. . . . The underlying assumption that all sources of information should be centered on the library needs to be examined carefully." Robert Hayes (Ed.). *Universities, Information Technology, and Academic Libraries: The Next Twenty Years*, report of the Academic Libraries Frontiers Conference, Lake Arrowhead Conference Center, University of California at Los Angeles, December 13–17, 1981, 223.

23. The federal government can do more to encourage and support interlibrary cooperation and networking. The College Library Resources Program and the Interlibrary Cooperation Program are both able to fund cooperative arrangements among libraries, networking, and the use of computers for cataloging and text storage. The Library Career Training program can be used to support study in modern information technology. These programs have a combined operating budget of under $4 million. The level of funding should be increased. National Commission on Student Financial Assistance. *Signs of Trouble and Erosion: Report on Graduate Education* (New York: New York University Press, 1983), 55–56. The Reagan administration's Fiscal Year 1985 budget request eliminates all library support including support for research libraries, under the Higher Education Act, Title II–C, funded at $6 million in 1984.

24. The recommendation of the American Council on Education that funding for existing federal library support programs be increased does not go far enough. See their "A Higher Education Agenda for the 99th Congress," 9–10.

25. Michael J. Liebowitz. "National Security and Scientific Training," letter to the editor, *Science*, August 10, 1984, 566. There is also the vexing problem of language difficulty.

26. Federal support for graduate education peaked in 1969 when 80,000 stipends were distributed. About half that number are now made available each year, one-third in fellowships and two-thirds in research assistantships. The result has been a decline from 36.6 percent in 1969 to 22.8 percent in 1981 of graduate science students receiving primary support from the federal government. *Signs of Trouble and Erosion*, 1985, 38–39, and 67.

In 1982, 37,200 graduate science and engineering students received fellowships and traineeships. Of this number, 15,042 came from the federal government. That same year, 53,294 received research assistantships, 28,497 of which were federal. 57,893 relied primarily on teaching assistantships from their universities and 84,784 supported themselves. Abt Associates. *NSF-NIH Survey of Graduate Science and Engineering Students and Postdoctorates* (Cambridge, MA: Abt Associates, December 23, 1983), 8. Almost 100,000 graduate students receive support through college work/study. *Signs of Trouble and Erosion*, 1983, 47.

There is no major field in which the federal government is the predominant source for graduate student support. In fact, the university is the major source of support for most graduate students. Only in biology and chemistry does the federal government rank second. Otherwise, even for engineering and computer science, self-support is the secondary source of graduate support. National Research Council. *Summary Report 1981, Doctorate Recipients from U.S. Universities* (Washington, D.C.: National Research Council, 1982), 13–14.

There are other sources of support. Corporations were the primary supporters of

221

1 percent of the students awarded doctoral degrees in 1981. State support is smaller and difficult to calculate. Even California provided only 800 graduate fellowships. Foundation support accounts for the primary means of support for about 1 percent of all doctoral recipients. The Woodrow Wilson Foundation and the Danforth Foundation together support 21,000 students. *Signs of Trouble and Erosion*, 1983, 67–69.

A study using 1981 data showed that whites are more likely than minority groups to be primarily dependent on the federal government for graduate study support. Blacks are almost three times as likely to be primarily dependent on loans. All minority groups, except for Asians, are considerably more likely to rely primarily on their own efforts in financing their graduate education than are white students. These differences in part reflect different levels of participation in different fields. National Research Council. *Summary Report*, 1981, 19.

27. Estimates of the number of graduate and professional students borrowing under the Guaranteed Student Loan program in 1984 range from 410,000 to 522,000. *Signs of Trouble and Erosion*, 1983, 69.

28. The following changes in federal student aid programs have been proposed by the Reagan administration and most of them are expected to impact adversely on graduate students:

   1) Tighten restrictions on Guaranteed Student Loans. All students will be required to demonstrate need to be eligible. The maximum size of the loan will be determined by the size of the calculated need less any other aid received by the student. This will affect independent students, many of whom are graduate students, more than dependent students.

   2) Eliminate federal capital funding to the National Direct Student Loan (NDSL) Program and raise the interest rate to 8 percent. About 20 percent of NDSL loans go to graduate students each year, many of whom are minorities. In 1982–83, 50,000 graduate students received loan funds under NDSL.

   3) Eliminate the Graduate and Professional Study Grant Program (G*POP). This program, begun in 1977, is run by the Department of Education. The awards are grants to the institutions, which then award fellowships to students. Fiscal year 1984 funding for G*POP was $11 million. That year 1,324 fellowships averaging $8,400 each were awarded, primarily to minorities and women. The number of new fellowships has fallen. It fell from 550 to 213 between 1980 and 1981.

   4) Eliminate Public Service Fellowships, which go to students preparing for careers in public sector management. Currently, there are 243 students in the program, many of whom are needy women and minorities.

   5) Eliminate Legal Training for the Disadvantaged. Funding has fluctuated around $1 million per year over the past several years. It provides remedial training for marginally eligible prospective law students with annual fellowship support of $1,000. The program has produced 2,000 law school graduates thus far. Currently 550 fellows are in law school.

   6) The National Science Foundation's programs for graduate fellowships were slated for extinction in FY 1982. The Reagan administration in FY 1985 is supporting this program with a budget request of $21 million. That will assist 1,550 graduate

students, about triple the 515 students assisted in 1981. The National Science Foundation is also requesting $13.9 million for FY 1985 for 11,614 graduate research assistantships, a 15.5 percent increase over FY 1984.

7) Eliminate the National Health Service Corps scholarships and traineeships, and loans for nurses under the Nurse Training Act for FY 1985.

8) Eliminate the authorized (though unfunded) 450 annual awards under the National Graduate Fellowship Program (The Javits Fellowships).

National Association of State Universities and Land-Grant Colleges. *Joint Budget Analysis of Higher Education Programs in the Federal Budget for FY 1985* (Washington, D.C.: National Association of State Universities and Land-Grant Colleges, February 13, 1984).

29. In 1981, approximately 27,000 graduate students worked as research assistants in federally supported projects. The National Science Foundation supports about 9,600 students as research assistants each year. The National Institutes of Health supports about 10,000 graduate students and postdoctoral fellows in biomedical, clinical, and behavioral research. *Signs of Trouble and Erosion*, 1983, 45.

30. The American Council on Education is much broader in their recommendation that *all* federal graduate support programs be increased. See their "Higher Education Agenda for the 99th Congress," 8.

31. England has developed a New Blood program and Germany has set up a Heisenberg program to help keep up the flow of young scientists into academe. England created 395 new positions under this program in 1984–85, mostly in the sciences and engineering. Ngaio Crequer. "New Blood Under the Microscope" *The [London] Times Higher Education Supplement*, No. 583, January 6, 1984, 12; and Ngaio Crequer. "Universities Gain More New Blood Posts" *The [London] Times Higher Education Supplement*, January 6, 1984.

32. A list of 1984's recipients appears in "200 Scientists, Engineers, and Named Winners of First Presidential Young Investigators Award" *Chronicle of Higher Education*, March 7, 1984, 8. After the first year of operation, the National Science Foundation decided to tighten eligibility requirements from seven to four and a half years after the Ph.D. in an effort to recruit younger people. It also opened up a second nomination track for people still in graduate school. As of February 1985, only 50 percent of the first year's award recipients had met the requirement of a matching grant from industry. President Reagan wants to reduce the number of new awards by half for FY 1986.

33. The Carnegie Institution of Washington recognizes that current mechanisms of peer review are strongly biased toward the "safe and sound." It was only through the intervention of the Carnegie Institution that Barbara McClintock was able to spend the past four decades doing research for which she received a Nobel Prize in 1983. "[I]mportant problems are not confined to those in the mainstream of current theory." Carnegie Institution of Washington. *Report of the President, 1982–1983* (Washington, D.C.: The Carnegie Institution of Washington, 1984), 4.

Minority Recruitment and Retention Programs

IT IS DIFFICULT TO GENERALIZE about programs that successfully attract qualified minority students and motivate them to stay on and complete their degree requirements for professional careers. No single course of action is appropriate for all institutions and all minority communities. Diversity and flexibility continue to define the criteria for success. That is why the competitive proposal approach by which the Fund for Improvement in Postsecondary Education (FIPSE) stimulates new and innovative programs should be considered as part of a national implementation strategy.

Dr. Arthur Chickering of Memphis State University has identified the essential characteristics of effective minority recruitment and retention programs. They are outlined as follows:

ADMINISTRATION AND ORGANIZATION
Strong and continuous leadership
Top-level, open commitment to minority education
Centrality in institutional mission and values
Focus on student needs, not administrative efficiency
Clear priority of teaching
Direct student access to top administrators
Minority role models in administration
Small units within the organization
Residential experience for students
Clear locus of identity for minority students

ETHOS AND SENSE OF COMMUNITY
Commitment to personal change
Commitment to institutional improvement

225

Cooperative, pluralistic value orientation
A "critical mass" of minority students
A caring and supportive attitude toward students

TEACHING STYLE
Clear expectations of students' performance
Active student participation
Recognition of student strengths
Academic cooperation, not competition
Concrete applications of what is taught
Narrative evaluations of student progress
Individual tutoring
Recognition of achievement
Role model provided by teacher

CURRICULUM
Course content considered relevant by students
A common core of learning
Diverse course options
A clear understanding of required competencies
Hands-on experience

ORIENTATION AND EVALUATION
Pre-college, pre-semester orientation
Accurate advice and information concerning future education and
    work
Focus on exit criteria
Continuous monitoring and feedback
Regularly scheduled counseling and advising
Peer assistance
Individual crisis intervention

The programs described in this appendix are drawn from the literature, our own observations, and discussions we have had with educators and administrators. They are known to have successfully assisted in the recruitment, retention, and program completion of minority students in various courses of study in higher education. In their educational philosophy and procedure, they incorporate many of the features of the outline presented by Dr. Chickering.

This list is not meant to be exhaustive; many good programs are not included. The primary purpose of this list is to educate and inspire. Because many programs have similar characteristics and goals, only a few examples of each particular type of program is included.

The first section includes engineering and science programs. Such programs serve a special need, because certain minority students (blacks, Native Americans and Hispanics) are under-represented in engineering and science fields. Because of efforts like those of the decentralized, largely nongovernmental, programs listed below, minority participation in engineering and engineering-related fields has grown slightly in the last few years—a pattern not found in most other fields. (Scientific Manpower Commission. *Professional Women and Minorities*, Washington, D.C., August 1984; and The National Action Council for Minorities in Engineering. (N.A.C.M.E.) *1982/83 Annual Report: Meeting The Challenge*, New York, 1984.) Mr. Wayne Owens of The National Action Council for Minorities in Engineering Inc., New York City Office, generously provided much of the information on these programs. (N.A.C.M.E. *1984 Pre-College Program Directory*, New York, August 1984.)

One of the strengths of these programs is that they reach into junior and senior high schools to identify and encourage bright young students from minority backgrounds and begin training them in math and science. Another strength of these programs is that they have been launched without government assistance. They usually involve three partners: schools of engineering, secondary schools with large minority populations and the private sector. Each partner shoulders a share of the time, money and other resources for carrying out the program's objectives.

ENGINEERING PROGRAMS

COLORADO MINORITY ENGINEERING ASSOCIATION (CMEA)

University of Colorado
1100 Fourteenth Street
Denver, Colorado 80202

A private, non-profit organization funded entirely by industry and various foundations, CMEA operates a statewide pre-college program, starting in the seventh grade, and including tutoring, specialized counseling, role models, speakers, monetary incentives, science and engineering projects, as well as other means to enhance minority student involvement in science and engineering.

MATHEMATICS, ENGINEERING, SCIENCE ACHIEVEMENT PROGRAM (MESA-CA)

Lawrence Hall of Science
University of California
Berkeley, California 94720

Founded in 1970, MESA is one of the earliest minority intervention programs and the model for many other successful programs. It has a statewide organization in which nearly one hundred forty California secondary schools participate. There are over four thousand students presently involved in its 16 centers within the California university system. The MESA program provides tutoring, academic and career centers, scholarship incentive awards, and summer enrichment and employment programs. The organization is sponsored by over one hundred industrial and governmental organizations.

PHILADELPHIA REGIONAL INTRODUCTION FOR MINORITIES TO ENGINEERING (PRIME)

1831 Chestnut Street, Suite 6B
Philadelphia, Pennsylvania 19103

PRIME is governed by a board of representatives from business and industry, universities and colleges, governmental agencies, local public schools and professional societies. The PRIME program is comprehensive, involving the early identification of minority students interested in science and engineering, and placement of these students in special classes monitored by PRIME staff members. An integral part of PRIME is its Summer Program which consists, in part, of a five-year, month-long college enrichment program. PRIME also runs a week-long summer institute for teachers, which focuses on the updating of skills and the application of science and math to technological problems. There are presently about

228

2,000 students in various PRIME programs, of which one-quarter are college students.

SOUTHEASTERN CONSORTIUM FOR MINORITIES IN ENGINEERING (SECME)

c/o Georgia Institute of Technology
Atlanta, Georgia 30332

SECME operates in 156 secondary schools in Alabama, Florida, Georgia, North Carolina, South Carolina, Tennessee and Virginia. Approximately 12,000 students participate in the program. Students are assigned to special classes in science, mathematics and language. Initial surveys indicate that 26 percent of the high school graduates involved with SECME are studying in engineering fields, with an additional 30 percent in related fields. Engineering industries provide the budget of SECME.

MINORITY ENGINEERING PROGRAM (MEP)

California State University
Northridge, California 91330

Calstate/Northridge provides a comprehensive recruitment and retention program for minorities. MEP has a remarkably high retention and graduation rate due to its focus on tutoring, academic advancement, creating an espirit de corps among students, personal counseling, summer teaching in math, English, computer programming and general study, and a full-time commitment on the part of MEP administrators and faculty. (David McNary. "Hats Off to Calstate/Northridge" *Minority Engineering*, Winter 1982–83, 35–37, 69–70; Raymond B. Landis. "Retaining Minority Engineering Students: A Model Program" *Engineering Education*, April 1982, 714–718; *Minority Engineering Program 1982/ 83 California State University Northridge* (Newsletter), *CSUW School of Engineering and Computer Science, 1982–83 Annual Report*.)

The second section focuses on programs not exclusively devoted to improving minority participation in engineering fields. Varying degrees of attention in these programs is paid to general educational preparation, preparation specifically in mathematics and sciences, preparation to facilitate transfer from two-year to four-year institutions, preparation designed to overcome cultural and linguistic barriers to higher education, and preparation intended to stimulate interest and competence in the legal and health professions and in research careers.

NON-ENGINEERING PROGRAMS

UNIDAD: NATIONAL HISPANIC UNIVERSITY AND THE UNIVERSITY OF CALIFORNIA, BERKELEY

B. Robert Cruz, Director
National Hispanic University
Cientificos Program
255 East 14th Street
Oakland, California 94720

Designed to increase the number of Bay Area Hispanic students taking college preparatory programs in math and science fields, UNIDAD operates in Ells High School in Richmond, California. It has three components: the University/High School Master Teachers' Unit, in which master teachers from the high school work with faculty at the University of California, Berkeley; the school-based Mathematics/Science Honors Unit, involving 35–40 students; and the parent involvement and education unit.

PROFESSIONAL DEVELOPMENT PROGRAM

Dr. Robert E. Fullilove, III, Director
University of California
Berkeley, California 94720

This program offers a summer academy for approximately two hundred high-achieving minority high school students. Almost all of these students later attend college, about half go to the University of California at Berkeley. At the undergraduate level, workshops in math and science are offered. Each year about 100 women and minority students take part. Also,

230

academic counseling, career advising, and support is given to minority female students planning to apply to medical school.

IMPROVED EDUCATIONAL OPPORTUNITIES FOR HISPANIC WOMEN

Edenia Guillermo, Director
Hood College
Frederick, Maryland 21701

Hood College undertakes special recruitment activities to attract Hispanic women and offers programs to improve their communication skills in both English and Spanish. Hood also strives to create an atmosphere supportive of Spanish culture.

SOLIDARIDAD HUMANA

Dino Pacio Lindin, President
107 Suffolk Street
New York, New York 10002

Solidaridad Humana is a community-based comprehensive learning center located on the lower east side of Manhattan. Using bi-lingual instruction, this project provides intensive preparation for college-bound Hispanics, many of whom are recent immigrants. It has a good record at placing its graduates in local colleges.

MONTCLAIR STATE COLLEGE

Marilyn Frankenthaler, Project Director
Montclair State College
Normal Avenue and Valley Road
Upper Montclair, New Jersey 07043

Montclair has a program that identifies, selects, and provides support services for minority and disadvantaged students interested in legal careers. Support services and role models are used to instruct and guide the students through legal reasoning, problem solving, and hands-on courtroom experience.

231

Ann Poskocil, Director
Project Discovery
P.O. Box 2868
Roanoke, Virginia 24001

This program operates primarily in rural communities and largely with black students. Its goal is to enhance students' awareness of attending college as an option in their life. Students are involved in workshops on college campuses where they learn to set goals, to study, to take tests, to meet admissions requirements, to qualify for financial aid, and to adapt to other aspects of college life.

TWO-PLUS-TWO AGRICULTURAL PROGRAM IN KERN COUNTY, CALIFORNIA

Dan Carlos, Agricultural Department
Bakersfield College
1801 Panorama Drive
Bakersfield, California 93305

This is a three-way program run by Bakersfield College, the Kern County Community College District, and the Kern High School District. It provides a four-year technical arts degree in agriculture. The first two years are taught at the high-school level and the final two years are completed in the community college. The schools serve an area wherein minority groups are heavily concentrated.

HIGH SCHOOL FOR THE HEALTH PROFESSIONS (HSHP)

Dr. William A. Thompson
Center for Allied Health Professions
Baylor College of Medicine
1200 Moorsund Avenue
Houston, Texas 77030

Baylor operates a program called High School for the Health Professions (HSHP), which is a four-year high school run in conjunction with the public school administration. Over three-quarters of its students are ethnic minorities. Almost all graduate and go on to post–secondary school.

PROJECT PLUS MATH

Dr. Elias Toubassi, Director
University of Arizona
Tucson, Arizona 85721

This program at the University of Arizona tracks students' progress in math from ninth through twelfth grades. Students are recommended by their high school teachers. The program draws upon university faculty and personnel from local high technology industries who tutor students, participate in workshops with student families, and offer career guidance. In some cases, it has quadrupled the rate at which minority high school students graduate and go onto college.

RESEARCH MENTORSHIP PROGRAM

Edmond J. Keller, Associate Dean
Graduate Division
University of California
3117 Cheadle Hall
Santa Barbara, California 93106

Santa Barbara runs a mentorship program that brings graduate students, undergraduates from under-represented minority groups and faculty together to work in research teams. The program strives to include more minority students in research projects in order to develop more highly their research skills at an earlier stage, and to infect minority students with enthusiasm for research.

FACULTY MENTORING OF MINORITY GRADUATE AND PROFESSIONAL STUDENTS

Dr. John Martinez, Director
University of California
Irvine, California 92717

233

This program aims to improve the retention and academic success of minority graduate students. Faculty are sensitized to the needs of minority students; administrative impediments are minimized; close cooperation between minority graduate students and faculty is institutionally supported.

FIORELLO H. LAGUARDIA COMMUNITY COLLEGE

Sheila C. Gordon
Associate Dean for Development
31–10 Thompson Avenue
Long Island City, New York 11101

LaGuardia Community College operates a program to increase the rate of transfer of students (including minority students) from community college to four-year colleges and universities. This program has attracted corporate support and has forged a special tie with Vassar College. It provides students with information on transfer possibilities and counsels them on how best to make the transition. (Networks [Ed.]. *New Initiatives for Transfer Students: Urban Community College Transfer Opportunities Program*, sponsored by the Ford Foundation, New York, June 1984.)

TRANSFER OPPORTUNITIES PROGRAM

John T. Greb, Director
Miami Dade Community College
Northcampus
11380 Northwest 27th Avenue
Miami, Florida 33167

This program tries to identify the problems that students encounter when they transfer to an upper division institution and to help them overcome these problems. Services include preparing students before they transfer and maintaining links with them after they have transferred to a four-year institution. (*Ibid.*)

COLLEGE ASSISTANCE MIGRANT PROGRAM (CAMP)

Randy S. Safady, Director
St. Edward's University
Austin, Texas 78704

CAMP is unusual insofar as it is directed at the children of migrant and seasonal farmworkers. Eligible students are recruited nationwide and the majority come from Texas and Florida. CAMP facilitates access to and successful completion of at least two semesters of college work for a section of the population that otherwise would have few options in life outside migrant labor. Their success rate is close to 90 percent.

BROWN-TOUGALOO EARLY IDENTIFICATION PROGRAM

Dr. McGinnis, Director
Tougaloo College
Tougaloo, Mississippi 39174

Reverend Baldwin
Chaplain
Brown University
Providence, Rhode Island 02912

Since the mid-1970s, Brown University's Medical School has cooperated with Tougaloo College in selecting two sophomores per year to a program for early admission to the Medical School upon completion of degree requirements at Tougaloo. In the summer of their junior year, students go to Brown to join in a research project with a faculty member. The following summer they take pre-admissions courses to overcome any academic weaknesses. The success rate has been high, with some students being admitted to and choosing to attend other medical schools. A similar program with Boston University has recently been created.

Dr. Enrique R. Lamadrid and
Dr. Michael Thomas, Co-Directors
Northern New Mexico Community College
P.O. Box 250
Espanola, New Mexico 87532

Conexiones provides an exceptional way to improve Hispanic recruitment to college by enhancing cultural interconnections between New Mexico and the greater Hispanic social and historical traditions in the southwestern United States and Mexico. This international component builds upon the existing humanities curriculum, so as better to acculturate Hispanic and Native American students into the college environment.

CHICANO HEALTH CENTERS INSTITUTE (CHCI)

Juan H. Flores, Executive Director
CHICANO HEALTH POLICY DEVELOPMENT
2300 West Commerce/Suite 304
San Antonio, Texas 78207

CHCI is a clearinghouse of information and direct health career service for Mexican-American students in Texas. Assistance is provided through a network of those four-year and two-year colleges with large enrollments of Mexican-Americans linked to health professional schools. Specific pilot projects demonstrate innovative approaches to prepare Mexican-Americans for the health professions.

BIBLIOGRAPHY

ACTIVE LEARNING

Alverno College Faculty. *Liberal Learning at Alverno College*, 2nd ed. (Milwaukee, WI: Alverno College, 1981).

Bergman, Charles A. "Writing Across the Curriculum: An Annotated Bibliography" *Current Issues in Higher Education, 1983–1984*, no. 3, 33–38.

Berry College. *Report on Student Work Programs Leadership Conference, October 4–5, 1982* (Mount Berry, GA: Berry College, 1982).

Chickering, Arthur W. "Education, Work and Human Development" in T.C. Little (Ed.). *Making Sponsored Experiential Learning Standard Practice, New Directions for Experiential Learning*, no. 20 (San Francisco: Jossey-Bass, 1983).

Chickering, Arthur W. and Associates. *The Modern American College* (San Francisco: Jossey-Bass, 1981).

Coulter, Xenia and Laurie Johnson. "The Use of the Undergraduate Teaching Assistant at Stony Brook," Report No. 21 (Stony Brook, NY: Research Group for Human Development and Educational Policy, State University of New York, 1984).

Downey, Ronald G. "Long-term Outcomes of Participation in Student Government" *Journal of College Student Personnel*, 1984, 245–250.

Duley, John S. "Nurturing Service-Learners" *Synergist*, Winter 1981, 12–15.

Duley, John S. and Jane Szutu Permaul. "Participation in and Benefits from Experiential Education" *Educational Record*, Summer 1984, 18–23.

Dye, G. G. and J. B. Stephens. "Learning Ethics through Public Service Internship— Evaluation of an Experimental Program" *Liberal Education*, October 1978, 341–356.

Ender, Steven C. and Roger B. Winston, Jr. (Eds.). *Students as Paraprofessional Staff*, New Directions for Student Services No. 27 (San Francisco: Jossey-Bass, 1984).

Endo, Jean J. and Richard L. Harpel. "The Effect of Student/Faculty Interaction on Students' Educational Outcomes" *Research in Higher Education*, vol. 16, no. 2, 115–138.

Eyler, Janet and Beth Halteman. "The Impact of a Legislative Internship on Students'

Note: A more extensive bibliography including works used as background but not cited in the footnotes or included here is available from The Carnegie Foundation for the Advancement of Teaching upon request.

Political Skillfulness and Sophistication" *Teaching Political Science*, Fall 1981, 27–34.

Gansneder, Nancy J. and Paul W. Kingston. "University Year for Action Internships and Post-Graduate Career Choice: A Retrospective Study," Undergraduate Internship Program, University of Virginia, MS, n.d.

Gryski, Gerard S. and Others. "Undergraduate Internships: An Empirical Review," Paper delivered at the annual meeting of the American Society for Public Administration, Denver, CO, April 10, 1984.

Keeton, Morris T. and Associates. *Experiential Learning: Rationale, Characteristics, and Assessment* (San Francisco: Jossey-Bass, 1976).

Kolb, David. *Experiential Learning* (Englewood Cliffs, NJ: Prentice-Hall, 1984).

Lewis, Morgan V. and Others. *High School Work Experience and Its Effects* (Columbus, OH: National Center for Research in Vocational Education, January 1983).

MacVicar, Margaret L. A. and Norma G. McGovern. "Not Only Engineering: The MIT Undergraduate Research Opportunities Programme," commissioned by the Society for Research into Higher Education, Ltd. at the University of Surrey, Guilford, England for its 1984 annual conference, "Education for the Professions," January 1984.

McKenzie, Douglas. "Student Employment and Persistence" *The Journal of Student Financial Aid*, May 1981, 38–42.

Mentkowski, Marcia and Austin Doherty. "Abilities That Last a Lifetime: Outcomes of the Alverno Experience" *AAHE Bulletin*, February 1984, 5–6, 11–14.

Milton, Ohmer. *Alternatives to the Traditional* (San Francisco: Jossey-Bass, 1972).

Mortimer, J. T. and J. Lorence. "Work Experience and Occupational Value Socialization: A Longitudinal Study" *American Journal of Sociology*, 1979, 1361–1385.

Overbye, Dennis. "Space Science for the People" *Discover*, February 1982, 36–38.

Sexton, Robert F. (Ed.). *Dimensions of Experiential Education* (Washington, D.C.: National Society for Internships and Experiential Education, 1981).

Smith, Virginia B. and Alison R. Bernstein. *The Impersonal Campus: Options for Reorganizing Colleges to Increase Student Involvement, Learning and Development* (San Francisco: Jossey-Bass, 1979).

Study Group on the Conditions of Excellence in American Higher Education. "Involvement in Learning: Realizing the Potential of American Higher Education," reprinted in *The Chronicle of Higher Education*, October 24, 1984.

Whitham, Michelle with Albert Erdynast. "Applications of Developmental Theory to the Design and Conduct of Quality Field Experience Programs: Exercises for Educators," PANEL Resource Paper #8 (Washington, D.C.: National Society for Internships and Experiential Education, 1982).

238

CIVIC FRAGMENTATION

Altheide, David L. *Creating Reality: How TV News Distorts Events* (Beverly Hills, CA: SAGE, 1976).

Committee for the Study of the American Electorate. "Non-voter Study '84–'85," Washington, D.C., 1984.

Cooperative Institutional Research Program. *The American Freshman: National Norms for Fall* (Los Angeles: University of California, December 1981, 1982, 1983).

Cornell University. *CIVITAS Annual Report 1982–83* (Ithaca, NY: Cornell University, 1984).

Dornbusch, Sanford M. and Catherine Gray. "The New Families" in S.M. Dornbusch and M. S. Strober (Eds.). *Feminism, Children, and the New Families* (New York: Guilford Press, 1985, forthcoming).

Etzioni, Amitai. *An Immodest Agenda: Rebuilding America Before the 21st Century* (New York: New Press, A Division of McGraw-Hill, 1983).

Fields, Cheryl M. "College Found to Have Little Impact on Student's Social, Political Views" *The Chronicle of Higher Education*, May 9, 1984, 1, 14.

Gais, Thomas L., Mark A. Peterson, and Jack L. Walker. "Interest Groups, Iron Triangles and Representative Institutions in American National Government" *British Journal of Political Science*, vol. 14, 161–185.

Greenberger, Ellen. "Children, Families and Work" in N. D. Reffucci, L. A. Weithorn, E. P. Mulvey, and J. Monahan (Eds.). *Mental Health, Law, and Children* (Beverly Hills, CA: SAGE, 1983).

Hacker, Andrew. *A Statistical Portrait of the American People* (New York: Penguin Books, 1983), 233–254.

Hage, Dean R., Cynthia L. Luna, and David K. Miller. "Trends in College Students' Values Between 1952 and 1979: A Return of the Fifties?" *Sociology of Education*, October 1981, 263–274.

Keene, Karlyn. "American Values: Change and Stability" *Public Opinion*, December/January 1984, 2–3.

Ladd, Everett Carl, Jr. and Seymour Martin Lipset. "Anatomy of a Decade" *Public Opinion*, December/January, 1980, 2–9.

Levine, Arthur. *When Dreams and Heroes Died* (San Francisco: Jossey-Bass, 1980).

Lipset, Seymour Martin and William Schneider. *The Confidence Gap: Business, Labor, and Government in the Public Mind* (New York: The Free Press, 1983).

McIntosh, John L. *Suicide Among Children, Adolescents, and Students 1980–1984: A*

Comprehensive Bibliography, Public Administration Series: Bibliography (Monticello, IL: Vance Bibliographies, December 1984).

Miller, Arthur. "Is Confidence Rebounding?" *Public Opinion* June/July 1983, 16–20.

National Assessment of Educational Progress. *Education for Citizenship: A Bicentennial Survey*, Citizenship/Social Studies Report No. 07–CS–01 (Denver, CO: NAEP, November 1976).

Sorauf, Frank J. "Accountability in Political Action Committees" *Political Science Quarterly*, Winter 1984–85, 591–614.

Thanksgiving Statement Group. *Developing Character: Transmitting Knowledge*, A Thanksgiving Day Statement by A Group of 27 Americans (Posen, IL: Thanksgiving Statement Group, November 21, 1984).

Veroff, Joseph, Elizabeth Douran, and Richard A. Kulka. *The Inner American: A Self-Portrait from 1957–1976* (New York: Basic Books, 1981).

Walker, Jack L. "The Origins and Maintenance of Interest Groups in America" *The American Political Science Review*, June 1983, 390–405.

Wolfinger, Raymond E. and Steven J. Rosenstone. *Who Votes?* (New Haven: Yale University Press, 1980).

Wuthnow, Robert. "Indices of Religious Resurgence in the United States" in Richard T. Antoun and Mary Hedland (Eds.). *Religious Resurgence in Comparative Perspective* (Syracuse, NY: Syracuse University Press, 1984).

———. "Religious Movements and Counter Movements in North America" in James A. Beckford (Ed.). *New Religious Movements and Rapid Social Change* (Paris: United States Education Social and Cultural Organization, 1984, forthcoming).

Yankelovich, Daniel. *New Rules: Searching for Self-Fulfillment in a World Turned Upside Down* (New York: Random House, 1981).

CIVIC LEARNING

Antaeus Report. "A Symposium on Public Life and Civic Literacy," Fall 1983.

Bellah, Robert N., Richard Madsen, William M. Sullivan, Ann Swidler, and Steven M. Tipton. *Habits of the Heart: Individualism and Commitment in American Life* (Berkeley: The University of California Press, 1985).

Bok, Derek. *Beyond the Ivory Tower* (Cambridge, MA: Harvard University Press, 1983).

Boyer, Ernest L. and Fred M. Hechinger. *Higher Learning in the Nation's Service* (Washington, D.C.: The Carnegie Foundation for the Advancement of Teaching, 1981).

Carnegie Council on Policy Studies in Higher Education. *Giving Youth a Better Chance— Options for Education, Work, and Service* (San Francisco: Jossey-Bass, 1979).

Cohen, Eliot A. *Citizens and Soldiers: The Dilemmas of Military Service* (New York: Cornell University Press, 1985).

Collins, Michael L. (Ed.). *Teaching Values and Ethics in College. New Direction for Teaching and Learning*, Number 13 (San Francisco: Jossey-Bass, March 1983).

Committee for Economic Development. *Stimulating Technological Progress* (New York: Committee for Economic Development, 1980).

Couto, Richard A. *Streams of Idealism and Health Care Innovation* (New York: Teachers College Press, 1982).

Crosson, Patricia H. *Public Service in Higher Education: Practices and Priorities* (ASHE/ERIC, Report No. 7, 1983).

Eberly, Donald J. "The Educational Integrity of Community Service and the Need for Federal Support" *New Directions for Higher Education*, Summer 1977, 53–63.

————. "A National Service Model Based on Experience and Research," prepared for the American Political Science Association Annual Meeting, Washington, D.C., August 31, 1984.

Eberly, Donald J. and Michael W. Sherraden (Eds.). *National Service: Social, Economic and Military Impacts* (New York: Pergamon Press, 1982).

Etzioni, Amitai. "A Remedy for Overeducation—A Year of Required National Service" *Change*, May/June 1983, 7–9.

Foley, Jonathan, Meryl Maneken, and Jeffrey Lee Schwartz. *National Service and America's Future: Special Report* (Washington, D.C.: Youth Policy Institute, January 1984).

Gorman, Margaret and Others. "Service Experience and the Moral Development of College Students," paper (Boston: Boston College, 1982).

Janowitz, Morris. *The Reconstruction of Patriotism: Education for Civic Consciousness* (Chicago: The University of Chicago Press, 1983).

Lacy, James L. "Military Manpower: The American Experience and the Enduring Debate" in Andrew J. Goodpaster and Others (Eds.). *Towards a Consensus on Military Service* (New York: Pergamon Press, 1982).

————. "National Service: The Origins and Evolution in Theory and Practice," unpublished MS, 1981.

Mathews, David. "The Liberal Arts and the Civic Arts" *Liberal Education*, Winter 1982, 270.

McGehee, Larry T. "Public Virtue & Higher Education Purpose," paper presented at Florida Endowment for the Humanities Meetings, April 12, 1984.

Moskos, Charles C. "Citizen Soldier and an AVF GI Bill," unpublished MS, October 1982.

O'Connell, Brian (Ed.). *America's Voluntary Spirit, A Book of Readings* (New York: The Foundation Center, 1983).

Paul, Richard. "Critical Thinking, Fundamentals on Education for a Free Society" *Education Leadership*, September 1984, 4–14.

Payton, Robert L. "Philanthropic Values," prepared for the Wilson Center Colloquium, October 2 and 3, 1982, unpublished MS.

Wells, Richard S. "The Problems of Civic Learning," Paper presented to the Annual Meeting of the Association of Graduate Liberal Studies Program, Los Angeles, California, October 11–13, 1984.

CREATIVITY

Amagile, Teresa. *The Social Psychology of Creativity* (New York: Springer Verlag, 1983).

Bastress, Frances K. *Teachers in New Careers: Stories of Successful Transitions* (Bethesda, MD: Career Development Services, 1985).

Chambers, Jack A. "College Teachers: Their Effect on Creativity of Students" *Journal of Educational Psychology*, 1973, 326–334.

Dreydahl, J. E. "Factors of Importance for Creativity" *Journal of Clinical Psychology*, 1956, 21–26.

Frederiksen, Norman, William Ward, and Charlotte Kiefer. "New Tests of Scientific Creativity Show Promise" *Findings: Educational Testing Service*, 1975, no. 4, 5–8.

Getzels, J. W. and M. Csikszentmihaly. *The Creative Vision: A Longitudinal Study of Problem Finding in Art* (New York: Wiley-Interscience, 1976).

Getzels, J. W. and P. W. Jackson. *Creativity and Intelligence* (New York: Wiley, 1962).

Guilford, J. P. "Creativity" *American Psychologist*, 1980, 444–454.

Heath, Roy. *The Reasonable Adventurer* (Pittsburgh: University of Pittsburgh Press, 1964).

Heist, Paul (Ed.). *The Creative College Student: An Unmet Challenge* (San Francisco: Jossey-Bass, 1968).

Holton, Gerald. *The Scientific Imagination: Case Studies* (Cambridge, England: Cambridge University Press, 1978).

Karlsson, Jon L. *Inheritance of Creative Intelligence* (Chicago: Nelson-Hall, 1978).

242

Kirton, Michael. "Adaptors and Innovators: A Description and Measure," *Journal of Applied Psychology*, 1976, 622–629.

Lytton, Hugh. *Creativity and Education* (New York: Shocken Books, 1972).

MacKinnon, Donald W. "Characteristics of the Creative Person: Implications for the Teaching-Learning Process" *Current Issues in Higher Education*, 1961, 89–92.

———. "Identifying and Developing Creativity" in *Selection and Educational Differentiation* (Berkeley: Field Service Center for the Study of Higher Education, University of California, 1960), 75–89.

Novak, Joseph D. "Metalearning and Metaknowledge: Strategies to Help Students Learn How to Learn," version of a paper presented at the International Seminar on Misconceptions in Science and Mathematics, Cornell University, June 21, 1983.

Prince, George M. "Synectics: Twenty-Five Years of Research Into Creativity and Group Process" *American Society for Training and Development*, 1982, 91–103.

Simonton, Dean Keith. *Genius, Creativity and Leadership: Historiometric Inquiries* (Cambridge, MA: Harvard University Press, 1984).

Stein, Morris. *Stimulating Creativity*, 2 vols. (New York: Academic Press, 1974, 1975).

Taylor, Calvin W. and Robert L. Ellison. "Searching for Student Talent Resources Relevant to All—United States Department of Education Types of Giftedness" *Gifted Child Quarterly*, Summer, 1983, 99–105.

Torrance, E. Paul. *Rewarding Creative Behavior: Experiments in Classroom Creativity* (Englewood Cliffs, N.J.: Prentice-Hall, 1965).

Wallach, Michael A. "Psychology of Talent and Graduate Education," in Samuel Messick and Associates (Ed.). *Individuality in Learning* (San Francisco: Jossey-Bass, 1979), 178–220.

Wilkes, John M. and Others. "The Hacker Challenge: Artistry, Addiction or Subversion?" a paper presented to the Eastern Sociological Association Annual Meeting, Boston, Massachusetts, 1984.

Willingham, Warren W. and Hunter M. Breland. *Personal Qualities and College Admissions* (New York: College Entrance Examination Board, 1982).

Wilson, K. *A Review of Research on the Prediction of Academic Performance After the Freshman Year* (Princeton, NJ: Educational Testing Service, 1983).

Zak, Paula M. and Others. "Several Factors Associated With Success As An Undergraduate Chemistry Major" *College and University*, Spring 1983, 303–312.

Zmolek, Jean. "Correlation Between Creativity and Academic Success in Student Groups from South High School and the University of Utah," unpublished MS, Department of Psychology, University of Utah, December 1984.

243

Zuckerman, Harriet. *Scientific Elite: Nobel Laureates in the United States* (New York: The Free Press, 1977).

ECONOMY

Baily, Martin. *Workers, Jobs, and Inflation* (Washington, D.C.: The Brookings Institution, 1983).

Baldwin, Robert and Anne Krueger (Eds.). *The Structure and Evolution of Recent U.S. Trade Policy* (Chicago: The University of Chicago Press, 1984).

Bell, Daniel. *The Coming of Post-Industrial Society* (New York: Basic Books, 1976).

Bergsten, C. Fred. "What to Do About the U.S.-Japan Economic Problem" *Foreign Affairs*, Summer 1982.

Birch, David. "Who Creates Jobs?" *The Public Interest*, Fall 1981, 3–13.

Bluestone, Barry and Bennett Harrison. *The Deindustrialization of America* (New York: Basic Books, 1982).

Botkin, James, Dan Dimencescu, and Ray Stata. *Global Stakes: The Future of High Technology in America* (Cambridge, MA: Ballinger Publishing Company, 1982).

Business-Higher Education Forum. *America's Competitive Challenge: The Need for a National Response* (Washington, D.C.: Business-Higher Education Forum, April 1983).

Calder, Kent and Ray Hofheinz, Jr. *The Eastasian Edge* (New York: Basic Books, 1982).

Choat, Pat. *Retooling the American Work Force: Toward a National Training Strategy* (Washington, D.C.: Northeast-Midwest Institute, July 1982).

Committee on Science and Technology and the Committee on the Budget. United States House of Representatives. 98th Congress. First Session. *Joint Hearings on Technology and Employment*, June 1983.

Congressional Budget Office. United States Congress. *Dislocated Workers: Issues and Federal Options*, Washington, D.C., July 1982.

Duchin, Faye and Wassily Leontief. *The Future Impact of Automation on Workers* (New York: Oxford University Press, 1985, forthcoming).

Galbraith, John Kenneth. *The New Industrial State* (New York: New American Library, 1968).

Ginzberg, Eli. "The Mechanization of Work" *Scientific American*, September 1982, 67–75.

Gordus, Jeanne Prial and Others. *Plant Closing and Economic Dislocations* (Kalamazoo, MI: W. E. Upjohn Institute for Employment Research, 1981).

Hansen, John A. and Robert T. Lund. *Connected Machines, Disconnected Jobs: Technology and Work in the Next Decade.* (Cambridge, MA: Center for Policy Alternatives, Massachusetts Institute of Technology, April 1983).

International Monetary Fund. *World Economic Outlook* (Washington, D.C.: International Monetary Fund, 1983 and 1984).

Kuttner, Bob. "The Declining Middle" *The Atlantic Monthly*, July 1982, 60–72.

Laurence, Robert. *Can America Compete?* (Washington, D.C.: The Brookings Institution, 1984).

Magaziner, Ira and Robert Reich. *Minding America's Business* (New York: Vintage Books, 1982).

Mansfield, Edwin. "International Technology and Trade Flows" *Indicators of International Technology and Trade Flows*, vol. 1 (Washington, D.C.: National Science Foundation, 1982).

Office of Technology Assessment. United States Congress. *Automation and the Workplace: Selected Labor, Education, and Training Issues*, Washington, D.C., March 1983.

Organization for Economic Cooperation and Development. *Economic Outlook*, semiannual (Paris: Organization for Economic Cooperation and Development, 1984).

Personick, Valerie. "The Job Outlook Through 1995: Industry Output and Employment Projections" *Monthly Labor Review*, November 1983, 24–36.

Rumberger, Russell W. *Overeducation in the U.S. Labor Market* (New York: Praeger, 1981).

Russell, Louise. *The Baby Boom Generation and the Economy* (Washington, D.C.: The Brookings Institution, 1982).

Schultze, Charles. *Industrial Policy: A Debate* (Washington, D.C.: The Brookings Institution, 1982).

United States Bureau of the Census. *Projections of the Population of the United States: 1977 to 2050*, Current Population Reports Series, Washington, D.C., June 1977, 25, 710, 704.   •

————. *Projections of the Population of the United States: 1982 to 2050* (Advance Report), Current Population Reports Series, No. 922, Washington, D.C., October 1982, 25.

World Bank. *World Development Report* (Washington, D.C.: World Bank, 1984).

Yankelovich, Daniel and Others. *Work and Human Values: An International Report on Jobs in the 1980s and 1990s* (New York: Aspen Institute for Humanistic Studies, 1983).

Zysman, John and Laura Tyson (Eds.). *American Industry in International Competition* (Ithaca, NY: Cornell University Press, 1983).

American Council on Education. *What We Don't Know Can Hurt Us*. (Washington, D.C.: American Council on Education, 1984).

Association of American Colleges. "Internationalizing the Curriculum" *The Forum for Liberal Education*, March 1984, 3–6.

Backman, Earl L. (Ed.). *Approaches to International Education* (New York: American Council on Education and the Macmillan Publishing Company, 1984).

Barrows, Thomas S. *College Students' Knowledge and Beliefs: A Survey of Global Understanding*, Final Report of the Global Understanding Project (Princeton, NJ: Educational Testing Service, 1981).

Burn, Barbara B. *Expanding the International Dimension of Higher Education* (San Francisco: Jossey-Bass, 1980).

―――. "Research in Progress: Does Study Abroad Make a Difference?" *Change*, March/April 1985, 48–49.

Change. "Special Issue: Educating for the World View," May–June 1980.

Collinan, Terrence. "Attitudes of Returning Peace Corps Volunteers Concerning Impact of Peace Corps Interlude on Subsequent Academic Work," Report No. 4 (Menlo Park, CA: Interlude Research Program, December 1969).

Consortium of Social Science Associations and Others. *Education and Economic Competitiveness Abroad*, papers presented at a congressional seminar on July 19, 1983 (Washington, D.C.: Consortium of Social Science Associations, 1983).

Council for International Exchange of Scholars. "The Fulbright American Scholar Program: How It Compares with Other Grant Programs," n.d.

Council on Learning. *Education for a Global Century: Hardbook of Exemplary International Programs*, Volume III of *Education and the World View* (New Rochelle, NY: Change Magazine Press, 1981).

Forum for Liberal Education. "Programs for Intercultural Understanding," January 1979.

Groennings, Sven. "The American Democracy in the Global Community: The Second Triad," ITT Key Issue Lecture Series, Fiftieth Anniversary of The College of Public and International Affairs, The American University, March 2, 1984.

McCaughey, Robert A. *International Studies and Academic Enterprise* (New York: Columbia University Press, 1984).

Nash, Dennison. "The Personal Consequences of a Year of Study Abroad" *Journal of Higher Education*, March/April 1976, 191–203.

National Advisory Board on International Education Programs. *Critical Needs in Inter-*

national Education: Recommendations for Action, A Report to the Secretary of Education, Washington, D.C., December 1983.

Pyle, Cassandra. "Our Shortfall in International Competence" *AGB Reports*, March/April 1984.

Simon, Paul. *The Tongue-Tied American: Confronting the Foreign Language Crisis* (New York: Continuum, 1980).

Smith, Ester Gottlieb and Others. *The Impact of Peace Corps and VISTA Service on Former Volunteers and American Society*, Draft Final Report prepared for ACTION (Belmont, MA: CRC Education and Human Development, Inc., 1978).

Starr, Jerold Martin. *Cross-Cultural Encounter and Personality Change: Peace Corps Volunteers in the Philippines*, Ph.D. dissertation, Brandeis University, 1970.

Winslow, E. A. *A Survey of Returned Peace Corps Volunteers as of January 1977* (Washington, D.C.: Office of Special Services, Action/Peace Corps, 1978).

MINORITIES

American Council on Education. Forum of Educational Organization Leaders, Institute for Education Leadership. *Demographic Imperatives: Implications For Educational Policy*, Report of the June 8, 1983 Forum on The Demographics of Changing Ethnic Populations and their Implications for Elementary, Secondary and Postsecondary Educational Policy. n.p., n.d.

————. *Minorities in Higher Education*, Second Annual Status Report of the Office of Minority Concerns for the American Council on Education. ACE Annual Meeting, Toronto, Canada, October 1983.

Association of American Medical Colleges. Office of Minority Affairs. *Minority Students in Medical Education: Facts and Figures II* (Washington, D.C.: Association of American Medical Colleges, March 1985).

Astin, Alexander W. *The College Environment* (Washington, D.C.: American Council on Education, 1968).

————. *Minorities in American Higher Education* (San Francisco: Jossey-Bass, 1982).

Blackwell, James A. *Mainstreaming Outsiders: The Production of Black Professionals* (Bayside, NY: General Hall, 1981).

Bouvier, Leon F. and Cary B. Dairs. *The Future Racial Composition of the United States* (Washington, D.C.: Demographic Information Services Center of the Population Reference Bureau, 1982).

Brown, George H., Nan L. Rosen, Susan T. Hill, and Michael A. Olivas. *The Condition of Education for Hispanic Americans* (Washington, D.C.: National Center for Education Statistics, May 1980, revised July 1980).

De los Santos, Alfredo G. and Others. "Chicano Students in Institutions of Higher Education: Access, Attrition, and Achievement" *Aztlan-International Journal of Chicano Studies Research*, 1983, 79–110.

Franklin, Paul L. *Helping Disadvantaged Youth and Adults Enter College: An Assessment of Two Federal Programs* (Washington, D.C.: College Board, 1985).

Green, Kenneth C. *Government Support for Minority Participation in Higher Education*, AAHE/ERIC Research Report (Washington, D.C.: American Association for Higher Education, 1984).

Hines, Judith A. *Hispanic Participation in Higher Education: A Focus on Chicanos and Other Hispanics in California*, a study for the James Irving Foundation (Princeton, NJ: The Woodrow Wilson National Fellowship Foundation, June 1982).

Hodgkinson, Harold. *Guess Who's Coming To College? Your Students in 1990*, a research report from the State-National Information Network for Independent Higher Education (Washington, D.C.: National Institute of Independent Colleges and Universities, January 1983).

Kent, Laura. *Puerto Ricans in U.S. Higher Education: Current Status and Recent Progress* (Los Angeles: Higher Education Research Institute, 1982).

Landis, Raymond, Enrique Ainsworth, Don Dorsey, and Mercilee Jenkins. "Training Faculty to be Effective Advisors, Mentors, and Counselors of Ethnic Students," Dissemination Document for Faculty Advisors for Minority Students (FAMES) Program, California State University, Northridge 1980–83. Funded by California State University Chancellor's Office, Academic Program Improvement.

Massey, Douglas S. *The Demographic and Economic Position of Hispanics in the United States: 1980*, Report to the National Commission for Economic Policy, Washington, D.C., March 1982.

——. *Patterns and Effects of Hispanic Immigration to the United States*, Report to the National Commission for Employment Policy, Washington, D.C., March 1982.

McNary, Dave. "Hats Off to Cal State/Northridge" *Minority Engineer*, Winter 1982/83, 35–37, 69–70.

Nettles, Michael T., A. Robert Thoeny, Erica J. Gosman, and Betty A. Dandridge. *The Causes and Consequences of College Students' Performance: A Focus on Black and White Students' Attrition Rates, Progression Rates, and Grade Point Averages*, Draft (Nashville, TN: Higher Education Commission, April 17, 1984).

Olivas, Michael A. *The Dilemma of Access: Minorities in Two-Year Colleges* (Washington, D.C.: Institute for the Study of Educational Policy, Howard University, 1979).

248

Population Reference Bureau. "Fastest Growing Minority: Hispanics in the United States" *Interchange: Population Education Newsletter*, October 1983.

Tinto, V. and R. H. Sherman. *The Effectiveness of Secondary and Higher Education Intervention Programs: A Critical Review of the Literature* (New York: Teachers College, Columbia University, 1974).

Williams, Melanie Reeves and Laura Kent. *Blacks in Higher Education: Access, Choice, and Attainment* (Los Angeles: Higher Education Research Institute, 1982).

RESEARCH AND TECHNOLOGY

Abernathy, William and James Utterback. "Patterns of Industrial Innovation" *Technology Review*, June/July 1978, 41–47.

Achilladelis, B., P. Jervis, and A. Robertson. *Project SAPPHO: A Study of Success and Failure in Industrial Innovations* (Brighton, England: Science Policy Research Unit, University of Sussex, 1971).

American Assembly. *Final Report of the Sixty-Fifth American Assembly on Improving American Innovation* (New York: American Assembly, November 17–20, 1983).

Association of American Universities. *The Nation's Deteriorating University Research Facilities* (Washington, D.C.: Association of American Universities, July 1981).

————. *The Scientific Instrumentation Needs of Research Universities*, Report to the National Science Foundation (Washington, D.C.: Association of American Universities, June 1980).

Baer, Walker S. *Strengthening University-Industry Interactions* (Santa Monica: The RAND Corporation, January 1980).

Bagwall, Roger. *Report from the Subcommittee on User Needs*, Report to the Presidential Task Force on Information Processing (New York: Columbia University, October 28, 1983).

Battin, Patricia. "The Library: Center of the Reconstructed University" *Colleges Enter the Information Society*, Current Issues in Higher Education, no. 1 (Washington, D.C.: American Association for Higher Education, 1983–84), 25–31.

Branscomb, Lewis M. "Opportunities for Cooperation Between Government, Industry, and the University" *Annals of the New York Academy of Sciences*, December 14, 1979, 211–227.

Bush, Vanevar. *Science: The Endless Frontier* (Washington, D.C.: Government Printing Office, 1945).

Butler, Meredith. "Electronic Publishing and Its Impact on Libraries: A Literature Review" *Library Resources and Technical Services*, January/March 1984, 41–58.

249

Commission on Human Resources. *Research Excellence Through the Year 2000: The Importance of Maintaining a Flow of New Faculty into Academic Research* (Washington, D.C.: National Academy of Science, National Research Council, 1979).

Committee for Economic Development. *Stimulating Technological Progress* (New York: Committee for Economic Development, 1980).

Congressional Budget Office. United States Congress. *Federal Support for R & D and Innovation*, Washington, D.C., April 1984.

Department of Commerce. President's Private Sector Survey on Cost Control. *Task Force Report on Research and Development* (Washington, D.C.: United States Department of Commerce, December 8, 1983).

Eveland, J. D. and William Hetzner (Eds.). *Development of University/Industry Cooperative Research Centers: Historical Profiles* (Washington, D.C.: National Science Foundation, May 1982).

Fakstorp, Jorgen and G. M. Idorn. "University-Industry Relations in Europe" *Research Management*, July 1978, 34–37.

Gilpin, Robert. *Technology, Economic Growth, and International Competitiveness*. A report to the Subcommittee on Economic Growth of the Joint Economic Committee, Congress of the United States. Washington, D.C., 1975.

Hayes, Robert M. (Ed.). *Universities Information Technology, and Academic Libraries: The Next Twenty Years*, Report of the Academic Libraries Conference, University of California, Los Angeles, Lake Arrowhead Conference Center, December 13–17, 1981.

Lancaster, Frederick W. "The Evolving Paperless Society and Its Implications for Libraries" *International Forum on Information and Documentation*, October 1982, 3–10.

Langfitt, Thomas, Sheldon Hackney and Others. (Eds.). *Partners in the Research Enterprise: University-Corporate Relations in Science and Technology* (Philadelphia: The University of Pennsylvania Press, 1983).

McCulloch, Rachel. "International Indicators of Science and Technology: How does the U.S. Compare?" *Scientometrics*, 1980, 355–367.

Mensh, Gerhard. *Stalemate in Technology: Innovations Overcame the Depression* (Cambridge, MA: Ballinger Publishing, 1979).

Mogee, Mary Ellen. "The Relationship of Federal Support of Basic Research in Universities to Industrial Innovation and Productivity" in Joint Economic Committee of the United States. *Special Study on Economic Change: Research and Innovation*, December 29, 1980, vol. 3, 257–279.

Morgan, Robert P. and Others. *Science and Technology for Development—The Role of U.S. Universities* (New York: Pergamon Press, 1979).

Morton, Herbert C. *Scholarly Communication and Technology: A Proposal*, Revised version (New York: American Council of Learned Societies, August 1983).

National Commission on Research. *Funding Mechanisms: Balancing Objectives and Resources in University Research*, Washington, D.C., May 1980.

————. *Industry and the Universities: Developing Cooperative Research Relationships in the National Interest*, Washington, D.C., August 1980.

National Enquiry into Scholarly Communication. *Scholarly Communication* (Baltimore: Johns Hopkins University Press, 1979).

National Governors' Association. *Technology and Growth: State Initiatives in Technological Innovation*, Final Report, Washington, D.C., 1984.

National Research Council. *International Competition in Advanced Technology: Decisions for America* (Washington, D.C.: National Academy Press, 1983).

————. *Outlook for Science and Technology: The Next Five Years* (San Francisco: W. H. Freeman, 1982).

National Science Board. *Science Indicators 1982: An Analysis of the State of U.S. Science, Engineering, and Technology* (Washington, D.C.: National Science Foundation, 1983).

————. *University/Industry Relations: Myths, Realities, and Potentials* (Washington, D.C.: National Science Foundation, 1983).

————. *University/Industry Research Relationships* (Washington, D.C.: National Science Foundation, 1982).

National Science Foundation. *Academic Research Equipment in the Physical and Computer Sciences and Engineering*, Universities and Nonprofit Institutions Studies Group, Division of Science Resources Studies, Washington, D.C., December 1984.

Norman, Colin. *The God That Limps: Science and Technology in the Eighties* (New York: N. W. Norton, 1981).

Office of Technology Assessment. Congress of the United States. *Commercial Biotechnology: An International Analysis* (Washington, D.C., January 1984).

Roberts, Edward and Donald Peterson. "Commercial Innovation from University Faculty" *Research Policy*, April 1981, 109–125.

Rosenzweig, Robert M. and Barbara Turlington. *The Research Universities and Their Patrons* (Berkeley, CA: The University of California Press, 1982).

Sahal, Devendra. *The Transfer and Utilization of Technical Knowledge* (Lexington, MA: Lexington Books, 1982).

Shapero, Albert. "University-Industry Interactions: Recurring Expectations, Unwarranted Assumptions and Feasible Policies" (Ohio: Ohio University Working Paper Series 79–85, October 1979).

251

Smith, Bruce L. and Joseph L. Karlesky. *The State of Academic Science: The Universities in the Nation's Research Effort* (New Rochelle, NY: Change Magazine Press, 1977).

Terleckyj, Nester E. (Ed.). *The State of Science and Research: Some New Indicators* (Boulder, CO: Westview Press, 1977).

United Nations, Department of Social Affairs. *The Role of Patents in the Transfer of Technology to Developing Countries* (New York: United Nations, Department of Economic and Social Affairs, 1964).

United States General Accounting Office. *The Federal Role in Fostering University-Industry Cooperation*, Washington, D.C., 1983.

United States House of Representatives. Committee on Science and Technology. *Summary and Analysis of Hearing on "Improving the Research Infrastructure at U.S. Universities and Colleges,"* Washington, D.C., July 1984.

———. Committee on Science and Technology, Subcommittee on Science, Research and Technology. *Hearings on Government and Innovation: University-Industry Relations*, Washington, D.C., 1979.

———. House Republican Research Committee. Task Force on High Technology Initiatives. *Targeting the Process of Innovation*, Washington, D.C., May 1984.

Wilson, John T. *Academic Science, Higher Education, and the Federal Government, 1950–1983* (Chicago: The University of Chicago Press, 1983).

STUDENT AID

Ahart, Gregory J. *The National Student Loan Program Requires More Attention by the Office of Education and Participating Institutions* (Washington, D.C.: General Accounting Office, June 1977).

Aleamoni, Lawrence M. and John Bowers. "The Evaluation of a Special Educational Opportunities Program for Disadvantaged College Students" *Research in Higher Education*, 1974, 151–164.

American Council on Education. "Policy Brief: Rates of College Participation 1969, 1974, and 1981" (Washington, D.C.: American Council on Education, April 1984).

———. "Who Gets Student Aid: A 1983–84 Snapshot," Summary of a Policy Seminar held July 19, 1984, Washington, D.C.

Applied Systems Institute. *Work Patterns of Full-Time College Students in 1974 and 1981*, prepared for National Commission on Student Financial Assistance (Washington, D.C.: Applied Systems Institute, May 5, 1983).

Astin, Alexander W. *Financial Aid and Student Persistence* (Los Angeles: Higher Education Research Institute, 1975).

252

————. *Preventing Students from Dropping Out* (San Francisco: Jossey-Bass, 1975).

Astin, Alexander W., James Henson, and C. E. Christian. *The Impact of Student Financial Aid Programs on Student Choice* (Los Angeles: Higher Education Research Institute, 1975).

Beal, Philip E. and Lee Noel. *What Works in Student Retention* (Boulder, CO: National Center for Higher Education Management Systems and the American College Testing Program, 1980).

Bean, John P. "Student Attrition, Intentions and Confidence: Interaction Effects in a Path Model" *Research in Higher Education*, 1982, 291–320.

Bella, Surjit K. and Mary E. Huba. "Student Part-time Jobs: the Relationship between Type of Job and Academic Performance" *Journal of Student Financial Aid*, November 1982, 22–27.

Berger, M. Betsy and Donald D. Zielke. "Educational Progress of Basic Educational Opportunity Grant Recipients Compared to Non-Recipients" *The Journal of Student Financial Aid*, February 1979, 19–22.

Bohn, Martin J., Jr. "Personality Variables in Successful Work-Study Performance" *Journal of College Student Personnel*, 1973, 135–140.

Brugel, J. F., G. P. Johnson, and L. L. Leslie. "The Demand for Student Loans in Higher Education: A Study of Preferences and Attitudes" *Research in Higher Education*, 1977, 65–83.

Burkheimer, Graham J., Jr. and Others. *Evaluation Study of the Upward Bound Program: A Second Follow-up, Final Report* (Durham, NC: Center for Educational Research and Evaluation, Research Triangle Institute, November 1979).

Carlson, Daryl E. *Student Access to Postsecondary Education: Comparative Analysis of Federal and State Student Aid Programs* (Washington, D.C.: Office of Education, Department of Health, Education, and Welfare, May 27, 1980).

Chapman, Randall G. and Rex Jackson. "The Influence of No-Need Financial Aid Awards on the College Choices of High-Ability Students: A Summary of Main Findings," MS, prepared for the College Board, October 1984.

Crawford, Norman C., Jr. *Effects of Offers of Financial Assistance on the College-Going Decisions of Talented Students With Limited Financial Means*, Reports, vol. 3, no. 5 (Evanston, IL: National Merit Scholarship Corporation, 1967).

Credit Research Center. *The Role of Educational Debt in Consumer's Total Debt Structure* (Lafayette, IN: Credit Research Center, Purdue University, January 31, 1983).

Cummings, Donald Lloyd. *Army ROTC: A Study of the Army's Primary Officer Procurement Program, 1962–1977*, unpublished Ph.D. dissertation, Department of Political Science, The University of California, Santa Barbara, 1982.

253

Davis, J. and Others. *The Impact of Special Services Programs in Higher Education for Disadvantaged Students* (Princeton, NJ: Educational Testing Service, 1975).

Davis, Jerry S. "Brief Descriptions of State-Supported College Work-Study Aid Programs," A Report Based on the Results of the 1984–85 Surveys of the National Association of State Scholarship and Grant Programs (Harrisburg, PA: Pennsylvania Higher Education Assistance Agency, November 1984).

Davis, Jerry S. and Kingston Johns, Jr. "Low Family Income: A Continuing Barrier to College Enrollment?" *The Journal of Student Financial Aid*, February 1982, 5–10.

Fenske, Robert H. and J. P. Boyd, "The Impact of State Financial Aid to Students on Choice of Public or Private College" *College and University*, Winter 1971, 98–607.

Fenske, Robert H., Robert P. Huff and Associates (Eds.). *Handbook of Student Financial Aid* (San Francisco: Jossey-Bass, 1983).

Fields, Charles R. and Morris L. LeMay. "Student Financial Aid: Effects on Educational Decisions and Academic Achievement" *Journal of College Student Personnel*, September 1973, 425–429.

Fife, Jonathan D. and Larry L. Leslie. "The College Student Grant Study: The Effectiveness of Student Grant and Scholarship Programs in Promoting Equal Educational Opportunity" *Research in Higher Education*, 1976, 317–333.

Flaner, H. J., P. H. Horch, and S. Davis. *Talented and Needy Graduate and Professional Students: A National Survey of People Who Applied for Need-Based Financial Aid to Attend Graduate and Professional Schools in 1980–81* (Princeton, NJ: Educational Testing Service, April 1982).

Frances, Carol. *Basic Facts on College-Going Rates by Income, Race, Sex, and Age, 1970 to 1980* (Washington, D.C.: National Commission on Student Financial Assistance, October 22, 1982).

Frederiksen, Norman and W. B. Schrader. *Adjustment to College: A Study of 10,000 Veteran and Nonveteran Students in Sixteen American Colleges* (Princeton, N.J.: Educational Testing Service, 1951).

Fuller, W. C., C. F. Manski, and D. A. Wise *The Impact of the Basic Educational Opportunity Grant Program on College Enrollments*, Number 94D (Cambridge, MA: John F. Kennedy School of Government, Harvard University, July 1980).

Fuller, William S. "Student Financial Aid—A Phase-in Approach" *AGB Reports*, May/June 1984, 39–40.

Gillespie, Donald A. and Nancy Carlson. *Trends in Student Aid: 1963 to 1983* (Washington, D.C.: College Board, December 1983).

Gladieux, Lawrence E. "The Future of Student Financial Aid" *The College Board Review*, Winter, 1982–83, 2–12.

254

Grass, Emily and Arthur Hauptman. *Closing the Information Gap: Ways to Improve Student Awareness of Financial Aid Opportunities,* A Report to the National Student Aid Coalition, Washington, D.C., April 1984.

Hammes, Judith F. and Emil J. Haller. "Making Ends Meet: Some of the Consequences of Part-time Work for College Students" *Journal of College Student Personnel,* 1983, 529–535.

Hansen, Janet S. "Creative Financing for Education Loans" *Change,* January/February 1983, 28–34.

———. *The State Student Incentive Grant Program* (Washington, D.C.: College Entrance Examination Board, November 1979).

Hartle, Terry W. and Richard Wabnick. "Discretionary Income and College Costs" (Washington, D.C.: National Commission on Student Financial Assistance, August 6, 1982).

———. *The Educational Indebtedness of Graduate and Professional Students* (Princeton, NJ: Educational Testing Service, July 1983).

Hesseldent, Jon and David Stockham. "National Direct Student Loan Defaulters: The Ability to Repay" *Research in Higher Education,* 1982, 3–14.

Higgins, A. Stephen. "Student Financial Aid and Equal Opportunity in Higher Education" *College and University,* Summer 1983, 349–361.

Hilton, T. *Persistence in Higher Education* (Washington, D.C.: The College Board, 1982).

Hirshorn, M. A. *Study of the Relationship of Types and Amounts of Work, Academic Achievement and Persistence of Students in College and University Work-Study Programs,* unpublished dissertation, University of Connecticut, 1975.

Hochstein, Susan K. and Robert R. Butler. "The Effects of the Composition of a Financial Aid Package on Student Retention" *Journal of Student Financial Aid,* February 1983, 21–26.

Horch, Dwight. *Estimating Manageable Educational Loan Limits for Graduates and Professional Students* (Princeton, NJ: Educational Testing Service, 1978).

Iwai, Stanley I. and William D. Churchill. "College Attrition and the Financial Support Systems of Students" *Research in Higher Education,* 1982, 105–113.

Jackson, Gregory A. "Financial Aid and Student Enrollment" *Journal of Higher Education,* 1978, 548–574.

———. "How Students Pay for College: Temporal and Individual Variation" *Higher Education,* 1980, 619–632.

Jackson, Rex and Randall G. Chapman. *The Influence of No-Need Financial Aid Awards on the College Choices of High Ability Students* (Washington, D.C.: The College Board, October 1984).

Jensen, Eric L. "Financial Aid and Educational Outcomes: A Review" *College and University*, Spring 1983, 287–302.

———. "Student Financial Aid and Persistence in College" *Journal of Higher Education*, 1981, 280–294.

Kohen, Andrew I. and Others. "Factors Affecting Individual Persistence Rates in Undergraduate College Programs" *American Educational Research Journal*, Spring 1978, 233–252.

Lee, John. "Changing Characteristics of Student Aid Recipients, 1969, 1974, 1981," prepared for National Commission on Student Financial Assistance (Washington, D.C.: Applied Systems Institute, Inc., March 9, 1983).

Lee, John and Others. *Changes in College Participation Rates and Student Financial Assistance, 1969, 1974, 1981*, prepared for National Commission on Student Financial Assistance (Washington, D.C.: Applied Systems Institute, Inc., January 28, 1983).

Leslie, Larry L. *Higher Education Opportunity: A Decade of Progress*, ERIC/Higher Education Research Report No. 3 (Washington, D.C.: American Association for Higher Education, 1977).

Leslie, Larry L., G. P. Johnson, and J. Carlson. "The Impact of Need-Based Student Aid Upon the College Attendance Decision" *Journal of Education Finance*, Winter 1977, 269–285.

Manski, Charles F. and David A. Wise. *College Choice in America* (Cambridge, MA: Harvard University Press, 1983).

McCreight, Keith and Morris Lemay. "A Longitudinal Study of the Achievement and Persistence of Students Who Receive Basic Educational Opportunity Grants" *Journal of Student Financial Aid*, February 1980, 11–15.

Melia, Patricia K. *The Effects of Financial Aid on Student Access, Choice, Persistence, and Satisfactory Progress, An Annotated Bibliography* (Washington, D.C.: American Council on Education, May 1983).

Merritt, R. "Academic Performance of Work-Study Students" *Journal of College Student Personnel*, 1970, 173–176.

National Commission on Student Financial Assistance. *Guaranteed Student Loans: A Background Paper, Report No. 1* (Washington, D.C.: National Commission on Student Financial Assistance, March 1982).

National Student Aid Coalition. *Student Aid: Four Suggestions for Improvement*, Washington, D.C., October 1983.

Nichols, Edward E. "Financial Aid Awards-Predictors of GPAs" *Journal of Student Financial Aid*, November 1980, 33–43.

Ostberg, Kenneth R. "An Examination of the Relationships Between Various Methods

256

of Financing College Costs and Academic Achievement" *Journal of Student Financial Aid*, November 1982, 7–15.

Pantages, Timothy J. and Carol F. Creedon. "Studies of College Attrition: 1950–1975" *Review of Educational Research*, Winter 1978, 49–191.

Pascarella, Ernest T. and Patrick T. Terenzini. "Interaction Effects in Spady's and Tinto's Conceptual Models of College Persistence" *Sociology of Education*, October 1979, 197–210.

————. "Predicting Freshman Persistence and Voluntary Dropout Decisions From a Theoretical Model" *Journal of Higher Education*, 1980, 60–75.

Peng, Samuel S. and William B. Fetters. "Variables Involved in Withdrawal During the First Two Years of College: Preliminary Findings From the National Longitudinal Study of the High School Class of 1972" *American Educational Research Journal*, Summer 1978, 361–372.

Pyecha, J. N. and Others. "A Study of the National Upward Bound and Talent Search Programs," Final Report, Vol. III, *Descriptive Study of the Talent Search Program* (Durham, NC: Center for Educational Research and Evaluation, Research Triangle Institute, December 1975).

Ramist, Leonard. *College Student Attrition and Retention*, Research Report (Princeton, NJ: Educational Testing Service, 1984).

Riccobono, John A. and George H. Danteman. *National Longitudinal Study of the High School Class of 1972: Preliminary Analysis of Student Financial Aid* (Durham, N.C.: Center for Educational Research and Evaluation, 1975).

Rice, Lois D. (Ed.). *Student Loans: Problems and Policy Alternatives* (New York: College Entrance Examination Board, 1977).

Roper Organization, Inc. *A National Study on Parental Savings for Children's Higher Education Expenses* (Washington, D.C.: National Institute of Independent Colleges and Universities, January 1984).

Rosen, David Paul. *The Effects of Phasing Out Social Security Student Benefits* (Oakland, CA: David Paul Rosen and Associates, March 1983).

Rouche, John E. and J. R. Snow. *Overcoming Learning Problems* (San Francisco: Jossey-Bass, 1977).

Sanford, Timothy R. "The Effects of Student Aid on Recent College Graduates" *Research in Higher Education*, 1980, 227–243.

————. "Residual Effects of Self-Help Aid on the Lives of College Graduates" *Journal of Student Financial Aid*, November 1979, 3–6.

Smith, Pat and Cathy Henderson. "Federal Student Aid: Who Receives it and How is it Packaged?" (Washington, D.C.: American Council on Education, 1977).

257

Spies, Richard R. *The Effect of Rising Costs on College Choice* (New York: College Entrance Examination Board, 1978).

Stampen, Jacob O. *Student Aid and Public Higher Education: A Progress Report* (Washington, D.C.: American Association of State Colleges and Universities, January 1983).

Stedman, James. *The Experience with Loan Forgiveness and Service Pay Back on Federal and State Student Aid Programs* (Washington D.C.: Congressional Research Service, January 1983).

Stephenson, Stanley P., Jr. "Work in College and Subsequent Wage Rates" *Research in Higher Education*, 1982, 165–178.

Terenzini, Patrick T. and Ernest T. Pascarella. "Toward the Validation of Tinto's Model of College Student Attrition: A Review of Recent Studies" *Research in Higher Education*, 1980, 271–282.

Terkla, Dawn Geronimo. *Financial Aid and Undergraduate Persistence*, unpublished dissertation, Harvard University, 1983.

Terkla, Dawn Geronimo and Gregory A. Jackson. *The State of the Art in Student Choice Research* (Cambridge, MA: Harvard University, January 1984).

Tierney, Michael L. "The Impact of Financial Aid on Student Demand for Public/Private Higher Education" *Journal of Higher Education*, 1980, 527–545.

Tinto, Vincent. "Dropout From Higher Education: A Theoretical Synthesis of Recent Research" *Review of Educational Research*, Winter 1975, 89–125.

Touche Ross and Company. *Study of the Cost and Flows of Capital in the Guaranteed Student Loan Program*, Final Report, prepared for the National Commission on Student Financial Assistance (Washington, D.C.: Touche Ross and Company, March 1983).

———. *Study of the Cost to Borrowers of Participating in the Guaranteed Student Loan Program*, Final Report (Washington, D.C.: National Commission on Student Financial Assistance, March 1983).

United States General Accounting Office. *Students Receiving Federal Aid are Not Making Satisfactory Academic Progress: Tougher Standards are Needed*, Report to the Chairman, Committee on Labor and Human Resources, United States Senate. Washington, D.C., December 3, 1981.

Wabnick, Richard. *Indebtedness to Finance Postsecondary Education* (Washington, D.C.: Education Policy Research Institute, October 1981).

Wagner, Alan P. and Nancy Carlson. *Financial Aid for Self-Supporting Students: Defining Independents* (Washington, D.C.: College Entrance Examination Board, April 1983).

Weinschrott, David. *Demand for Higher Education in the United States: A Critical Review of the Empirical Literature* (Santa Monica, CA: The RAND Corporation, December 1977).

258

Wenc, Leonard M. "The Role of Financial Aid in Attrition and Retention" *The College Board Review*, Summer 1977, 17–21.

TECHNICAL MANPOWER

Ailes, Catherine P. and Francis W. Rushing. *The Science Race: Training and Utilization of Scientists and Engineers, U.S. and USSR* (New York: Crane Russak and Company, 1982).

American Association of Engineering Societies, American Association of Mechanical Engineers, and American Society for Engineering Education. "Data Related to the Crisis in Engineering Education," prepared by a Task Force, Robert H. Page, Chairman (Washington, D.C.; AAES, March 1981).

American Association of Engineering Societies and American Society for Engineering Education. *Catalogue of Industrial Programs to Aid Graduate Engineering Education*, by Project on Engineering College Faculty Shortage, John W. Geils, Executive (Washington, D.C.: AAES, May 15, 1983).

————. *Catalogue of Professional Society Programs to Aid Graduate Engineering Education*, by Project on Engineering College Faculty Shortage, John W. Geils, Executive (Washington, D.C.: AAES, June, 1983).

————. *Catalogue of State Initiatives*, by Project on Engineering College Faculty Shortage, John W. Geils, Executive (Washington, D.C.: AAES, October 22, 1982).

————. *Engineering College Faculty Shortage Project*, Final Report (Washington, D.C.: AAES, November 1983).

————. *A Working Plan for Treating the Engineering Faculty Shortage Problem*, prepared by a Special Task Force (New York: AAES, May 1983).

American Electronics Associations. *Technical Employment Projections of Professionals and Paraprofessionals 1983–1987* (Palo Alto, CA: American Electronics Association, 1983).

Atelsek, Frank J. *Student Quality in the Sciences and Engineering: Opinions of Senior Academic Officials*, Higher Education Panel Reports Number 58 (Washington, D.C.: American Council on Education, February 1984).

Babco, Eleanor L. *Salaries of Scientists, Engineers, and Technicians: A Summary of Salary Surveys, Eleventh Edition* (Washington, D.C.: Scientific Manpower Commission, November 1983).

Berryman, Sue E. *Who Will Do Science? Minority and Female Attainment of Science and Mathematics Degrees: Trends and Causes*, A Special Report (New York: The Rockefeller Foundation, November 1983).

Blanpied, William A. "Recent Trends in the Education of Scientists and Engineers" in *National Science Foundation Annual Science and Technology Report to the Congress* (Washington, D.C.: National Science Foundation, 1981), 88–95.

Committee on the Quality of Engineering Education. *Report on the Quality of Engineering Education* (Washington, D.C.: National Association of State Universities and Land-Grant Colleges, November 7, 1982).

Engineering Manpower Commission. *Engineering and Technology Degrees* (Washington, D.C.: Engineering Manpower Commission, 1984).

National Association of State Universities and Land-Grant Colleges. *The Quality of Engineering Education*, A Report by the Committee on the Quality of Engineering Education, Commission on Education for the Engineering Profession (Washington, D.C.: National Association of State Universities and Land-Grant Colleges, November 7, 1982).

National Science Foundation. *Projected Response of the Science, Engineering, and Technical Labor Market to Defense and Nondefense Needs: 1982–1987 Special Report*, Washington, D.C., January 1984.

———. *Scientific and Technical Work Force in Trade and Regulated Industries Shows Major Shift in Occupational Composition: 1979–82*, Washington, D.C., May 1984.

———. *Selected Data on Graduate Science/Engineering Students by Racial/Ethnic Background, Fall 1982*, Washington, D.C., January 1984.

———. *Women and Minorities in Science and Engineering*, Washington, D.C., January 1984.

National Society of Professional Engineers. *Engineering Education Problems: The Laboratory Factor*, a Pilot Study by the Professional Engineers in Education Practice, Division of the National Society of Professional Engineers, Washington, D.C., September 1982.

Vetter, Betty. *Supply and Demand for Scientists and Engineers* (2nd ed.) (Washington, D.C.: Scientific Manpower Commission, 1982).

INDEX

Access to higher education, xvi, 69-70, 72, 187n9

ACTION's University Year for Action (UYA), 197n39, 198n42

Active learning, xviii, 60-68, 86-87, 178n18, 180n37, 181n42, 182n50

Aetna Life Insurance Company, 166n32

Agency for International Development (AID), 102, 107-8, 210n30

Alice Lloyd College, 199n47

Alverno College, 184n58

American Association for the Advancement of Science, 218n1

American Chemical Society, 195n27

American Council of Education, 37, 43, 198n40, 203n10, 221n24, 223n30

Applied research, 138-40, 143, 218n32

Arizona, University of, 233

Asian Americans, 95

Association of American Universities, 147

Atomic Energy Commission, 114

Austin (Stephen F.) State University, 197n39

Automation, 21-22, 23-24, 166n32

Autonomy in higher education, 10-12, 160n17

Bakersfield College, 232

Barnes, Michael, 210n29

Baylor University, 232-33

Beaver College, 65

Bell, Terrel, 195n27

Bennington College, 184n58

Berea College, 80, 97, 199n47

Berry College, 80, 87, 199n47

Bethune-Cookman College, 199n47

Billington, James, 172n30

Biomedical Research and Support Grant, 219n6

Blackburn College, 199n47

Blacks. *See* Minorities

Blackwell, James, 202n7

Bloch, Erich, 215n11

Bloom, Allan, 58

Bloom, Benjamin S., 175n4

Bluffton College, 199n47

Boston College, 182n46

Boyer, Ernest, 57

Brazil, 167n39

Brooklyn College, 66

Brown University, 65, 80, 182n52, 183n53, 193n23, 235

Brown-Tougaloo Early Identification Program, 235

Bush, Vanevar: *Science: The Endless Frontier*, 113-14

California State University at Northridge, 97, 229

California, University of: at Berkeley, 204n14, 228, 230-31; at Irvine, 233-34; at Los Angeles, 37; at San Diego, 114; at Santa Barbara, 217n30, 233

Career education, 37, 39

Carnegie Commission on Higher Education, 179n21

Microelectronics and Computer Technology Corporation (MCC), 133
Middle Income Student Assistance Act (1979), 72
Minnesota, University of, 80; at Duluth, 193n23
Minorities: access to higher education for, 69; Asian Americans as, 95; corporations and education of, 96, 97; distribution by field, 91, 95; enrollment, 89-90, 95-96, 200n3; faculty, 202n8; National Opportunity Fund for, xix-xx, 98; outreach programs for, 96-98; professional careers for, 89-98, 202n7-8; recommendations about, xix-xx, 98; recruitment and retention programs, 225-36; and student aid, 77, 191n17, 205n18, 206n18, 222n28; suicide among, 169n13; and technical manpower, 174n10; voting patterns of, 170n22
Minority Engineering Program (MEP), 229
Moll, Richard, 177n14
Montclair State College, 231

National Academy of Engineering, 213n19
National Action Council for Minorities in Engineering, 96
National Bipartisan Commission on Central America (Kissinger Commission), 102, 210n29
National Direct Student Loan Program, 154, 189n12, 222n28
National Graduate Fellowship program (Javits Fellowships), 223n28
National Health Service Corps, 196n36, 223n28
National Hispanic University, 230
National Institute of Education, 160n13
National Institute of Mental Health, 168n9
National Institutes of Health, xxi, 134, 148, 149, 219n10, 220n18, 223n29

National Opportunity Fund, xix-xx, 98
National Research Council, 43, 204n12
National Science Foundation: applied research role of, 139, 218n32; and block grants, 160n13; instrumentation concerns of, 146, 147, 148, 149, 219n10; manpower study of, 45-46; and minority institutions' awards, 205n18; mission of, 217n27; and peer review procedures, 11, 160n15-16, 214n7; politicalization of, 159n6; Presidential Young Investigator's Award, 155, 223n32; recommendations about, xx-xxi, 143, 149, 154-55; science indicators, 115; and student aid, 154-55, 196n32, 222n28, 223n29; university/industry centers, 142-43, 215n14, 217n30
National Service Corporation: City Volunteer Corps, 194n24
National Technology Foundation Act, 217n27
New York, City University of, 83
North Carolina State University, 142
Northeastern University, 199n45
Northern New Mexico Community College, 236

O'Connor, Sandra Day, 172n30
Oakwood College, 199n47
Oberlin College, 184n58
Ohio State University, 142, 183n52
Operation Crossroads Africa, 210n28
Organization for Economic Cooperation and Development, 167n38

Pace University, 199n45
Panetta, Leon, 84
Passive learning. See Active learning
Payton, Robert, 172n30, 175n1
Peace Corps, 197n39, 198n42
Peer review process, 11, 160n15-16, 214n7
Peer tutoring, 66

266